READING MINDS

READING MINDS

A Guide to the Cognitive Neuroscience Revolution

Michael Moskowitz

KARNAC

First published in 2010 by
Karnac Books Ltd
118 Finchley Road, London NW3 5HT

British Library Cataloguing in Publication Data

A C.I.P. for this book is available from the British Library

ISBN 978 1 85575 714 1

Edited, designed and produced by The Studio Publishing Services Ltd
www.publishingservicesuk.co.uk
e-mail: studio@publishingservicesuk.co.uk

www.karnacbooks.com

CONTENTS

ABOUT THE AUTHOR

Michael Moskowitz, PhD, a psychoanalyst and organizational consultant in NYC, is an adjunct associate professor in the NYU School of Social Work and Associate Director of the IPTAR Organizational Consultation and Executive Coaching Program. His past positions include CEO and Publisher, Other Press; Publisher, Jason Aronson; Director of the City University of New York Graduate School and Medical School Counseling Offices; and Team Leader, Operation Outreach Vietnam Veterans Center, New Haven. He is author of articles and chapters on psychoanalytic theory, organizational dynamics, morality, and race and ethnicity; a co-editor of three text books, including *Reaching Across Boundaries of Culture and Class: Widening the Scope of Psychotherapy*; and the co-editor of the journal *Organisational and Social Dynamics*.

Introduction

I hope you will accompany me on a trip through the exciting new field of cognitive neuroscience. The landscape is vast and the particular paths I have chosen—based on my particular training and passions—will show only part of it. But, as we go along, you will see ways of approaching other areas you may choose to explore in greater depth later on.

I have been a psychotherapist now for nearly forty years, and a psychoanalyst for over twenty. I have been fortunate to be able to work with many people in a variety of settings: people with chronic schizophrenia in hospital back wards; traumatized soldiers and their families in their communities; autistic children in their homes; students in campus counselling centres; executives in organizations; individuals, couples and families of all sorts in my private practice. I have also always had a least one foot in academia, teaching at a number of universities and psychoanalytic institutes. As a clinician, I felt enriched by the academic literature—whether in developmental psychology, learning theory, neuroscience, anthropology, linguistics, and more—convinced it offered additional perspectives from which to view my patients and my practice. However, like most clinicians, I was often frustrated by the refusal of many academics' (researchers, in particular) to address the complexity of human nature and the limits of their discipline.

Academics—like most everyone these days—are under enormous pressure to produce and earn their keep; which for them means publishing as many papers as possible and getting as much grant money as possible. Too often their careers and self-esteem are built on gaining recognition, not on addressing tough questions or doing what they think is right.

Many researchers live in their laboratories. Most have never treated a patient, a person in pain, suffering the hurt of their circumstances, someone who might shock them back into seeing narrowness of their vision. Moreover, academics rarely read journals outside their area of interest and often actively chose to ignore obviously related research if it threatens to make their own work seem less special. This struck me hard as an idealistic graduate student. I was able to take a course at another university with an esteemed researcher whose work I then greatly admired. I was, for a time, quite thrilled. My disillusionment came when I enthusiastically expressed the opinion that his general conclusions were supported by the work of another psychologist who was studying the same subject with different methods. "I don't know his work," he said, shaking his head and grimacing with disgust. It was as if I had asked him to taste something horrible. I guess I had.

This book is my attempt to bring things together and to connect what I can of this vast new field before us in order to better understand human nature, and especially what leads to our self-imposed inhibitions and self-inflicted mental pain. It offers a view from a practical perspective that addresses central clinical questions: what keeps us from fully realizing our capacities to understand ourselves and others, and what can be done to change this?

I do not claim great expertise in research design, statistics, or the interpretation of brain scans, but I believe I have learnt enough to exclude the merely sensational. I have chosen not to present controversies in the interpretation of MRI data, although I know they exist, because I know we are far from the end of the story. Some findings will remain accepted and others will not. I have tried to present the work of reputable researchers that has gained support, either through replication or by virtue of fitting in with a pattern of related studies. I do not privilege brain science over social science, or from what we gather from the clinical encounter. I believe we have to struggle to see how it all fits in order to better understand what it means to be human. I hope you will bear with me through some occasional bouts of over-enthusiasm which may border on hyperbole, and not lose me on my side paths and digressions. I can get carried away. I only wish to convey my excitement about the possibilities ahead.

CHAPTER ONE

Reading minds

A Svengali in geek's clothing

On Monday 21 July 1980, in his cluttered new office in suburban Seattle, twenty-four-year-old Harvard dropout computer geek Bill Gates answered his phone in sleep-rumpled clothes. It was Jack Sams, a mid-level middle-aged IBM executive, calling from Boca Raton, Florida. He wanted to meet. Gates offered a time the following week. Sams pushed for the next day and Gates agreed. On Tuesday, Sams appeared at Gates's office, flanked by two corporate watchdogs. Waiting in the reception area in their conservative blue suits and wing-tipped shoes, they looked as out of place as friars at a fraternity house.

"I knew Bill was young," Jack Sams recalls, "but I had never seen him before. When someone came to take us back to the office, I thought the guy who came out was the office boy. It was Bill."

Sams's first order of business was to have Gates sign IBM's infamously one-sided non-disclosure agreement. Gates recalls, "IBM didn't make it easy. You had to sign all these funny agreements that sort of said IBM could do whatever they wanted, whenever they wanted, and use your secrets however they felt"

(Cringely, 1996). Most business people consult their lawyers. Gates didn't hesitate; he signed immediately. IBM was just checking out the scene, Sams explained, and without revealing anything more, he pumped Gates for ideas and information. Gates talked freely. At the end of the meeting, Sams told Gates not to expect anything, not even a phone call.

At the time, personal computers were in their infancy. Breadbox-sized microcomputers had just been transformed from near impossible-to-use nerd toys to affordable home appliances. Radio Shack led the way, soon followed by Apple, but there were dozens of other companies. There was no compatibility between systems and each required different software.

Bill Gates's expertise was computer languages. Computer languages are the codes programmers use to write software for all the applications we use like word processors and spreadsheets. Each language has to be adapted to work on each new kind of computer. Most of us do not know what language our programmes use and could not care less. Tweaking languages takes place in an esoteric arena populated by maths whizzes and puzzle freaks. Bill Gates was both. He had spent most of his two years at college pirating the Harvard mainframe computer to write code he could sell to small companies. Microsoft Basic was his baby.

Had Bill Gates stayed in computer languages, you probably would have never heard of him. Like some Silicon Valley pioneers, he might have made a few million and retired, or, like many others, he might have been supplanted, gone bankrupt, and faded from the scene. Before the IBM deal, he had said no to several proposals from other small companies, and had turned down a multi-million dollar buyout offer from Ross Perot, the then reigning software king. Perot—best known as an eccentric billionaire presidential candidate—had made his fortune computerizing the US government's Medicare records. Bill's mother wanted him to consider Perot's offer but, as she recalls, "I don't think he gave it any serious thought at all."

Gates says about the meeting with Perot, "I was very bowled over by their size and everything, but when we talked about the product vision it was very strange. They *weren't really thinking about it*" (*ibid.*).

One month after his first visit, Sams was back in Seattle, this time with three associates, including a lawyer. IBM did not want to be on the sidelines of the personal computer explosion. Sams told Gates about IBM's top-secret project to bring out a cheap personal computer that would blow away competitors and dominate the market. It had to be out in less than a year. To meet the deadline, Sams, the head of the project, was breaking with IBM's do-every-thing-itself tradition and contracting with outside suppliers for hardware and software. Sams asked Gates if he could provide an operating system.

Gates immediately saw an opening. It was no secret that Microsoft's niche was computer languages, not operating systems. Either Sams had not done his homework and did not know this about Microsoft, or he did not *want* to know it. Maybe he felt comfortable with Gates and was intent on working with him no matter what. In either case, Gates felt confident enough of his position to make a bold move: he told Sams that someone named Gary Kildall had an operating system ready to go.

Then, with Sams looking on, Gates phoned Kildall: "Gary, I'm sending some guys down. . . . Treat them right, they're important," he said (*ibid.*).

A programming legend, Kildall was a brilliant, bearded, long-haired, pot-smoking academic. When the IBM contingent arrived at his home office, he was not there. Distrustful of authority, not inter-ested in making deals, he left it to his wife to run the company, and the meeting. One of the IBM executives recalls, "It was an unfortu-nate situation—here you are in a tiny Victorian House, it's overrun with people, chaotic." After hours of uncomfortable discussion, Kildall's wife refused to sign IBM's non-disclosure agreement. Sams claims that subsequent phone calls to Kildall went nowhere. Kildall claims he never got any. Sams never wanted to deal with Kildall or his associates again. The feeling was mutual.

The IBM crew returned to Microsoft. Sams was desperate. Competition was mounting daily and he feared IBM developers would take too long to come up with an operating system. Sams practically begged Gates to take it on and pledged his full support. Could Gates and Microsoft do it? Gates said yes.

On 30 September, just two months after the initial meeting, a characteristically scruffy Gates and two colleagues, after flying all night from Seattle, changing in the Miami men's room, and stop-ping to buy Bill a tie, arrived thirty minutes late to a meeting with

IBM at Boca Raton. The meeting changed corporate history. Following a stunning technical presentation, Gates confidently proposed a new deal: there would be no sale of software to IBM. Instead, IBM would pay a substantial upfront fee for a non-exclusive licence. In addition, they would pay a royalty of $1–$15 dollars for each computer or software package they ever sold (Manes & Andrews, 1994, p. 162). IBM could not sub-license the languages or operating system, but Microsoft would be free to make similar deals with anyone else.

Did Gates know that Sams would return on bended knee? I think he did. Bill Gates's real expertise is reading minds, knowing what people want, and knowing what he could get away with giving them. He had no doubt that he had to sign the IBM non-disclosure agreement in order to establish a relationship, and he knew signing immediately without consulting a lawyer made him seem trusting, egg-headed, and naïve; a persona reinforced by his rumpled, geek-scientist appearance and distracted demeanour. His appearance belied his background. Gates's father was a prominent corporate lawyer; his mother sat on the boards of corporations and philanthropies. Gates grew up with people like Sams. He knew that Kildall and Sams would mix like oil and water. He knew Sams liked him and wanted to treat him like a son. Gates read Sams' mind and took advantage of it. Sams, on the other hand, misread Gates: completely blind to Gates's ruthless, competitive side, he ended up giving away what could have belonged to IBM, dominance of the personal computer software market.

To most observers, Gates's proposal in Boca Raton might have seemed like a wild gambit. But he understood the IBM corporate world and the kinds of minds that made it home; and he understood the new silicon valley cyberworld and its creative, eccentric characters. Most importantly, in arranging the meeting of Sams and Kildall, he understood there could be no meeting of minds, no possibility of connection. Gates knew each would run from the other, and Jack Sams path would be straight back to his door.

What Sams and IBM did not know was that Microsoft did not yet have an operating system, and had no plans to write one. Gates knew that besides Kildall's there was only one usable system out there. He knew there was little chance IBM would know about it, but to be certain, just before the Boca Raton meeting, Gates paid a few thousand dollars for an option to buy it. In total, he paid its unsuspecting developer, Tim Paterson, $75,000 for an operating system called DOS. DOS became industry standard, and Windows was later built on top of it. For nearly thirty years, Bill Gates has received a royalty on every computer sold with his operating system installed—more than 95% of the computers ever made.

Bill Gates has been described as coming late to the party and then making himself the centre of attention. It's true. Gates did not become the richest man in America by brilliant technical innovation. Microsoft's products, while competent, are often technologically rather humdrum and sometimes badly flawed. Gates's genius is in reading minds, knowing what people want, and providing them with something close enough. Even if he cannot provide it when they want it, he holds their attention with promises; and if what he provides is not great, he convinces them it is as good as they will get.[1]

In both business and personal relationships, Gates has flirted with the edge. He has manipulated good friends, but most remained friends. He rarely reads people incorrectly and has carefully selected and surrounded himself with some of the brightest and most loyal people to be found anywhere. To be fair, there is no evidence Gates treats his friends or family the way he treats his competition. Quite the opposite; his personal relationships have been caring and long lasting. He is devoted to his family. This seems all the more reason to marvel at the flexibility of his mind.

Bill Gates is celebrated as a computer genius, and he is, but his real brilliance is his ability to grasp quickly and accurately what others are thinking. A Svengali in geek's clothing, Bill Gates is a master mind-reader. How people like Bill Gates read minds so well and how we can all learn to do it better is one subject of this book.

Reading minds is in our nature

Though we often do not think about it consciously, we read minds every day. Before we pass another car, we read the intentions of the driver; before we leave a tip, we read the expectations of the waiter; and before we allow a child who says she is sick to stay home from school, we read her motive—is she really ill, or is she trying to avoid a test she hasn't studied for?

Real mind reading is no parlour trick. It is an essential skill. Mind-reading is a form of social communication like language; and, like language, unless something goes obviously wrong and we experience a mind-reading stammer or block and feel totally lost, or suffer the consequences of an obvious mind misread, we take this remarkable gift for granted.

Other social animals understand each other in limited ways, but they do not read minds. A chimp can read another chimp's expressions or gestures and anticipate its behaviour. If it is hungry, it will look for food. If it is angry, it is likely to fight. People look at another person and wonder, "Why is she angry? Why is she hungry? What is on her mind?" That is because what a person does is determined by what she is thinking: Maybe she looks angry because she failed a test; maybe she looks hungry because she is on a diet. How we respond will depend on what we think is on her mind, and the success of all of our relationships will depend on how accurate we are in thinking about what others are thinking, in reading their minds.

Social cognition is the scientific study of our ability to read minds. Researchers in social cognition have determined that a "theory of mind" is the main ingredient in mind reading. It is called theory of mind because we try to understand each other by coming up a theory of what is on another persons mind. Theories of mind are very similar to scientific theories. In scientific theories, scientists make a best guess—in technical terms, formulate a hypothesis— to explain something they observe. The force of gravity explains why objects fall to earth. The structure of DNA explains how traits are inherited. People's private thoughts, their minds, explain their behaviour. A "theory of mind" is an explanation of behaviour based on thoughts, motivations, and beliefs. The better our theories, the more accurately we can predict what others will feel, do, and say.

Even infants think about other minds. By fourteen months, they have some important ideas about other minds, but it is not until they are around five that they know the basics of mind-reading, in other words, have a theory of mind. Psychologists test a person's theory of mind by describing or illustrating a particular kind of social situation: a boy is sitting on the couch and eating cookies. He hides the cookies under the couch before running outside to play.

While he is outside, his mother finds the cookies and puts them in the cupboard. When the boy comes back, where will he look for the cookies?

If children younger than around five are asked, they will answer, "In the cupboard." The reason: young children are incapable entering another person's mind and taking another person's point of view. If asked, "Why do you think the boy will look in the cupboard?" A typical four-year-old will answer, "Because they are there!"

The great psychologist Jean Piaget described the young child's thinking as egocentric, meaning she or he is incapable taking another person's point of view. Before the age of around five, children think everyone thinks just like they do. If confronted with the fact that others think differently they cannot explain it and may become frustrated. Then a major transformation occurs, a pre-programmed developmental advance (Wellman, Cross, & Watson, 2001). At around age five, a light goes on and children suddenly understand, "other minds are different from mine".

This understanding, bringing with it the ability to read minds, is part of our evolutionary heritage. All primates are social animals, but humans are far more social than others. For chimps, the typical group size is less than ten. The average chimp has three close chimp friends. How does that compare to the number of people you regularly see—neighbours, co-workers, family, fellow worshippers, friends? Think of all the people you deal with only occasionally, all the people you interact with only once. Some of those occasional and singular social contacts can be quite important—such as the doctor in the emergency room, or the stranger on the dark street—and these contacts are unique to human social groups. Chimps maintain social connection by grooming each other. They are in nearly constant physical contact. People maintain social connection by reading minds.

The complexity of human social life rewards good mind reading. From the time we venture beyond our immediate family, we interact with people we do not know. Who is safe and who is dangerous? Who wants to help and how? Understanding what others think and feel provides a great adaptive advantage both in leading us into beneficial experiences and in avoiding painful ones.

Please explain

Why is the sky blue? Why do people die? Why are boys and girls different? Where did I come from? Why do I have to go to bed? Why are you arguing? Starting around the age of three, children ask for explanations. Often they question incessantly and will not stop until their curiosity is satisfied. Some of their questions can be simply answered, but many of their questions—for instance, about love and death—have no easy answer, and are asked and answered repeatedly in different ways over the course of a lifetime. When children's questions are met with evasions, they make up their own fantasy-filled explanations.

This drive to understand the world, to demand and invent explanations, is at the core of human nature and paved the way for humankind's greatest cultural achievements: theories—theories that help us navigate the physical world, which I call theories of matter, and theories that help us navigate the social world, theories of mind.

Reading minds is in the brain

Queen Square is at the epicentre of the new science of the mind. Here, at University College London, researchers at the Institute of Cognitive Neuroscience first demonstrated that mind reading is not a magician's trick or sleight of hand, but, rather, an innate property of the human brain (Gallagher et al., 2000). In 1999, a dozen mostly twenty-something graduate students came to the Institute for a brain scan—but one with an unusual twist. Researchers would not be using the MRI to look for a problem, a disease, or disorder. Researchers would be looking to locate the very centre of our social being, the area in our brain responsible for our ability to know what others are thinking and feeling, the place in the brain where we read minds.

At a pre-scan briefing, the volunteers were told that during the experiment two stories would appear on screens inside the MRI machines. They were instructed to read the stories to themselves and to answer the question at the end of each—once again, to themselves. The first tale, about a nervous burglar, was specifically designed to elicit a mind-reading response. To answer the question at its end, volunteers would have to step inside the burglar's head and try to understand his motivations during the incident described in the story, which read as follows.

> A burglar has just robbed a shop and is making his getaway. As he runs to his car, a policeman, unaware of the robbery, sees the burglar drop a glove. "Hey, there—stop!" shouts the policeman, thinking he is helping an absent-minded passerby. To his astonishment, the burglar throws up his arms and abruptly blurts out, "I surrender!"

> Why did the burglar confess?

The second story, about a battle between two mythical armies, was followed by a question that called for a different intellectual response: analysis. This story read:

> Two enemy powers have been at war for a very long time. The Blue army is stronger in foot soldiers and artillery; its opponent, the Yellow army, in air power. On the day the two forces meet to fight a decisive battle, it is raining heavily.

> Why did the Yellow army lose the battle?

Only the volunteer inside the MRI could see which story was on the screen, but the Institute investigators, who were positioned at a bank of scanning monitors a dozen feet away, found that they also had a visual cue. Whenever a subject stepped inside the nervous burglar's mind and attempted to understand why he surrendered (in other words, whenever a subject began to read the burglar's mind), a specific region of the brain, in this case the medial prefrontal cortex, lit up on the scanning monitors. Conversely, when a subject was analysing the reasons for the Yellow Army's surrender (and analysing is a non-mind-reading task), the region remained grey, a sign that the medial cortex was not in use.

For the first time there was proof that mind reading is an innate human ability, an ability that evolution has built into our brains. Our mind-reading centre is, in fact, the apex of human evolution. Located deep in the prefrontal cortex, humankind's most advanced biological structure, it connects to all other parts of the brain, integrating a myriad of abilities to help us better understand our

increasingly complex social world. Gut reactions, adaptive unconscious processes, perceptions of facial expression and body
language, responses to tone of voice and even smells, and our vast
storehouses of cognitions and memories are all brought together in
the service of reading minds.

In 1955, Noam Chomsky opened a new era in the study of the
mind. He proposed that the essence of language is not learnt; rather,
it is a unique biological structure found only in the human brain.
He argued that there is no other way to explain the universality of
language in humans, its seeming absence in all other creatures, and
the commonplace observation that children learn new languages so
easily without formal instruction. Move a young child from Shang-
hai to Chicago, or vice versa, and he or she will learn a new
language in a matter of months. Fifty years of research have confirmed Chomsky's ideas. Thirty years of research have also shown
that the ability to read minds, like language, is a basic and unique
aspect of human nature.[2] Now we know the ability is built into the
human brain.

Navigating the social world

Reading minds is an essential skill for navigating the social world.
In our personal relationships, we assume that much is understood
without being said. People often want their intimate companions to
read their minds. They want their wishes and fears to be understood even when, perhaps especially when, they have trouble
putting thoughts into words. You know the pleasure of being
understood: receiving just the gift you wanted; being taken to a
movie or a given a book that perfectly fits your mood; hearing the
right words at a time of distress; being set-up on a date with someone you actually like. Just as important is the pleasure that comes
with understanding, getting it right, the gift, the movie, the words,
the date, or whatever fulfils the unspoken desires of someone you
care about.

You also know the pain of being misunderstood, when someone
close does not read, or misreads, your mind. Why didn't he or she
know that you wanted to go out, wanted to have sex, wanted to be
left alone, even though you could not say what you wanted,

perhaps did not quite know what you wanted yourself? The converse is true as well. You feel bad when you miss or misunderstand what a friend is thinking.

Reading minds is a relationship. That is the single most important rule of reading minds. Reading minds involves a relationship between two people, someone reading and someone being read. Mind reading is not like taking an X-ray. It involves interaction. If you forget that, you are lost. Even understanding something about a person's mind by observing her dress and demeanour involves relating; what a person wears and how he moves is a communication, whether he knows it or not. Trying to understand that communication is a relationship, just like listening to someone talk. (Forensic profilers view a criminal's behaviour as a communication to his potential captors.) Just as different kinds of relationship call for different ways of listening and talking, different types of relationships call for different approaches to reading minds.

Often in personal relationships, and almost always in other relationships, people do not want their minds to be read. This may be the case even when we desire closeness. Unfortunately, sometimes the closeness is feared even more than it is desired, and, consequently, there is a need to avoid letting the other person read your mind. At times like that, if you feel someone is moving too close, you can say or do something to push him away. Keeping others from reading their minds becomes an art in itself for some people. They become especially alert to mind-reading attempts and especially adept at blocking these attempts.

Poker offers the starkest examples of competitive mind reading and many have found playing it an excellent way to practise their skills. When dealt a good hand, a player will typically try to hide his excitement. Feigning disappointment doesn't work because it is an old trick and easy to spot. One poker champ says when he gets a good hand, he thinks about mowing the lawn. Good players usually ignore overt signs of emotion because they are easy to fake; they look for subtle signs, called "tells", that an opponent is unaware he is showing. Player A has determined that player B taps his index finger almost imperceptibly when he has a bad hand; it is a sign of impatience that B thought he had suppressed. B notes that A seems to know when he has a bad hand—he raises and calls his bluffs. He then observes A glancing at his hand after each deal and realizes A has discovered his tell. On his next good hand, B taps his finger and bets heavily. A thinks he is bluffing and calls his bet and loses. Signalling the opposite of what you feel is not confined to poker. People act disappointed at a good offer in order to get a better deal. People act excited with their lovers in order to hide their boredom and the discovery of an illicit affair.

What stands in our way?

Though evolution has made us all natural-born mind readers, research shows that most of us are not very good at it. We trust people we should mistrust; we fall in love with people we should avoid; we think we are hated when we are loved, misunderstood when we are understood, deceived when we are told the truth, rejected when we are accepted. We misread the intentions and motives of our children, our spouses, our lovers, our friends, and our colleagues at work.

Mind misreads can undermine our judgement, deprive us of critical information, and lead us to behave inappropriately. A common example of this last point is the man who misreads his date's mind and makes an unwanted advance; another is the parent who misreads her child's mind and makes a false accusation. Faulty mind reading is behind many of life's most unpleasant surprises. Think of all the husbands who have been shocked by the announce-ment, "I want a divorce," or all the people who have been surprised by Donald Trump's signature line: "You're fired."

Poor theories

The most common problem is formulating an incorrect theory of mind. Scientists test their theories by making predictions. If their predictions are wrong, they should reject the theory and look for a better one. Sometimes, however, for a number of reasons, scientists cling to a poor theory. They may refuse to reject an unsupported theory because it fits their personal or religious beliefs, or they may be ashamed to be wrong; or sometimes there is simply no better theory. It took a long time to give up the theory that the sun revolved around the earth, despite tons of evidence against it, because it was core religious belief. It took a long time to give up the idea that spicy foods or stress causes ulcers, because no one had yet theorized that the bacteria were the real cause.

Limited information. "You never get a second chance to make a first impression" is a wise folk expression that points to how easy it is for initial misunderstanding based on limited information to set the course of a relationship. Some people are so taken by status, money, and good looks that they do not look further or overlook what they see. An awkward or arrogant first impression is sometimes hard to live down. So many career orientated self-help books contain detailed descriptions of how to make a good first impression that experienced human resource professionals now discount the usual signs—open smiles, good eye contact, forward leaning posture, and the like. Not taking those signs to mean what they used to is, by the way, a good example of a cognitively based mind read.

Preconceptions. Ordinary folk, just like scientists, are often loath to give up a theory once they have developed it. Racial and ethnic stereotyping is the most obvious example. It is very difficult for people to change their prejudiced views. Often, people deny they have stereotypes, or are unaware of them and think they are being objective. Psychiatrists, for example, are generally unaware that they often give black men more serious psychiatric diagnoses and see them as more hostile and paranoid than white men who have exactly the same symptoms. People are even less aware of some non-race-related stereotypes, since they are not a frequent topic of discussion: fat people are viewed as less diligent, women as less scientific for example. These distortions are often subtle, but still significant. Project Implicit has brought together researchers from around to study unconscious biases.[3] They found that nearly all people, including the researchers themselves, have negative reactions to various social groups even when they honestly believe they are not prejudiced. You can examine your own biases—privately and confidentially—by visiting the Project Implicit website (www.implicit.harvard.edu).

Transference. Until recently, psychologists thought that transference—the unconscious compulsion to fit new relationships into the familiar patterns of old relationships—was confined to patients in psychotherapy, but we now know that transference is universal in new relationships and occurs without awareness (Andersen, Reznik, & Manzella, 1996). For instance, you might immediately like and feel safe with a new acquaintance who calls to mind a caring parent. On the other hand, you might feel wary of a new person who reminds you of a critical older sibling. Transferences can lead people to feel certain they understand someone based on a brief initial interaction. Sometimes, such impressionistic theories prove correct, as Malcolm Gladwell's book *Blink* (2005) amply demonstrates, but often they prove wrong.

First impressions can trigger transference. Gates's rumpled demeanour signalled boyish unconcern, not ruthless competitiveness. Gates might not have dressed for effect, but he was aware of how he was perceived. An adept mind reader will try to be aware of how she is being read by a new acquaintance and either try to correct a misunderstanding or use it to her advantage. Jack Sams had a transference response to Bill Gates. Gates reminded Sams of his son. Gates knew it and used it.

Most people do not pay much attention to the transferences that their appearance trigger, while some carefully dress the part they want to play in the minds of others. When he was sixteen, Frank Abagnale, Jr, whose character was portrayed by Leonardo Di Caprio in *Catch Me if You Can*, had his first breakthrough as a successful impostor when he noticed that pilots were treated with great respect, and that bank tellers, who were then mostly young women, went weak at the smile of a handsome man in uniform (Abagnale, 2005). In pilot's garb, Abagnale was rarely asked for identification when cashing a cheque. Not only were his bad cheques accepted—2.5 million dollars worth—but many women fell in love with him. On the other hand, if a teller or bank official did not react in the usual ways, even if she just seemed unimpressed or unfriendly, Frank knew to be careful. If you have a good sense of how you usually come across to others, you can pay particular attention to people who react differently. It is not always something to worry about, but it usually something worth thinking about—what might be going on in the mind of someone who experiences you in an unusual way?

Love blinds. Different kinds of love blind in different ways. When in the thrall of passion, it is hard to be objective about the person who is turning you on. Our theories of mind bend to desire and we come up with rationalizations, reasonable explanations for the self-ish, uncaring, or otherwise difficult behaviour of the person we yearn for. Even when a friend sees the truth and tells us, we often misread his motivation—he is envious; he is shallow—in order to continue to deny what he sees.

Not only does sexual desire distort theory formation, it affects perception. The folk wisdom immortalized in the song, "Don't the Girls All Get Prettier at Closing Time", has been confirmed by social psychologists (Pennebaker et al., 1979). The fewer the choices, the better each one looks. Morning light often changes the view.

In our most intimate love relationships, it is easy to confuse our beloved's mind with our own. In romance, we want so much to feel that we are at one with our lover and share the same thoughts that it is difficult to see when we do not. With our children, we want so much for them to be what we wish them to be that is difficult to see that they have wishes of their own.

Group pressure. For over fifty years, social psychologists have demonstrated how group pressure can influence an individual's thinking and judgement. It is very difficult for most people not to go along with their group's prejudices and preconceptions. Now neuroscientists have shown that not only does thinking and emotion bend to the will of the group, a person's actual perception of reality can be changed in the brain (Berns et al., 2005); even thinking about going against the group's opinion activates the amygdala—the part of the brain responsible for telling us when to be afraid.

Deception and lies. Theories built on lies are bound to lead us astray. Yet people are not well attuned to detecting deception and lies. Humans evolved in small communities in which care and mutual concern were expected and wrongdoers had no place to hide. Lies were used primarily in socially positive ways—to avoid confrontations and to shield others from fear. Our brains have still not caught up with the complexity of a social world in which deception is a weapon and some people treat others as prey.

If anything, we seem to be ever less concerned about lies. Lying is commonplace, and there are myriad forms of deceit. Most lies seem benign, the white lies of social lubrication. Yet even these small lies can create distance in intimate relationships, producing a vague feeling of distrust that keeps people apart. Of course, we are familiar with the suffering caused by big lies and deceit. Headlines daily bring us news of personal infidelities, business frauds, and political corruption, lies uncovered only after too much damage has been done. Though it does not come naturally, it is not difficult to learn to detect some kinds of lies, as we will discuss in Chapter Seven.

Inhibitions

While our ability to read minds is part of our nature, like all natural abilities it can be improved or inhibited. It is similar to other natural abilities, such as the ability to speak, to draw, to run, to sing, to dance, to play. In the absence of severe disability, everyone can do these things to some degree. Not only can we do them, we have a need to do them. Before something stands in his way, every child will speak, draw, run, sing, dance, and play without hesitation. Depending on temperament, some will perform exuberantly and some will be more restrained. These abilities are so much a part of our nature that people will develop alternative pathways for their expression if the usual ones are blocked. People speak with their hands, draw with pencils in their mouths, and run marathons in their wheelchairs. Some people will practise incessantly, turning natural abilities into exceptional skills. Some will become inhibited by painful feelings of anxiety or shame and cease to draw, sing, or dance; others become afraid to speak.

It is the same with reading minds. Its expression is affected by the individual's inborn temperament, which can range from outgoing to shy. Outgoing children interact with others enthusiastically and their theories of other minds tend to be based on emotional interactions. Shy children interact cautiously and their theories of other minds tend to be based on thoughtful reflection. Most children fall somewhere in between, understanding others through both emotion and thought. Whatever their temperament, some will practise and become adept; others will become inhibited.

Inhibitions are primarily caused by anxiety, shame, and other difficult emotions. Intense anxiety makes it difficult to think straight; if severe enough, the mind goes blank. Even moderate anxiety distorts mind reading. Anxiety can be experienced as fear or excitement and can amplify other emotions. Anxiety can turn a small concern into a raging worry. It can turn a mild attraction into blinding passion. In anxiety-arousing organizations, particularly those that employ young adults, such as emergency rooms, start-up companies, and the army, people often mutually misread their own and one another's anxiety as sexual arousal, often with embarrassing results; occasionally, the consequences can be calamitous, as at Abu Ghraib in Iraq, where anxiety-amplified adolescent arousal transformed unsupervised soldiers into sadistic pornographers.

Anxiety can intensify other emotions, such as guilt. Think of the nervous burglar's reaction in the mind-reading story earlier in this chapter. What made him surrender was not the policeman's "Stop!" If the burglar had read the policeman's mind correctly, he would have seen the intention of the cop was to be helpful, but his anxiety and guilt caused him to misread what was intended to be helpful as an accusation. Guilt-ridden people regularly make that misread. Everyone is seen as an accuser, and even helpful comments are experienced as criticisms.

Anxiety can also stop people from looking at things that may be frightening. How many husbands and wives fail to notice obvious signs of a spouse's infidelity because they do not want to experience the pain of betrayal or think about the consequences of divorce? Even when reality can no longer be denied, people often inhibit their emotions and act as if they do not really care. Severe inhibition of thoughts and emotions can lead to people to experience life as meaningless, empty, or even unreal.

Shame can inhibit reading minds. Shame is a painful feeling of being exposed as inadequate or bad. Children are often made to feel shame for asking about private matters adults do not want to discuss. In the same way, adults can feel ashamed for wondering about the private thoughts of others who are important to them. "How dare you accuse me of that? You should feel ashamed", is often a ploy used by the accused to stop the accuser from reading further into his mind.

Improving mind-reading skills

Skilful mind readers come from all walks of life. Some, like undercover detectives and hostage negotiators, use their skills to manage difficult circumstances; others, like Bill Gates, to achieve success in business and professional life; and others to engage in rich and satisfying personal lives. What they have in common is the ability to balance their "gut" emotional reactions with their cognitive assessment of available information. By balancing emotion and cognition, feeling and thinking, they are able to:

- understand the perspective of others;
- feel powerful emotions without surrendering critical judgement;
- distinguish their own feelings from the emotions of others and not be swayed by emotional appeals or the contagion of crowds;
- know when to trust an intuition and when to verify the intuition with an assessment of the facts;
- know when to ask for help in assessing a situation; and knowing whom to ask.

A fortunate few may excel at what they do by accident of nature and nurture, but nearly everyone has the capacity to do well. Researchers have studied master performers in a wide variety of fields, including athletics, music, chess, science, and writing, and determined the most important factor by far in becoming an expert in nearly anything is time spent practising (Anders Ericsson, Krampe, & Tesch-Römer, 1993). Talent and innate ability count for little by comparison.

Bill Gates practised mind reading from early on. He played highly competitive board games through childhood and high stakes poker in college and—not very many people seem to know this— was in psychotherapy for a year and a half when he was eleven. Perhaps the most important part of his therapy was understanding how he misread his parents minds. At the time, Bill was a scholastic underachiever. He thought he was in a battle for control with his parents, a battle he could only win by refusing to succeed. In therapy he recognized, "It's a fake battle. It's ridiculous . . . They love you and you're their child. You win" (*Playboy* Magazine, 1994). From then on he immersed himself in learning whatever he could; he became adept at finding people he could trust, and he picked his battles carefully, engaging in competition only when he could read his opponents with precision.

Bill Gates is an expert mind reader. He is also an expert computer programmer and poker player. These are all skills that he learnt, not magical abilities or genetic endowments. Perhaps not everyone can become as skilled at reading minds as Bill Gates, but most people can get eighty to ninety per cent of the way there. I have seen interpersonally clueless students become perceptive clinicians. I have seen people who had no idea how to think about children become sensitive parents. I have seen spouses understand each other for the first time. What is required is a willingness to practise in way that allows you to see what you are doing wrong so that you can correct it; researchers call it deliberate practice; folk wisdom calls it learning from mistakes.

Any amount of practice is better than none. Research has shown that that while it takes a great deal of practice to become expert, it takes much less to become quite good, and skills can improve dramatically in very little time. Repetition and experience are not the same as practice. It does not help to do the same thing over and over, especially if you are doing it wrong. I am an ardent golfer and have spent a lot of time on golf driving ranges. I see many people labour away for hours, sweating week after week, and never getting better. Some of them continue to play devotedly, with good humour about their ineptitude, but most eventually quit. For some reason, they imagine they should know what to do without any instruction, without ever having read a guide to technique. Many have no idea how to think about the golf swing. If they had learnt just a little about the elements of the stance and the swing and— this is a point many coaches miss—how to apply what they had learnt to their particular body type and tempo, they could have become excellent golfers.

The same is true for reading minds. In the chapters to come, you will learn how to think about reading minds. You will read about exciting research in the new field of cognitive neuroscience, showing how nature and experience together determine each person's unique approach to the world. You will learn about the elements that go into reading with your head and reading with your heart and gut, and you will learn how to formulate better theories of mind.

Some people are balanced knowers, adept at using and integrating both feelings and thoughts in making judgements about others. Later, we will discuss why many people lean toward one approach or the other, why emotional knowers prefer to make judgements based on their gut reactions, and why cognitive know-ers prefer to reflect on the facts. You will see that there is no one right way to do it—to improve mind-reading—as with almost any skill—you can focus on building your strengths or correcting your weaknesses, but either way, it really helps to know what your strengths and weaknesses are.

Notes

1. How many Microsoft developers does it take to change a light bulb? None. Microsoft will convince people darkness is industry standard.
2. I think Chomsky implies that theory construction is uniquely human. See in particular, Chomsky (1987).
3. http://www.projectimplicit.net

Rock, paper, scissors: it pays to have a theory

Takashi Hashiyama, president of a major Japanese electronics company, could not decide. Would he pick Christie's or Sotheby's to auction his company's $20 million art collection? "As both companies were equally good and I just could not choose one, I asked them to please decide between themselves and suggested . . . rock paper scissors." This is not an unusual business strategy in Japan, where rock, paper, scissors originated. To pick one competitor over another when they both seem good could leave hard feelings.

In this game, played throughout the world, each opponent chooses a weapon and hurls its symbol at his opponent. Rock smashes scissors, scissors cuts paper, paper smothers rock. In the playground, hand-signals are used—fist for rock, open palm for paper, fingered V for scissors. In Hashiyama's boardroom, words were written on paper.

"The client was very serious about this, so we were very serious about it, too," said Jonathan Rendell, deputy chairman of Christie's America. Kanae Ishibashi, the president of Christie's Japan, researched the psychology of the game, reported the *New York Times* (Vogel, 2005), but it was Alice and Flora, the eleven-year-old twin daughters of Nicholas Maclean, international director of Christie's Impressionist and Modern Art department, who came up with the strategy. The girls played the game at school, "practically every day".

"Everybody knows you always start with scissors," said Alice.

"Rock is way too obvious, and scissors beats paper," Flora piped in. "Since they were beginners, scissors was definitely the safest," she added.

If the first round was a tie, you should still stick to scissors because, "Everybody expects you to choose rock," Alice explained.

Sotheby's took a different approach. Blake Koh, an expert in Impressionist and Modern Art at Sotheby's in Los Angeles told reporters, "This is a game of chance, so we didn't really give it that much thought. We had no strategy in mind."

Rock, paper, scissors, shoot! Christie's – scissors; Sotheby's – paper. Christie's wins.

In order to succeed at rock, paper, scissors, you need to be able to read your opponent's intentions, while trying to get your opponent to misread yours. If you play against a computer making random throws, it is a lottery, a game of pure chance. Had he been playing against a computer, Blake Koh's "no strategy" was as good as any. But Blake was not playing against a computer. He was playing against two eleven-year-old girls.

Here's what Flora and Alice were thinking:

1. They imagined playing against a thoughtful, rational adult, someone like their father.

2. "Everyone expects rock": that is, if you stop to think about it, you realize that rock is the obvious first choice. Rock is strong and hard; it's thrown with a fist; and it is first on the list. In fact, rock is chosen on average more than 40% of the time. If Flora and Alice thought they were playing an inexperienced child, they would have chosen paper. Instead, they assumed that their father's opponent at Sotheby's was thoughtful enough to expect rock and, thinking that he was playing a novice, would choose paper to counter rock.

3. They also probably knew, though maybe not consciously, that people like their father, academics and intellectuals, tend to favour paper.

4.   "Everybody knows you always start with scissors" is Flora's shorthand for: experienced players like her think that scissors is the best first move when playing inexperienced but thoughtful players.

In other words, Flora and Alice formulated a theory of their opponent's mind that predicted he would choose paper, and they were right. Their theory assumed that their opponent would also have a theory of mind, that is, he would be thinking about what was on his opponent's mind, and they were right about that as well.

Blake Koh's statement that he had no strategy cannot be true. Humans simply cannot choose randomly.[1] Every decision we make reflects our preferences and our understanding of the world. Takashi Hashiyama understood this when he decided he could not choose, because a choice would indicate a preference and he did not want either competitor to feel slighted.

Koh might have used something other than a human mind to pick randomly-thrown dice, a lotto ball machine, for instance, but he did not. "We really didn't give it that much thought," he said. But once he gave it any thought, he formulated a theory of mind, whether he knew it or not. Koh apparently did not know what was on his mind, but Alice and Flora did. They had a better idea of what he was thinking than he did.

Alice and Flora might have been wrong. No theory is perfect. Brett Koh might have acted impulsively and chosen rock; he might have thought like the girls and chosen scissors; he might have formulated a theory about what the girls were thinking, and responded with rock. What we do know is that people who give some thought to what others are thinking and who consciously and actively formulate theories of mind understand others better than those who do not. Formulating a theory allows you to test it, see the results, and learn from the experience. It's a cliché, but still true: too often people do not learn from their mistakes. They see their misjudgements as personal flaws or, like Brett Koh, discount them as quirks of fate, rather than as data that can be used to test and adjust their theories. If Brett Koh had analysed the data, he might have concluded that "don't give it much thought" is not the best competitive strategy.

Many games, like rock, paper, scissors, involve competitive mind-reading: chess and other board games, and poker and other card games. In some, like chess, chance plays no role; it is all a matter of outwitting your opponent. In others, like poker, much depends on luck, but with all of these games, the best players are master mind readers.

The intentional stance: it don't mean nothing

"It don't mean nothing" was one of the favourite expressions of the Vietnam Veterans I worked with soon after the war ended. It was shorthand for their feeling that the indifferent and sometimes cruel treatment they received when they returned home was not purely accidental; it meant something, not nothing. They had different theories about its meaning. Some thought it was due to the liberal media brainwashing people into seeing them all as drug addicts or murderers. Some saw it as an expression of the national feeling of guilt and shame. But all saw it as meaning something; it was intentional.

If you see a ball roll across the room and end up behind the armchair in the corner, you might think that the cat was playing with it and let it get away, or that someone kicked it while walking by. You don't wonder why the ball put itself there. On the other hand, if you saw the cat run across the room and dive behind the chair, you might think it is hiding from the dog; and if you saw your five-year-old do the same thing, you would almost definitely assume she was hiding for a reason.

We assume that people and animals act with the intention of reaching goals, and that the way they try to attain their goals is meaningful. Darwin scholar Daniel Dennett named this assumption the *intentional stance.* He proposed that understanding others as acting with intention, with purpose and meaning, evolved as an essential part of human nature that provided us with an enormous evolutionary advantage and opened new vistas in understanding the social world. The intentional stance is the foundation of building a theory of mind, and evolution has built it into the human brain.

Rock, paper, scissors in the brain

In 2002 researchers at the University College London observed volunteers playing rock, paper, scissors inside a PET scanner

(Gallagher, Jack, Roepstorff, & Frith, 2002). Their goal was to locate the intentional stance in the brain. Functional neuroimaging, MRI, and PET scans have opened new vistas in brain research. The MRI has been refined to the point that it can create detailed three-dimensional images of the entire body, and, most important for the study of mind reading, when combined with computer technology, the MRI can show how blood flows in the brain. This is a measure of the brain's function, or fMRI.

When blood flows to a particular area, it means that area is working harder. Before the invention of the MRI, our knowledge of brain function came primarily though lesion studies. Scientists could discover the function of a part of the brain only when it was lesioned, that is injured, through disease, accident, or surgery. Unfortunately, bullets, motorcycle accidents, a lifetime of heavy drinking, and even surgery can devastate large areas of the brain. Before the development of functional neuroimaging, we could tell that if someone lost a large chunk of frontal lobe, their judgement became impaired and their morality loosened, or that the wobbly elderly alcoholic who couldn't remember your name or the date and told long, made-up stories about his past had sustained damage to his thalamus. But identifying the location of something as subtle as a thought or a way of thinking was beyond our capacity until now.

Like the fMRI, the PET scan measures blood flow in the brain. But it is more invasive, requiring the injection of a radioactive tracer. The amounts of radioactivity are small, but ethics boards limit the number of times someone can be scanned for the sake of science. MRIs have, for the most part, replaced PET scans in brain research, but PET scans have a few advantages. Unlike MRIs, they do not require the subject to lie perfectly still, so they are good for monitoring someone playing a game.

During odd hours at the University College London when the expensive equipment was not being used for medical diagnosis, volunteers came to play rock, paper, scissors. Inside the scanner, subjects viewed a computer screen and held a keyboard, on which they could choose their weapon. When signalled, the subject and his opponent choose. The winner was displayed on the screen. Subjects were told they would be playing three different opponents: (1) a normal human, namely, one of the experimenters sitting with her own keyboard and monitor in another room, (2) a not-too-clever computer playing a very simple strategy such as, make your next move your opponent's last move, and (3) a random number generator. They were told they would receive a signal indicating which opponent they were about to play. Notice, and this is the main point of the study, only opponent number one requires that the subject take the intentional stance. Only opponent one is an agent with beliefs, desires, intentions. Opponents two and three are machines. And it was only when playing opponent one, while taking the intentional stance, that a specific region of the brain lit up like a beacon— the anterior paracingulate cortex was switched on by a sudden rush of oxygen-rich blood.

When you think someone is thinking, that part of your brain comes alive. When you face an opponent in the schoolyard, or across the poker table, your anterior paracingulate cortex is telling you to take the intentional stance and think about what your opponent is thinking. It is not telling what he or she is thinking, but it is an important start. Even one-year-old babies can take the intentional stance.

Bouncing baby balls

In central Budapest, in the baby lab of the Hungarian Academy of Sciences, a one-year-old infant intently observes an unfolding animated drama. On screen, a little ball and a big ball gaze longingly at each other, across an open field. A low wall cuts across the field, a barrier to their connection. Big Ball inflates, then shrinks, as if breathing a sigh. Little Ball answers with a sigh of its own. Little Ball rolls up to the wall, stops and sighs again. Big Ball sighs too. Little Ball turns, and slowly rolls away. Abruptly, Little Ball turns back and, now moving faster, leaps over the wall. Little Ball nuzzles next to Big Ball. Finally touching, they sigh together.

Year-old babies are initially excited by this simple cartoon and happy when the two balls meet. But babies bore easily, and after watching a few times, they lose interest. If the wall is removed, and Little Ball rolls happily towards Big Ball, babies barely pay attention. But if the wall is removed and Little Ball continues to leap as if the wall were still there, the babies perk up and stare, as if to say, why is it doing that? By the time they have reached their first birthday, babies are trying to read minds (Gergely, Nádasdy, Csibra, & Bíró, 1995). They assume that others, even cartoon balls, act with a purpose in mind, that they have a goal, and that their actions reflect their intention to reach that goal. The Little Ball jumps over the wall intending to reach its goal: contact with Big Ball.

Taking the intentional stance is a baby's first step toward reading minds, but it cannot stop there. Babies see everything as having intention, even simple cartoon balls. Children have to learn that only people and perhaps some animals have intention. Balls and other objects, machines, computers, and fate, do not.

The sense that we act for a reason is a basic building block of the conscious mind. Babies become aware of their actions when they act for a reason. Babies turn towards the breast to be fed, lift their arms to be held, smile to be smiled at, cry to be soothed. The behaviours that are responded to and lead to their intended goals become the core of our sense of self. Unintentional and unacknowledged actions do not feel as much a part of our selves.

As adults, we may no longer think that things have minds, but our sense of self is still defined by our intentions. We do not pay much attention to our unintentional actions, our tics, our odd movements, our mannerisms. If they are pointed out, they can become a source of embarrassment. Our most intensely felt unintentional actions, those we cannot avoid paying attention to, bodily urges and arousals, can become the focus of our desire for self-control and our fear of loss of control as we struggle to make them subject to our intention.

For most of human evolution, adults too assumed that things had intentions, that nearly everything had a mind or was controlled by a mind. Some groups believed trees were spirits who could fall on those they wished to harm; others believed that gods drew the sun across the heavens in a chariot in order to light the sky. Almost every culture told a story in which powerful beings created life for a reason.

The intentional stance is so basic and built-in that it is difficult even for adults to accept that often things do not happen for a reason. How common are the laments of the injured, "it doesn't make sense", and "it isn't fair". Only intending beings can make sense, be fair or unfair. Nature and fate have no motives. Yet mourners and others who have lost a great deal can get caught in their need to make sense of their loss, to look for justice in the random cruelty of nature, while those who escape tragedy, relieved and guilt-ridden onlookers, devise reasons for the others' misfortune, sometimes blaming the victim, sometimes invoking the will of God.

The intentional stance is at the core of our nature and the core of building theories of mind. Just as humans are unique in having evolved languages of infinite variability, we are unique in building theories of infinite varieties. Humans, by nature, are speaking, theorizing primates driven to understand and to articulate their understanding. The intentional stance is our first theory. Little Ball jumps over the wall in order to get to Big Ball. The sun god Helios rides westward so he can float home on the eastward flowing river Oceanus. The sun stops shining during an eclipse because the sun god is abandoning the earth. These explanations are based on our theories of mind.

Theories of matter and mind

Explanations of natural events in terms of the intentions of unseen beings are attempts to understand the world, but they are not scientific because they cannot be tested. How do you find out if a god is pulling the sun? What makes a god angry enough to cause a storm? What charm will entice a spirit to cure an illness? Based on their reading of imagined minds, the answers of priests and shamans were various and invariably wrong. At some level they must have recognized they were whistling in the dark, since nearly all mythologies try to prevent testing of their explanations. In ancient Greek myth, questioning the power of a god is hubris, excessive pride, and leads to destruction. In most religions questioning god's power, even if it does not lead to tragedy in life, will lead to punishment in the afterlife. The human desire to make sense of things is so great that for most of history we have clung desperately to unsupported explanations, often at great cost. It is sad to think about how many have been sacrificed to expiate angry gods.

Pre-scientific explanations are attempts to apply theories of mind to things that have no mind. They are sensible attempts in as much as the first most important thing for a child to understand is his mind and the minds of his caretakers. What delight is greater than learning how to make mummy smile? What dread greater than seeing her turn away? What relief and joy in finding ways to bring her back! Much of childhood is spent thinking about what others think, including what is good and what is bad, what questions can be asked and what questions must never be asked. Understanding other minds is essential to survive in our complex social world. Being in the presence of others whose minds are closed to us or whose thoughts are alien, is frightening. It is no surprise that we apply our theories of mind to things we do not understand.

Practical theories

"There is nothing so practical as a good theory" was the motto of Kurt Lewin, the father of social psychology. Many people—Americans in particular—are suspicious of theory. Americans see themselves as practical, and see theories as theoretical—but theoretical in the sense of mere opinion, as in "What's your theory about the stock market? My broker's theory seems to change every day"; or—particularly if they have taken badly taught courses in postmodernism—they think of theory as mind-numbing academic discourse, originally written in French. That's not what scientists like Lewin mean by theory; and it is not what I mean by theory when I talk about "theory of mind".

A theory is simply a proposed explanation that can be tested.[2] "The stock market always goes down after an election", and "Mary always starts crying three days before her period", are both theories, the latter also being a theory of mind; both can be tested. Let's say you happen to live with Mary. You make note of Mary and her menstrual periods for six months and discover that four of the six times she started crying three days before her period. That does not mean your theory is wrong. When it comes to psychology—and other sciences dealing with complex systems such as meteorology and economics—a theory working two out of three times isn't bad. A pharmaceutical company is delighted if a new antidepressant works for two out of three patients; a poker player is thrilled if he can call an opponent's bluff two-thirds of the time.

But that does not mean you need to be content with knowing that Mary starts crying three days before her period, two-thirds of the time. There is a second part to Lewin's motto, "Nothing contributes more to good theory than practice", meaning that theories are developed through repeated interactions and observations. If you observed carefully, you might have noted that the one of the times Mary didn't start crying was when you were on vacation together. You weren't sure about the other time, but you know you were not on vacation, so it could be that whatever happened then also happened during the vacation. In a flash of inspiration, you make a connection: "Mary doesn't start crying before her period if I spend time with her and we feel close", you theorize. During the next few months, you test your theory and it works, perhaps illustrating another of Lewin's maxims: "If you want to truly understand something, try to change it". You might now amend your theory of Mary's mind to, "Mary starts crying three days before her period if she feels alone and uncared for". You might further wonder about those times that Mary gets upset for what seems to be no reason. You now know that people do not do anything without a reason. What is your theory of why Mary gets upset?

If you were a social scientist, you might begin to think more broadly about how psychological factors influence premenstrual distress. You know that feeling alone and uncared for are signs of depression, so you theorize, "Depression increases premenstrual distress". If you thought that, you would be right. In looking at the scientific literature, you would find other scientists have tested your theory. You might be satisfied with that or you might want to test it again or test it in a different way. The point of this illustration is that ordinary folk and scientists theorize in much the same manner.

Your mind-reading skill depends on your theories of other minds. Scientists improve their theories by stating them clearly and testing them in light of the evidence. If you want to improve your mind-reading skills, you should do those things as well. Bill Gates theorized that Jack Sams wanted to work with him no matter what. Flora and Alice theorized that a thoughtful novice like Brett Koh would choose paper. They were right. But it is important to bear in mind that any theory is better than no theory. When confronted with someone's behaviour that seems baffling, or if you want to predict what someone will do, come up with a theory of what is on his mind. You might be right. If you are wrong, you can refine your theory and have a better chance of being right the next time. As we go along you will also learn what to look for to improve the chances that your theories of mind will be right the first time.

Some might object that skilful mind readers seem to do it naturally, without giving it thought. That is partly true. Some people develop their skills during childhood, without much conscious awareness. But to improve your skills in any area, whether athletic, creative, or social, you must become conscious of what you are doing, become aware of what you are doing wrong, and deliberately practise doing it right. People who read minds for a living—poker players, secret service agents, and psychotherapists, for example—improve by thinking about what they are doing and practising all the time. Well-practised skills eventually feel, look and become natural.

Some of the theories of social cognition, such as "love is blind", or "first impressions count", seem like obvious folk wisdom, and they are; but they are bits of folk wisdom that have been clearly stated and rigorously tested. Other bits of obvious folk wisdom, such as "women have superior intuition", or "people don't really change", or "opposites attract" have been tested and shown to be incorrect. For thousands of years people observed fruit falling and birds flying and came up with folk wisdom to explain what they saw; and much of it was wrong. Isaac Newton's testable theory of gravity and motion enabled people to make practical devices to harness the forces of nature—the machines of the modern world. The section that follows shows how theories—of both matter and mind—have transformed our thinking and changed the course of human history.

Revolutionary theory

Science and business are both practical pursuits, concerned with observation and prediction. Thales, who lived in the Mediterranean city of Miletus in the sixth century BC, was a practical and observant man. One particular winter, after years of studying the cycles of the seasons, he predicted there would be a bumper crop of olives the following autumn. He kept the prediction to himself, but, using borrowed money, he bought every olive press he could find. When the predicted crop arrived, Thales leased the presses for great profit, becoming perhaps the first capitalist oilman. Now rich, he could devote his time to science.

Thales then publicly made a prediction: there would be a total eclipse of the sun the following year. Herodotus records that it did occur as predicted in 585 BC, fortuitously preventing a battle between the armies of two warring cities as the armies stopped in awe of what they took to be a sign from an angry god. Thales proclaimed that the event had nothing to do with gods; it was part of a natural cycle and could be mathematically predicted. So western science was born, with Thales as its acknowledged father.

Coming to grips with the cold unintentionality of the universe marked the beginning of science. The sun and the planets do not move in their particular way because someone intends them to; their movements are caused by unthinking natural forces. Using the scientific approach, the Greeks and the Romans made great advances, particularly in astronomy and engineering. The fall of the Roman Empire marked the beginning of the Middle Ages and the end of scientific progress for nearly a thousand years in the West. Without stable government, the infrastructure of education, schools, and libraries collapsed. Though the church kept literacy and scholarship alive in its monasteries and universities, theology was the subject of study, and little that could be called science was produced until the fourteenth century. Backed by the church, the clergy reasserted its position as the source of all wisdom, and God as the cause of all things. It was even declared heresy for laymen to own the Bible (Peters, 1980), for fear they might question the church's interpretation.

In the fourteenth century, the Black Death depopulated Europe, decimating the monasteries and halting even their limited scholarship. But that same Black Death undermined the authority of the church (Kelly, 2005), whose priests died like everyman. In fact, the plague seemed to prove the truth of Thales' science: there is no one out there to talk to. Nature neither intends nor cares. Relatively unencumbered by religion and nurtured by commerce, science blossomed again with vigour during the renaissance. The beauty of renaissance art was inspired by science. Filippo Brunelleschi, a Florentine architect and engineer, performed experiments that led to a mathematical theory of perspective. Artists studied optics and anatomy in order to more accurately portray the natural world. Copernicus, Galileo, and Kepler showed the Earth was not at the centre of the universe and changed our view of the world forever. Da Vinci's and then Vesalius's dissection and detailed drawings of the inside of the human body changed our view of ourselves.

Isaac Newton may have been the greatest scientist of all time. In 1687, he published a theory that explained the motion of all things, from the way pool balls interact to the way rockets fly to the way planets revolve around the sun. His theory provided the basis for physics and its applications, such as mechanics and engineering, and it determined our view of the universe until it was replaced by Einstein's theory of relativity in the twentieth century. Newton's universe is a machine like a clock. If you know its position now, you can predict its position in the future. On a practical level, you can predict the trajectory of a bullet, how much weight a bridge will bear, how fast a car can go.

How does this relate to reading minds? It relates in two ways. First, it tells us something important about theories: theories are never perfect; they can work quite well in some circumstances and not in others. Newton did not call his ideas theories. He called them "laws", which is unfortunate and has caused great confusion that continues to this day. Many people, for instance, think that Darwin's theory of evolution is less "true" than Newton's laws of motion. It isn't. Newton thought he had discovered God's laws, the rules that He used to set up the universe the way a clockmaker sets up a clock. He, God, then wound the clock-universe and off it went, no longer needing His intervention. Being God's laws, Newton thought, they were perfect and forever.

Newton was wrong. In 1887, in Cleveland, Ohio, at what is now Case Western Reserve University, Albert Michelson and Edward Morley were surprised to find that light did not follow Newton's laws. Other problems were soon discovered. In 1905, Einstein's theory replaced Newton's laws. We now know science cannot provide laws of nature; but it can provide theories, some of which work very well. Theories are ways of understanding that allow us to make predictions and test them. Newton provided a wonderful theory. For over two hundred years, all of its predictions were correct. Even now, to build a bridge or launch a rocket to the moon, you would use Newton's theory.[3] To build a nuclear device, launch a rocket to the nearest star, or look for wormholes to another universe, you need Einstein's. For reading minds, we need theories that make testable predictions and work well enough. They do not have to be perfect. Current research in psychology and neuroscience provides us with a good start.

The other way that Newton's approach applies to reading minds is this: while it ultimately fails as an approach to mind-reading, the attempt to apply Newton's theories to psychology did lead to greater understanding of just how complicated the mind is. In addition, there are findings that can contribute to improvement of skills if viewed with some knowledge about interpreting research results. Newtonian physics was the culmination of the project begun by Thales of Miletus in 585 BC: taking the intentionality out of scientific explanations. All motion in the universe was explained by impersonal forces acting on impersonal objects. Once God wound the clock-universe, it ran on its own. Physics, the Queen of Science, was so successful that, starting in the nineteenth century, it was used as a model for psychology. In fact, psychophysics was the name given to the new science in 1860. It is still a part of psychology today. Psychophysics tries to describe an exact relationship between the stimulus, what is out there in reality, and the response, what happens in the mind. What wavelengths are perceived as red? How loud does a sound have to be for it to be heard? The methods and findings of psychophysics proved useful in areas such as camouflage design and dashboard safety. But its theories proved limited in scope and could not address the more baffling relationships between reality and mind, such as what makes an event a trauma, or how much hugging does a baby need.

Behaviourism was another attempt to apply the model of physics to psychology. It tried to find clear relationships between events (stimuli) and behaviour (response). What makes a child act afraid of a rabbit? How can losing money lead to a gambling addiction? The mind was left out of the equation altogether because it was so troublesome to observe. While behaviourism's findings in the laboratory were impressive, especially with rats and pigeons, its practical application to teaching and therapy proved disappointingly limited. As much as behaviourists wanted to ignore it, the human mind kept getting in the way, altering the relationship between stimulus and response.

The hubris of behaviourism led to its fall. It defined psychology as the science of human behaviour. Modelled on Newtonian physics, it asserted that it could produce laws to predict and control human behaviour without any reference to intentional thinking minds. Many behaviourists, including the most famous behaviourist of all, Harvard's B. F. Skinner, even thought the brain was irrelevant to the science of psychology.[4] Skinner had the chutzpa in 1957 to publish a book on how children develop language that showed he knew little about either children or language. Noam Chomsky's devastating review of Skinner's book (1959) stands as a marker for the cognitive revolution that transformed American psychology. To Chomsky, defining psychology as the science of behaviour was like defining physics as the science of meter reading (Chomsky, Foucault, & Rajchman, 2006)—the numbers on an electric meter are produced by unseen matter, behaviour is produced by an unseen mind. Physics is the science that proposes and tests theories of matter, and psychology is the science that proposes and tests theories of mind.

Freud at first modelled psychoanalytic theory on Newtonian physics. He tried to explain the mind in the same way that Newton explained the universe, in terms of energy with varying force affecting structures of varying stability. For Freud, the energy was sex and aggression, and the structures were the id, ego, and superego. Though the model was brilliant, and still has some utility, Freud soon realized that human psychology required an agent acting with intention. Freud became a doctor of unfulfilled desire, examining the obstacles and conflicts that prevent people from reaching their goals. Freud saw that people were often not aware of their intentions and so felt as if they were not the initiators of their actions or the authors of their lives. In search of explanations, they attributed their state sometimes to the influence of others, sometimes to age-old imagined agents (gods, fates, and spirits), and sometimes to modern ones (genetics, chemical imbalances, and drugs). This is not to say that drugs, genes, and other people do not affect our lives. They surely do, but two people can take the same drug and have very different experiences, and two people with the same genes— identical twins—can have very different lives.

Powerful ideas. Our thoughts, our words, our culture, and all of our creations alter the environment to which we mould, evolve, and adapt. All creatures affect the environment of their family and their neighbours. An evolutionary change in one species can have enormous consequences for the entire planet. For example, over three billion years ago, a species of aquatic bacteria evolved photosynthesis, the ability to use water and sunlight to produce food and energy. It was a great leap forward for that species of bacteria that still thrives today, blue-green algae, the mother of all plants, but it led to the extinction of most other species then living. A by-product of photosynthesis, oxygen, was unlocked from water and released into the atmosphere for the first time. A highly reactive, corrosive molecule, oxygen causes metals to rust and pigments to fade. Concentrated in disinfectants like bleach and peroxide, it kills micro-organisms. In reacting with other elements, oxygen produces massive amounts of energy. Oxygen combined with carbon in food produces the energy that fuels our bodies; oxygen combining with carbon in coal and oil produces the energy the fuels the industrial world.

Oxygen killed most of the creatures it touched, but, at the same time, it provided the rich atmosphere in which complex, energy-consuming animals could evolve. If those ancient one-celled creatures had never developed photosynthesis, life would not have progressed beyond single cell, sluggish bacteria and the earth's entire ecosystem would resemble the bottom-most layer of a swamp.

When humans developed the capacity for language and theory, they created a new atmosphere, an atmosphere of culture and imagination, in which we now all evolve. Like oxygen, the by-products of this transformation have immeasurably increased the complexity and power of those who could use it while leaving most other creatures defenceless in its path.

Here's one example. For most of human evolution, we were prey. Six to ten per cent of early humans were killed by predators, about the same rate as antelopes and chimpanzees (Hart & Sussman, 2005). Human fossils show marks on bones, and holes in skulls into which sabre-tooth tiger fangs and hyena teeth neatly fit. Then we invented weapons and the tactics of the hunt and became predators to all. Some apes use tools, but their use is limited and repetitious. No ape could imagine propelling a spear with a dried intestine stretched on a stick, much less theorize the result. Once humans have an idea, it becomes subject to the infinite transformations of imagination, and the press for realization. Like the peak of Everest, the line between imagination and reality is under constant assault. Whatever is imagined, someone tries to achieve. Think of a weapon and you will probably find that someone has built it. Think of a sexual act and you will probably find it on the Internet. Recognizing that people often try to fulfil their fantasies without considering the possible consequences, every culture, in its own way, places restrictions on imagination. Imagining can be dangerous and, as Freud theorized, the structures of the mind are often used to inhibit rather than generate thought.

You can never know

When bacteria first produced oxygen, it did not suddenly flood the atmosphere. Its concentration grew gradually. As it was released, it first combined with metals, particularly iron. It was not until all the iron on earth was oxidized, turned to iron ore—essentially rust— that oxygen levels rose dramatically, reaching today's concentration of about 20% some 500 million years ago. Rising high into the atmosphere, oxygen formed the ozone layer and blocked harmful radiation from the sun, causing yet another great spurt in evolution. Protected from the sun, life could now venture out of the water on to land. New species proliferated.

The level of oxygen has stayed about the same since then, and that is a good thing. Had it not combined with iron, or had it increased even a bit more, ignited by lightning the atmosphere would blaze with constant fire, preventing or extinguishing all life on land and near the surface of the sea. The new atmosphere of theory, language, and culture that humans have spawned continues to increase in richness and density. We do not know where it will lead and what further bursts in evolution it will produce; nor do we know if we can contain the explosive forces that are triggered by the overwhelming complexity of the culture we have created.

For each of us, constructing ever more complex and accurate theories of other minds can lead to deeply experiencing psychic realities very different from our own. This has its practical benefits, but it will be powerfully moving, and sometimes frightening and overwhelming. I think it is a journey worth taking; you can never know where it might lead.

How to use psychological research

Inspired by the theories of Darwin, Freud, and many others, such as the famous Swiss child psychologist Jean Piaget, scientists have developed increasingly sophisticated approaches for studying the mind. Some, like the developmental psychologists at the Budapest baby lab, set up ingenious experiments that take us into the minds of babies and the unconscious minds of adults; others, like the neuropsychologists at the UCL imaging lab, devise techniques for seeing how thoughts occur in the brain.

Scientists are still a long way from being able to directly read the actual contents of people's thoughts. Though some tantalizing steps in this direction have recently been taken (Mitchell et al., 2008), the human mind is so complex and the forces acting on it so varied that any theory that tries to predict what a person will think or do based his history and current circumstances will often be wrong. Psychologists are pleased if a theory predicts better than tossing a coin. That is why researchers speak about groups and not individuals. Psychological studies are an average of many individuals' responses. So, when we consider, for example, studies that show that childhood adversity can lead to adult depression, it is important to know that while this is generally true, it is not true for every person. In the chapters ahead, I will discuss research about how innate temperament, security of attachment, trauma, and other experiences can affect an individual's mind. Familiarity with relevant research can help you both in understanding your particular style of reading minds, and in formulating theories of mind that are more likely to be right the first time. However, research can also lead us astray if generic truths cloud our experience of the individual. The goal here is to select the research findings that are useful in increasing the ability to read minds.

To know what a person will do, we need to know what is on her mind, what are her goals and conflicts; how does she understand the world? Freud was at first unsure what to make of the fact that patients reported memories of events that probably never happened, and had no memory of many events that certainly did occur; that some patients were scarred by childhood trauma and others healed with time. He came to realize that each person constructed her mind, moulding the raw material of reality with the tools of her talents and intentions. He called the resulting creation psychic reality. Our understanding another of another person's psychic reality is our theory of his mind.

Reading another person's mind involves striking a balance between what you know about that person with what you experience in direct contact with that person. Knowing a person's family background or psychiatric diagnosis and can lead to mind misreads in the same way that racial or gender stereotypes can. In clinical practice, I do not want to know a patient's diagnosis before I first see him. I want to have as little information as I can. I do not want my experience of him to be filtered though preconceptions. Later, I will want to have that information to compare with my impressions. I will be particularly interested in contradictions between my experience and previous assessments. Is there something that is leading me in wrong directions, or have I got in touch with something about the person's mind that others did not see?

Mr B, for example, was referred by a highly respected colleague, who said his practice was full. Mr B was an ageing accountant seeking help in controlling his anger. He had been warned that he would be fired if he could not control his temper. He was desperate to hold on to his job for one more year until he could retire. But he kept getting into petty fights with his boss, whom he felt overworked and abused him. He had violent fantasies about her. During our first meeting, he talked very little about that, but instead regaled me with stories about his adventures travelling alone to exotic places. He impressed me with his breadth of knowledge of literature and history. I saw him as a lonely, likable eccentric resigned to never finding love or friendship. He felt appreciated and connected, and we ended up working together with some success over a period of two years. After we had met a few times, I called my referring colleague. He confessed that he found Mr B abrasive and contentious and felt put off by his obesity and unkempt appearance. I confessed I had not really noticed his appearance. I also learned that a psychiatrist who had evaluated Mr B had given him the diagnosis of borderline personality disorder and did not feel he was likely to be helped by insight-orientated psychotherapy. (More about the dangers of diagnosis can be found in Chapter Eight.)

The fact that my perception of Mr B was so different from other professionals may seem odd, but it is really not an unusual experience. It is not unusual for someone to have a close friend that her other friends cannot stand. It is not unusual for the same teacher to be loved by some students and hated by others. I have discovered that I often see hurt and loneliness in a patient where others have seen anger or contempt, and there are patients I find difficult that other therapists do not.

Neither my colleague nor I had read Mr B incorrectly; we each saw his mind in relationship to ourselves. For a long time it was hard for me to admit that I could be perceived as arrogant and distant, despite being so told by some close friends. Seeing myself on tape during my training made it hard to deny. Not everyone saw me in that way, however. People who liked Mr B saw someone like themselves—a kindred spirit—who just beneath the surface was reserved and shy. Mr B felt comfortable enough with me to show me a part of his mind he did not usually reveal. If I had known too much about him before we met, I might not have been open to seeing that part of him, or he might have sensed wariness and kept away. It was important in establishing a relationship that I liked him and he felt comfortable, but I knew I had to take my colleague's perception seriously in order to help Mr B deal with the angry and provocative part of his mind. To read minds well you need to be aware not only of your preconceptions and inhibitions, you need to learn what you bring out in others, and when it is helpful to get another point of view. Not only is mind reading a relationship, it is sometimes a relationship in which what you see in another's mind depends on what the other sees in yours.

Notes

1. Humans cannot even construct a computer programme that picks numbers in a truly random way. The programme always reflects something about the mind of the designer.
2. For this discussion, we can ignore the difference between theory and hypothesis.
3. Einstein's would be more accurate, but not in any way that you would notice and the mathematics is much more complicated.
4. Skinner changed his opinion about the brain after he had a stroke, reports Temple Grandin (2004) in the first chapter of *Animals in Translation: Using the Mysteries of Autism to Decode Animal Behavior.*

CHAPTER THREE

What the brain tells us about the mind

Scientists methodically collect data to test the theories of their discipline. Science advances bit by bit. Data that does not support current theory fails to gather much attention at first; academic journals rarely publish studies that do not support a theory. Inevitably, too much data gathers that does not fit existing theories, too much that does not make sense, too much that cannot be explained. Then, in ways that are never predictable, the science shifts so dramatically in theory and methods, explaining what seemed inexplicable, that the previous version now seems odd and old-fashioned.[1]

In my parent's generation, Einstein's re-imagining of space, time, and matter overthrew Newton's "laws of nature", transforming physics and human history. In my lifetime, Watson and Crick's decoding of DNA revolutionized biology and opened the door to forms of reproduction and genetic change that had only been imagined in science fiction. Though the implications of these discoveries were immediately apparent, it took decades to develop their applications. Einstein published his first important papers in 1905, but the first controlled nuclear chain reaction was not achieved until 1942. Watson and Crick's two-page paper appeared in the journal

Nature in 1953, but it was not until 1982 that recombinant DNA produced useful medicine, and not until 1996 that the genetically cloned sheep, Dolly, was born. The full implications of these revolutions are still being imagined.

Some revolutions move more slowly—perhaps especially those that change the way we think about our place in the world. Darwin's first major work was published in 1859 and Freud's in 1895. Their theories were immediately attacked, and attacks continue. Both theories can be viewed as taking humans further from God and closer to nature. This has offended many who hold particular religious convictions, though many other religious individuals have embraced both evolutionary and psychoanalytic perspectives without conflict. Parts of each theory never worked, and both spawned followers who misused their ideas. Yet the central theories of Darwin and Freud are more solidly supported now than ever.

Darwin explained that all traits, psychological as well as physical, evolve in a particular environment. If traits persist, they do so because they have survival value. But environments change, and traits that were once adaptive can become liabilities while other traits that seemed useless become lifesaving. Freud showed us that we are much more than we can consciously know; that our minds are ever evolving dynamic systems constantly integrating personal history and personal experience. Personal history begins with a winning sperm joining a willing egg. Personal experience begins at the same time. Each person's psychic reality, starting in the womb, is unique and ever changing.

A revolution in cognitive neuroscience is now transforming our understanding of the human mind. Bringing together Darwin's theory of the evolution of species with Freud's theory of the development of the mind, the data and theories it has generated would not surprise either theorist. Central to both theories is an appreciation of diversity and change and an understanding of the continuity between culture and nature. Darwin explained that the more genetically diverse a species, the greater the chance that some individuals will adapt to unusual circumstances and help the species survive. Random changes—oddities and mutations rewarded—slowly accrue until a new life-form takes shape: a fish walks; an ape speaks.

"We shall assume that everyone is much more simply human than otherwise",[1] wrote American psychiatrist Harry Stack Sullivan (1953, pp. 32–33), starkly articulating a core premise of Freud's theory. Freud questioned rigid boundaries: boundaries between human nature and animal nature, between moral and immoral, dream and reality, memory and make-believe, man and woman, crazy and sane. There is no thought, fear, or desire that cannot be rehearsed in fantasy. Empathy with anyone is possible and we all can enter the mind of the serial killer and the saint. But much of what we could know is troubling, and we often stop wanting to know. We try not to think about what we fear we might do in different circumstances, in prisons and concentration camps, in famines and wars. When we do not acknowledge what troubles us about ourselves, we narrow the range of our understanding of others and place limits on our capacity for caring and love. Recognizing the malleability of each person's psychic reality was one of Freud's most important contributions. People are much more flexible than they know with respect to whom they can love, whom they can care for, and whom they can hate. Minds are easily swayed, and words alone, whether spoken by politician or prophet, preacher or psychotherapist, can change a person's mind and alter the structure of his brain.

This malleability, though often troubling of conscience, increases the chances of survival. Diversity and malleability are the hallmarks of human adaptation, allowing us to develop an infinite variety of skills and to thrive in an unsurpassed range of environments. In only 60,000 years since we left Africa, modern humans have colonized the planet.

As Einstein's theory shattered the rigid boundaries of energy and matter, showing how either one can be transformed into the other, Darwin and Freud shattered the boundary between mind and matter, thought and biological structure. Joseph LeDoux, director of the multi-university Center for the Neuroscience of Fear and Anxiety, writes,

One of the most important contributions of modern neuroscience has been to show that the nature/nurture debate operates around a false dichotomy: the assumption that biology, on one hand, and lived experience, on the other, affect us in fundamentally different ways. Research has shown that not only do nature and nurture each contribute (in disputable proportions) to who we are, but also that they speak the same language. Both achieve their effects by altering the synaptic organization of the brain. [LeDoux, 1998]

This cognitive neuroscience revolution, the belated brainchild of Darwin and Freud, offers a resolution to the age-old question: "Is it nature or nurture, genetics or environment?" With new technologies, scientists can see for the first time the structures of the brain in action, see what happens when we think and feel; see the brain transform as we grow and change. Innovative new experimental designs have given insight into the minds of babies and our primate kin. We now know that each individual is the product of a unique and ever changing interaction between biology and experience. The particular brain each of us is born with affects our thoughts and approach to understanding the world; our thoughts and experience in turn affect the biological structure of our brain.

More potential connections than atoms in the universe

The newly fertilized egg contains one undifferentiated cell. Before a month has passed, the foetus has an identifiable brain. Over the course of nine months in the womb, new brain cells, neurons, are produced at an average rate of 250,000 a minute; at key points sometimes as many as a half-million a minute. When a baby is born, its brain contains more than 99.9% of the 100 billion neurons it will ever have, yet weighs less than one pound. The adult brain weighs about three pounds. This three-fold weight gain is the result of an increase in the number and efficiency of connections between neurons. These connections are made by axons, long cable-like structures on neurons that branch out and grow. The central structure of a neuron, the cell body, can be measured in thousandths of an inch, but some axons are over three feet long. If all the brain's neurons and their connections were arranged in a line, they would stretch over two million miles.

The newborn's brain is relatively unwired, the neurons relatively unconnected to one another, but their potential for connection is vast. Synapses are tiny gaps between cells; cells come close to one another, but do not actually touch. Cells communicate with each other by releasing neurotransmitters, complex chemicals that travel across the gaps and influence other cells. Over twenty-five different neurotransmitters have been identified, and more are being discovered. Some neurotransmitters cause cells to fire and communicate with other cells; some inhibit communication. Caffeine, alcohol, and other recreational drugs work by affecting synaptic transmission, as do antidepressants and other psychiatric medications. Like alcohol, capable of revving you up in some situations and calming you down in others, certain neurotransmitters can both enhance and inhibit communication between neurons.

About 20% of the brain's connections are inhibitory: one neuron preventing another from sending a signal. LSD and other hallucinogens may work by turning off the inhibitory brain centres that work tirelessly to keep memories in the past, dreams in the night-time, and fantasies from feeling too real. Think about your most vivid dream: did you ever wake up thinking the dream had really happened? Did you ever wonder if you said something to someone yesterday or in last night's dream? Inhibitory neurons help keep us safely moored to reality. Can you imagine if dream imagery continued vividly in the daytime? Or if your muscles were not inhibited during dreaming? In fact, if dreaming is too often interrupted, it may continue in daydreams and turn our attention inward (Fiss, Ellman, & Klein, 1969). If movement is not sufficiently inhibited during dreams, we talk or scream or writhe or walk in our sleep. Over-inhibition of fantasy and emotion may be at the core of some kinds of depression, and antidepressants may work by lessening that inhibition.

Through the growth and branching of its axons, each neuron makes connections to an average of 10,000 other neurons and some connect to more than 100,000 others. There are many more potential connections in the brain than there are atoms in the universe (10 followed by a million zeros *vs.* 10 followed by only seventy-nine zeros). If you were to count one synapse per second, it would take more than thirty-two million years to count them all (Edelman, 1999). Imagine each neuron as a newly purchased computer. It has Internet capability, but to surf the web it has to be connected. To gather information, a computer has to communicate with other computers. There are billions of potential connections. Some offer websites. Some send email. Some send worms and viruses. In order to know what information another computer can provide, your computer must connect to it or to another computer that knows about it. Some websites provide information about other sites, which ones to connect to, which ones to avoid.

Many of the neurons in a baby's brain are not yet plugged into the brain's web of connections. The newborn's neocortex, the part of the brain that will read intention, formulate theories, make judgements and imagine other minds is offline entirely, disconnected from the rest of the brain. The Cognitive Emotional Network, or CEN (Fonagy, Gergely, Jurist, & Target, 2002, who refer to the network as the interpersonal interpretive mechanism and later as the interpersonal interpretive function) is the web of connections that develops between the mind-reading centres of the neocortex and the rest of the brain. Improved social awareness and mind-reading ability correspond to an increase in the capacity and efficiency of the CEN to gather and relay information, just as your access to useful information on the Internet increases with the number and efficiency of connections your computer makes to other computers.

As the baby grows, neural connections are constantly being made and unmade, blocked and unblocked. None of these changes occurs in a vacuum. All are subject to the sway of words and thoughts: the child's own fears and desires, the intentions of adults who educate, and myriad of other intentional and accidental influences. Subtle neural reorganization is continuous; massive reorganization corresponds to recognizable shifts in mental ability, marking what psychologists call new stages in development—for example, thinking in words, thinking about other minds, thinking logically, thinking abstractly.

During two periods, infancy and preadolescence, the brain makes overabundant connections. This surplus provides insurance against brain injury to which both infants and adolescents are vulnerable. The over-connected brain may also be the source of some typical infant and adolescent characteristics—difficulty in maintaining focus and rapidly shifting moods. Pruning—eliminating excessive, sometimes confusing neural connections—is a normal part of childhood and adolescence; when relationships with parents, educators, and peers can have their most profound impact in reshaping an individual's brain and personality. "Use it or lose it" seems to be the rule of neural connection. Children and adolescents experiment with different identities and ways of relating; most are discarded, but the ones that are most practised during these critical periods of development become ingrained in a person's character.

The baby's brain grows rapidly and by one year is half its adult size. The neocortex comes dramatically online between six months and one year, leading to rapid development in sociability and social cognition. Though babies display a social smile in the second month, it is an automatic response to faces, like a dog wagging its tail. At around eight months, babies begin to reserve their smiles for people they know well, while becoming fearful when approached by strangers. Before their first birthday, babies have taken the intentional stance and assume everything happens for a reason. Still the brain continues growing rapidly through adolescence. Neuronal reorganization can continue through old age.

A nerve is a bundle of neurons. If you cut a nerve in a finger, some neurons die and there may be a temporary loss of function or sensation, but new neurons will grow and the nerve will regenerate, restoring what was lost. Textbooks tell you that once a baby is born, no new neurons can be produced in the central nervous system. This "fact" explained why injuries to the brain and spinal cord do not heal as they do in the rest of the body. However, scientists have recently discovered new neurons continue to be created in the adult brain, particularly in the hippocampus, an area related to memory.[3] Some substances—marijuana is one—may increase that production; and some activities—social activities in particular—may not only help keep neurons alive in the elderly but also spur the birth of new ones. The field is new, but it seems likely that scientists will soon develop drugs and techniques to trigger the birth of new neurons in the central nervous system, potentially healing now-untreatable injuries to the spinal cord and brain.

All that is uniquely human

The neocortex, or new brain, is the seat of the cognitive style of knowing. It is where we remember, calculate, reason, and assess.

The neocortex is the seat of humankind's most glorious achievements—Newton's apple would have fallen to the ground unnoticed had not the neocortex seen it and transformed the fall into the laws of gravity. The neocortex is also what a detective uses to "read" the next move of a criminal by looking at the evidence, and a marketing executive to determine the reaction of a competitor by looking at the data.

The neocortex covers the mammalian brain in six folded layers of densely packed neurons, making it much larger and more complex than the brains of other animals. As a result, mammals are far more varied and flexible than other creatures. As every pet owner knows, furry animals, even gerbils, have personalities. Fish and reptiles seem one-dimensional by comparison. Birds are another story. Evolved for flight, bird brains are light, and have a different organization altogether. In terms of social organization and flexibility, they are probably more like mammals than reptiles.

In any case, the neocortex has proved so useful that it has increased in size by 125 times since mammals first appeared about 265 million years ago. Brain cells consume huge amounts of energy, and mammals with large brains must be resourceful hunters and gatherers. Animals that eat readily obtainable low-calorie vegetation tend to have smaller brains and longer intestines, hence the maxim small brain, big gut (think cows). Among land mammals, primates have by far the biggest brains in relation to their bodies. The enlargement is primarily in the neocortex, which makes up more than 80% of the human brain.

Large, complex brains take longer to develop, and big heads pass through the birth canal with difficulty. In consequence, more advanced primates, and especially humans, are born with brains that continue to grow and develop long after birth. These immature brains are especially flexible and susceptible to the influence of culture and education, and this exposure further increases the diversity and adaptability of the species.

Not only is the primate neocortex larger than that of other mammals, a outcropping of densely packed neurons has evolved on its front end, the prefrontal cortex, also called the frontal lobes. Since the first humans appeared about two million years ago, the prefrontal cortex has grown by over 50%. This rapid growth forced change in the shape of the human skull, pushing the sharply slanted forehead of our forbears into its modern vertical shape about 200,000 years ago. Our brain is still growing as we evolve. Some day we may have bulging foreheads like the alien intellects of science fiction.

Morality, motivation, and social connection

For a long time scientists could not determine the role of the prefrontal cortex. Unlike other parts of the neocortex, the prefrontal cortex is not directly connected to perception or movement. Damage to the visual cortex, a stroke for example, will impair vision. A stroke in the right parietal lobe or motor cortex will cause weakness or paralysis on the left side. What happens in the frontal lobes was not so clear until the mid-nineteenth century, when Phineas Gage, the twenty-five-year-old foreman of a Vermont railway construction crew, had a horrible accident. On 13 September, 1848, Gage was using an iron rod to compress an explosive charge deep inside rock, as he had done hundreds of times before, when he got distracted and made a careless error. The charge exploded prematurely, and the thirteen-pound iron rod, 3 feet 7 inches long tapering to 1¼ inches in diameter at one end, shot up like a bullet and entered Gage's face under his left cheek bone, exited through the top front of his head, and landed more than twenty-five feet behind him. Remarkably, Gage never lost consciousness and returned to work in a few months. However, as his friends reported, "Gage was no longer Gage."

Before the accident, his employer called Gage the company's best employee-conscientious, hardworking, liked by all. After the accident, while his memory and intelligence seemed unaffected, Gage became an unmotivated, irresponsible liar, hatching dubious schemes that he never followed through with. A previously proper citizen, he swore ceaselessly and had no respect for social convention. His doctor reported that he had lost "the equilibrium or balance, so to speak, between his intellectual faculty and animal propensities". Almost 150 years later, Dr Hanna Damasio and her associates used modern neuroimaging techniques to study Gage's skull, which had been honoured with a resting place at the Harvard Medical School. They concluded that the steel rod shot right through the middle of Gage's frontal lobes, leaving the rest of his brain entirely intact.

Gage's unfortunate accident showed that the prefrontal cortex was central to social functioning. Yet it was hard for scientists of the time to accept that a chunk of brain could control such lofty human functions—motivation, judgement, morality. As we saw in the guilty burglar experiment discussed in the first chapter, neuroscientists have discovered that the centre of our mind-reading abilities lies deep in the frontal lobes. Many now believe that all that is uniquely human—including language itself—evolved from the primary function of the neocortex: social connection.

All primates are social animals, but some have more complex societies than others. Robin Dunbar, an evolutionary anthropologist at University College London, discovered that the larger the neocortex, the larger and more complex the social network (Kudo & Dunbar, 2001). In other primates, grooming holds relationships together. Chimps spend about 15% of their time grooming the fifty or so other chimps in their social network. Based on the size of our neocortex, Dunbar (1993) theorized that the "natural" human group size is about 150; and 150 turns out to be a significant number in many ways. The average size of hunter–gatherer and primitive farming clans and villages was 148.4. The Hutterites, a separatist communal Christian sect, limit each colony to 150 members in the belief that that is the largest group that can be controlled by peer pressure alone; they have no need for a police force. Around 150 men is the basic military unit of all armies from Roman times to today, for much the same reason. Yet with a 150-member social group, if humans spent as much time grooming one another as chimps do, we would spend 42% of our time grooming; there would not be much time left for work and other activities.

Language and theory of mind

Dunbar and others believe that language developed as a way of maintaining contact in larger groups. In fact, about 62% of our conversations are devoted to gossip and other personal matters, but talking takes less time than grooming and we can talk to more than one person at a time. Along these lines, Noam Chomsky, along with two Harvard psychologists, recently made a startling proposal: language did not evolve from primitive forms of communication; in fact, language and communication are basically different (Hauser,

Chomsky, & Tecumseh Fitch, 2002). Even animals with tiny brains, such as insects, can communicate complex information. One bee can tell another bee where to find open blossoms. But animal communication is inflexible; its "sentences" are fixed and do not change from time to time or place to place.

Human language is infinitely flexible; there is no limit to the number of sentences that can be constructed. In some ways, sentences are like theories: you can try one out and if doesn't work—if it doesn't say what you want it to say—you can discard it and try another. It seems that language and theory making evolved together in order to help our ancestors cope with their increasingly large and complex social world. It is interesting to ponder that though we now use language to communicate, we can no longer communicate in the pure and precise manner of the bee. Words have many meanings and all sentences can be misunderstood. We are stuck with the paradox that language allows for both communication and miscommunication; theory of mind allows for both understanding and deceit.

The neocortex has become enormously effective at processing language but, perhaps because of the shear volume of information, much of the processing occurs outside of awareness. In a recent study (McLaughlin, Osterhout, & Kim, 2004), researchers at the University of Washington asked first semester French students to decide whether words were real French words or made-up nonsense words. After an average fourteen hours of French class, most students said they had no idea of which were which, and their conscious choices were little better than chance. In fact, the students had learnt a lot more than they thought they did. Brain wave measurements showed the cortex clearly knew which words were real and which were not. Lee Osterhout, one of the principle researchers, said,

> At first, I thought this was an impossible result. It seemed incredible that the brain could do this with such facility while the subjects could not do it consciously. When students were asked how they thought they performed on the task, many of them laughed and said that they were just guessing. [Schwarz, 2004]

After only fourteen hours, the students had learned profoundly important rules about the structure of French. But they didn't know what they knew. In this case there was no adaptive advantage for the students to be consciously aware of what they had learnt. They did not know enough French to make use of it in social interaction. If they continued studying to the point where their knowledge was useful, they would become aware of what they knew.

In the way that software directs the flow of information in a computer but does not alter the hardware, neuroscientists used to believe that learning produced functional but not structural changes in the brain. With new brain imaging technology, science has now conclusively demonstrated that experience changes the structure of the brain. For example, as a new language is learnt, grey matter in the inferior parietal region of the neocortex grows thicker with new connections (Mechelli et al., 2004). As athletic performance improves, the insulating myelin covering around the repeatedly exercised neurons grows thicker, improving their efficiency (Coyle, 2007).

Language and theory enabled humans to develop technologies of communication that allowed social networks to grow ever larger—drums, smoke signals, writing, the printing press, telegraph, telephone, radio, television, the Internet. Today many feel overwhelmed by information. Humans generally try to communicate by the most efficient means available, abandoning old technologies for newer ones in the process. The content of their communications does not change drastically but its quantity explodes. Whatever the medium, some will try to use it to convince, cajole, sell, and manipulate; others to extend their social network of shared interests and identities; and still others to tell stories and entertain. In the same way that bigger highways draw more cars that can trigger longer traffic jams, more efficient communication technologies draw more information that can snare and overwhelm its users. The human brain continues to grow larger and more complex (*Science Daily*, 2005), perhaps in response to the stress of coping with overwhelming information and constant social stimulation.

Fear is primal

The amygdala, a small almond shaped structure at the base of the brain, scares us because fear drives us from danger. From an evolutionary perspective, this is one of the most important functions of the brain. An organism that avoids danger gains an enormous adaptive advantage. An animal can be haphazard in its search for food or sex and still survive. An animal that does not avoid danger soon perishes. You can skip dinner or miss an opportunity to procreate and still have many more opportunities to eat and pass on your genes, but if you get eaten, it's over. The amygdala is ancient and ubiquitous. From the first fish to humans, all animals with spines have an amygdala. While people like Gage with damage to the frontal lobes cannot navigate social relationships, they still take care not to expose themselves or others to danger. People with amygdala damage are oblivious to danger and chronically risk injuring themselves and others (Bechara, Damasio, Damasio, & Lee, 1999).

Surfing near Bodega Bay in Northern California, Megan Halavais felt uneasy:

> The water was really glassy, really calm. You could see straight to the bottom . . . I felt, this is really sharky . . . It was just kind of an eerie feeling. Not just looking at the bottom and seeing shadows and freaking myself out, but the water felt shifty . . . Sometimes you just get a feeling like there's something in the water. I usually ignore it, because you don't want to freak yourself out, but this time I guess I was right. [Composite of three interviews: Doyle, 2005; Marcus, 2005, Dudas, 2005]

Megan is alive today because she sensed danger and prepared to fight. She never consciously saw the sixteen-foot great white coming, but when it grabbed her leg, she climbed on top of it and fought it off. Megan is alive because her amygdala, one of the most primitive parts of the brain, felt something and put her body on alert well before her thinking brain knew what was happening. Megan wasn't even aware that the shark had bitten her leg down to the bone until she was paddling back to shore.

With its vast array of connections, the neocortex can perform great feats of judgement, communication, intellect, and imagination, but disconnected from the amygdala, it is crippled. The amygdala sends raw feelings to the neocortex where they are assessed, integrated, regulated, and transformed into the language of emotion. Without the input of the amygdala, the mind would be a shadowy wasteland where love and hate, life and death mean nothing.

The amygdala is so important, so central to survival, that there are two paths of communication from the organs of perception—the eyes, the ears, and sensations from the body—to the amygdala.[4] One is the cortical, thoughtful high road; the other is the quick, thought-free, low road. The low road is twice as fast as the high road, twelve milliseconds faster in responding to a sound. It can mean the difference between life and death, eating and being eaten. In that twelve-thousandths of a second, while the amygdala is assessing how to emotionally categorize the sound and waiting for the cortex to deliver its thoughts, the amygdala puts the body on alert. In humans and most other animals that means orientating toward the sound with muscles tense, heart racing, breathing shallow, pupils dilated, prepared to flee or fight. This state of preparation is called freezing in fear, and freezing for a fraction of a second is an adaptive response. It keeps you from doing anything stupid and allows your cortex to assess the situation while remaining in a state of tense readiness. Freezing for a longer period might be adaptive if you are being stalked by a predator. But freezing for an extended period usually signifies helplessness, not having the information to know how to act or the resources to act effectively. For young animals, helpless freezing may be their best bet, keeping them in the same place, awaiting possible rescue. In adults, extended freezing is the last ditch response—most often seen in those suffering unrelenting, inescapable fear, in times of war and great disasters.

Reactions to some stimuli seem built-in. Rats are naturally frightened by the smell of cats. Humans appear to be naturally frightened of snakes and spiders. Imagine walking in the woods and unexpectedly hearing a faint rustling. If, when you freeze and turn, you see a snake or a snake-like stick, you will jump back even before the cortex has had its say. If it's a rabbit or a toad, you may relax and laugh. If it turns out to be a snake, in a few more milliseconds your cortex and your amygdala will collaborate though the CEN to determine the best course of action. Do you kill it or run? Your memory may be engaged to help determine if it is a poisonous snake. If it turns out to be a stick, your cortex will signal your amygdala, and you will sigh in relief and wipe the sweat from your brow.

In any case, it will take some time for your heart rate to slow, your muscles to relax, your breathing to deepen.

Emotions, by their nature, are slower to change than thoughts. *It's a snake! No, it's a stick* happens very fast. The feeling of apprehension and tension remain for minutes or even longer. The same is true of positive emotions. A good laugh can get you through much of the day. That's partly because certain neurotransmitters continue to circulate in the bloodstream and affect the body for some time after the amygdala stops triggering their release; and partly because the brain is constructed to give dominance to emotions—neural pathways from the amygdala to the cortex are much wider than pathways from the cortex to the amygdala.

The key to emotional knowing

The amygdala offers an important path to reading minds—emotional knowing. Through the amygdala we can sense and remember things emotionally without being aware of it. Experimenters flashed pictures of angry, threatening, or unfamiliar faces on a screen so quickly that the subjects had no conscious awareness of them. They simply did not "see" them. Yet brain scans showed the amygdala was activated and the subject's emotional reactions—increased heat rate, sweating—demonstrated that the faces were perceived unconsciously. These too-quick-to-notice dangerous faces were processed via the quick, thought-free, low road, but not the cortical, thoughtful, high road. The experimental subjects became anxious without knowing why. People can similarly become sexually aroused or soothingly calmed without consciously knowing what produced the emotions.

These direct-to-amygdala perceptions form the basis of many of those hard-to-describe funny and uncanny feelings; feeling someone is staring at you behind your back, feeling inexplicable discomfort or comfort, *déjà vu*, liking or disliking someone for no apparent reason, love at first sight. Some direct-to-amygdala perceptions are never processed consciously, yet, along with the emotions they triggered, are stored as unconscious memories. Evoked by a sensation, a sound, a smell, a bodily posture that is associated with the original perception, they are again processed by the amygdala bringing back old emotions without our knowing why.

Though small, the human amygdala is complex. While its role in anticipating danger is primary, it is involved in all emotional processing. The amygdala attaches emotion to perception. Whatever you see, hear, and touch is given its emotional charge by the amygdala, and it is the seat of emotional knowing. When something or someone feels just right or wrong; when some sixth sense tells us to avoid a person, to turn left instead of right, to reject a business proposition, to be wary or frightened; when we know by hunch and instinct and gut reaction, we know through the amygdala. Emotional knowledge originated as a survival mechanism. For prehistoric humans, the ability to react instantly—to freeze, fight or flee—constituted an important adaptive advantage, and that remains true today. When you hear a strange sound in the middle of the night, you call the police not because of the sound, a meaningless noise, but because the amygdala, sensing danger, produces a spike of fear. Emotional knowledge also gives us a sense of what others feel without them having to tell us. Sometimes the amygdala goes overboard and senses danger everywhere.

Connecting cognition and emotion

The neocortex and the amygdala are in constant communication with each other through the Cognitive Emotional Network (CEN). The amygdala gives thoughts emotional significance; the neocortex determines if the amygdala's reaction to events make sense. As we just saw in the example of the snake-like stick, emotional responses have priority. It is better to jump from the stick in fear and then find you are mistaken than to fearlessly approach the "stick" and be bitten by a snake. It is not just fear—the amygdala is constantly reacting emotionally to perceptions before the neocortex has its say; often the neocortex doesn't even get to make a judgment because so many of the amygdalae's perceptions occur outside of conscious awareness. That's one reason emotions often seem to occur for no reason—an angry glance, a seductive wink, or a momentary frown can get a response from your amygdala that changes your mood, and you may never know why.

You can take situations like this as opportunities to practise reading minds. Let's say you suddenly feel anxiety without any apparent cause. If you are with someone when it happens, you might wonder if his emotional state triggered yours. Do you see any signs that he might be angry or upset? If you know the person, you could ask him if anything is wrong. If he says yes, and asks how you know, you can decide whether or not to tell him you have read his mind.

The CEN connects the amygdala and mind-reading centre of the neocortex (the medial prefrontal cortex) not only to one another, but to numerous other structures in the brain as well. The hippocampus and mirror neurons are two worth remembering. The hippocampus is a storehouse of memories. When the amygdala sees something threatening—the snake-like object for example—it signals the hippocampus to search for similar images to send to the neocortex for evaluation. The hippocampus stores memories indefinitely. In situations of extreme danger, it can become over-stimulated by the amygdala and pour forth memories so quickly that your life seems to flash before your eyes.

Mirror neurons, since their discovery fewer than twenty years ago, have been the subject of great excitement and much debate in the neuroscientific world (Rizzolatti, Fadiga, Gallese, & Fogassi, 1996). Mirror neurons fire in the same pattern both when someone is performing an action and watching the same action; so if you watch someone wave goodbye or wave goodbye yourself, the same mirror neurons light up. Emotional states are mirrored as well—watching someone in ecstasy or being in ecstasy for example—activate the same pattern. Mirror neurons seem to be involved in many diverse and important processes such as learning by watching—mirror neurons may be why athletes love to watch their sport; vicarious pleasure—mirror neurons may be why pornography is so addictive; empathy—mirror neurons may allow us to feel what others feel by watching their expressions and body language. To experience empathy in this way, however, requires close and careful observation. It is something helping professionals can do, as can people in intimate relationships, but it may be awkward to attempt in less personal relationships.

Each individual's CEN is uniquely organized based on her particular temperament, experience, and interests, just as each person's computer is uniquely organized. Both are systems for storing, linking, separating, and retrieving information. In the CEN, there are neural pathways that connect particular memories to particular emotions, to particular thoughts and perceptions; other pathways inhibit and prevent connections. Pathways grow stronger with each use and weaker when forgotten. This growing, changing web of interconnections reflects your every emotional connection to your every thought and perception and gives rise to what Freud called "das Ich", the I—your sense of self in relationship with the world.

Since the brain is organized to give priority to emotions—the amygdala reacts faster than the neocortex can think and is sensitive to information that the neocortex cannot even see—it is reasonable to wonder why we are not all emotional knowers. Though there are no studies, I have no doubt more people tilt towards emotion than cognition. Yet cognitive knowers are far from rare and some people know almost nothing about emotion. The answer to this puzzle lies in the capacity of the neocortex to inhibit, to send out neurotransmitters that dampen the experience of emotion or block it altogether. Some of these inhibitions are selective and consciously chosen. For example, people who study snakes or jump out of aeroplanes can learn to block their fear.

In some people, emotional experience is inhibited, attenuated in varying degrees, sometimes cut off completely. Paradoxically, these are often individuals born with extraordinary emotional sensitivity. As infants they are so sensitive that they are easily overwhelmed an—unless the environment is just right—easily disorganized by their own emotions. To children with such temperaments, the neocortex can be their saviour. It can inhibit their emotional reactions and offer an alternative approach to understanding the social world.

Temperament

Some people are born placid, seek excitement, and charge ahead into life fearlessly. Others are born hyper-reactive, seek comfortable familiarity, and explore tentatively, fearful of being hurt or overwhelmed. Temperament, this quality of reactivity, can be predicted in the third trimester of pregnancy (Werner et al., 2007) and is readily apparent by the time a child is four months old. Not all babies respond to a noisy jack-in-the-box with glee. Some look terror-struck, burst into tears, and need to be soothed; some are mildly apprehensive and wary; and some bubble with excitement and joyful laughter and clap for an encore.

Frightened babies are called high-reactive or inhibited; bold babies are called low-reactive or uninhibited. High-reactive babies have an oversensitive amygdala. They are inhibited and shy. By age two, ten to twenty per cent of children are painfully shy. Low-reactive babies tend to become outgoing and uninhibited two-year-olds. Shy children usually become shy adults; and outgoing children tend to become outgoing adults.

In the womb, high-reactive foetuses are stressed by their mother's stress; low-reactive foetuses are not affected. Chronic maternal stress makes children more susceptible to future traumas. Repeated trauma increases amygdala sensitivity and makes the sufferer more fearful each time as well as more vulnerable to future trauma.

In an MRI study (Schwartz, Wright, Shin, Kagan, & Rauch, 2004), Harvard psychologist Jerome Kagan, the developer of modern temperament theory, and his associates compared adults who had been either inhibited or uninhibited as infants. Twenty-two young adults were shown pictures of familiar and unfamiliar faces. The thirteen who were inhibited as infants showed greater amygdala activity. However, only two of the thirteen had social phobia. The other eleven, though biologically prone to be fearful, had figured out a way to manage it, in the process building neural pathways that enabled the cortex to tell the amygdala to keep its feelings to itself.

Inhibited, shy children can be taught to explore the social world and become more outgoing. Research shows that parents of these shy children gently encourage them to meet new people and try new things. Aware of their children's sensitivities, they use mild discipline and are not overly critical, but they do not allow them to withdraw. Reactive, sensitive children can spend time alone day-dreaming and playing, often developing a rich imagination. By engaging in fantasy play with these children, parents, caretakers, and teachers can help turn daydreams into artistic and other creative pursuits. Success in these endeavours makes it easier to interact with others around shared interests.

High reactive and extremely shy

Brain imaging studies show that shy children, children with anxiety disorders (De Bellis et al., 2000) and children with autism have enlarged amygdalae (*ibid.*); the more severe the autism the greater the enlargement.[5] Scientists consider autism to be a spectrum disorder. In spectrum disorders there is no single defining symptom. Instead, there is a broad range of symptoms that vary from mild to severe; and mild forms of those symptoms can also be found in the normal population. Bipolar disorder and Foetal Alcohol Syndrome are other examples of spectrum disorders. People on the autistic spectrum range from low-functioning individuals who cannot live on their own to high-functioning individuals who can do well in life but appear odd and lack social skills. People with Asperger's Syndrome are on the high-functioning end of the spectrum and tend to be more social, but still odd. The most common autistic spectrum disorder symptoms are extreme shyness, social awkwardness, and an inability to read other people. These symptoms in milder forms are among the most common problems found in normal individuals as well.

The current theory of autism says that autistic people do not have a theory of mind, so they cannot take another persons perspective, or see that other people's minds are different from their own. This inability to have a theory of mind is felt to be the result of damage to some part of the CEN; many researchers think the mirror neurons are damaged. The problem with this theory is that it is wrong. Even in the first experiment that claimed to show that autistic people did not have a theory of mind, several autistic children did pass the theory of mind test, and several of the normal kids did not (Baron-Cohen, Leslie, & Frith, 1985). There may be more than one kind of autism, but I think that some people with autism have such extremely reactive temperaments that they are easily overwhelmed by stimulation, especially social stimulation.

These people with autism are not neurologically damaged; they are extremely shy. This idea is not new. Frances Tustin, a brilliant psychotherapist who helped many autistic children, had a similar view, as does Anni Bergman (Mahler, Pine, & Bergman, 1975), who filmed the therapy of one of her patients who started as an unapproachable autistic five-year-old who did not make eye contact or speak and is now a successful artist and mother of three. I think one of the reasons some of us see autistic persons as shy rather than brain damaged is that we have worked with them in psychotherapy for many years and have seen them get better. We have had an opportunity to know them well. Researchers see them briefly under stressful conditions. A theory of autism is, after all, a theory of mind, and as we have discussed before, what you see in someone's mind is different in different relationships. I will be spending some time discussing people with autism because they provide good illustrations of the relationship between temperament and style of knowing.

In normal development, the amygdala grows by about fifty per cent through adolescence until adulthood. In autism, the amygdala starts out larger and reaches adult size before adolescence.[6] Yet the frontal lobes are developing normally, which means much more slowly than the rest of the brain. In general, infants are especially vulnerable to trauma because their frontal lobes do not come online for about eight months, leaving them with no capacity to cognitively process their experience. Imagine now being a baby who is extraordinarily sensitive to stimulation; every new sight, sound, smell, taste comes like the shock of turning a corner and seeing a snake. Repeated trauma further sensitizes the amygdala, making the world progressively more frightening. You haven't yet learnt to crawl, so all you can do is close your eyes or turn away. If it gets to be too much you shut down, space out. Your caretakers sometimes try to get your attention by cooing, laughing, tickling, jiggling. The only thing that doesn't threaten to overwhelm you with its newness is your actions on your own body. The only thing you can count on to be soothingly the same is what you can do to yourself—moving, sucking your thumb, waving your fingers in front of your eyes.

A shy theory of mind

One way to think of autistic people is as extremely shy, on the most extremely inhibited end of the temperament continuum. This extreme shyness, starting so early in infancy, builds on itself. If you are scared of people, you don't interact with them; if you don't interact with them, you don't get to know them; and if you don't get to know them, you never get comfortable with them. Your theory of mind will reflect that discomfort. Many autistic people view normal folk—neurotypicals is their word—as odd creatures, irrationally dominated by their need for human contact. It is not unlike the experience of very shy people at work who rarely leave their cubicles, or shy college students who rarely leave their rooms. Popular sociable people, even if envied, are often seen as shallow, manipulative, irrationally driven by their need for friendship and approval.

The theories of outsiders who cannot cope with the normal social world, such as shy eccentrics and those on the autistic spectrum, are often interesting, perhaps limited, but not completely wrong. Increasingly, autists and aspes, as they sometimes refer to themselves, are challenging the idea that they have a psychiatric disorder and are in need of cure. Justin, a tenth-grader, is reported to have said, "People don't suffer from Asperger's. They suffer because they're depressed from being left out and beat up all the time" (Harmon, 2004). The webmaster of the humorous website of the fictitious Institute for the Study of the Neurologically Typical[7] offers observation about normality:

> Neurotypical syndrome is a neurobiological disorder characterized by preoccupation with social concerns, delusions of superiority, and obsession with conformity. Neurotypical individuals often assume that their experience of the world is either the only one, or the only correct one. NTs find it difficult to be alone. NTs are often intolerant of seemingly minor differences in others. When in groups NTs are socially and behaviorally rigid, and frequently insist upon the performance of dysfunctional, destructive, and even impossible rituals as a way of maintaining group identity. NTs find it difficult to communicate directly, and have a much higher incidence of lying as compared to persons on the autistic spectrum.
>
> NT is believed to be genetic in origin. Autopsies have shown the brain of the neurotypical is typically smaller than that of an autistic individual and may have overdeveloped areas related to social behavior . . . Tragically, as many as 9625 out of every 10,000 individuals may be neurotypical . . . There is no known cure.

Since some people on the autistic spectrum lack any sense of humour, the author goes on to explain to any of those who may be in his audience that he is joking. Clearly, he in some way understands that others think differently than he does, demonstrating that some autistic people have a nuanced theory of mind. Many individuals on the autistic spectrum are so frightened of social interactions that they never learn about other minds. Yet some, like this comic webmaster, and others, like the popular author Professor Temple Grandin, have been able to use their cognitive abilities to quell their fears, understand other minds, and cope with life.

A wide spectrum

Autism is on the rise and has been described as an epidemic. The chance of a child being diagnosed with an autistic disorder is nearly thirty times greater today than it was twenty years ago. Some researchers estimate that autism, Asperger's Syndrome, and other related disorders, what is known as the *autistic spectrum,* affect one per cent of the population, three million in the United States alone (The National Autistic Society, London, 2007). People on the autistic spectrum are deficient in three areas: social interaction, communication, and imagination.

A severe impairment of social connection is one of the defining features of autism. Looking someone in the eye or gazing at someone's face is emotionally powerful. Eye contact increases heart rate and respiration rates and often causes sweating and blushing. Normal mothers and babies gaze at each other for long periods, but when it becomes too intense, babies avert their gaze or shut their eyes. New lovers luxuriate in each other's gaze, but as the relationship wears on, mutual gaze declines. Staring at a stranger or looking directly in his eyes can be a sign of dominance and is often experienced as aggressive, but when two strangers look each other in the eye while shaking hands, it can be an acknowledgement of friendship and mutual respect. In most ancient cultures, making eye contact with the king was forbidden, and approach to authority had to be made with the head bowed. Looking at the face of the Old Testament god brought swift death; gazing at Jesus' face brought eternal love and grace.

The parent of an autistic child often first feels something is wrong when the child does not respond to her facial expression and does not look into her eyes, but instead looks away, averting her gaze. Autistic children avoid looking at faces. They also show impairment in what psychologists call "joint attention". Joint attention is using eye contact and pointing to share experiences with others. Recent research has looked at birthday party home videos and found that some children later diagnosed as autistic were already showing difficulties in looking at people and sharing experiences by their first birthday, the rest by their second. Some children look perfectly normal, even better than normal, at their first birthday, only to lose their social skills by their second birthday.

A specialized part of the brain, the fusiform face area, responds to faces but not to other objects. Neuroscientists initially concluded that this area was inactive in autistic people, that their brains processed faces as if they were inanimate objects. Recent, more detailed studies have shown that they can process faces normally, but only if the faces are of a very familiar family member (Pierce, Haist, Sedaghat, & Courchesne, 2004). This is evidence that people with autism are interested in people if they are comfortable with them; they find strangers frightening and feel overwhelmed by them—what looks like indifference to strangers is really fear and withdrawal, something like freezing.

People with Asperger's are different. They, too, find contact overwhelming. As one young Asperger patient reflected, "Really looking someone in the eye is the scariest thing in the world." But, unlike people with autism, those with Asperger's don't give up on people entirely. Many express a desire for a friend, someone they imagine will be a soul mate, but that wish is often undermined by social ineptitude and odd behaviour that can lead to cruel rejection. A young man with Asperger's wrote,

> I cannot make friends and need friends badly. When you have friends you get more support and you can ask a lot of things from them and they'll help because they're your friends . . . because I don't have friends it means that I'm cut off from help . . . I don't know how to socialize. [Attwood, 2007, p. 77]

Unless they have had years of intensive psychotherapy, even high functioning autists may express no desire for human relationships. Temple Grandin, a professor of Animal Science at Colorado State and bestselling author of books about her own experience as an autistic person, wrote, "Teasing hurts, the kids would tease me, so I'd get mad and smack 'em. That simple" (Grandin & Johnson,

2005, p. 2). She says that even as adult, personal relationships are something she just doesn't really understand. The thought of sex, one body touching another, deeply disturbs her, but she designed a folding mattress to sleep in because it soothes her to feel held.

Autistic children speak late, and many never speak at all. Those who do learn to speak, speak oddly—in a monotone with strange pitch, or very rapidly; they may use words in peculiar ways and repeat the same phrases interminably, or echo back exactly what has been said to them. About 70% of autistic children are also mentally retarded, making remediation all the more difficult and an independent life impossible. Others have normal or even genius IQs and some—high functioning autistics—are able to live full independent lives. Asperger's children show normal or even advanced language development, but their speech tends to be odd—often repetitive, pedantic, or stilted.

People on the spectrum are limited in how they play and their imagination and their focus is narrow. They can spend hours staring at one object or repeat the same action, or they can display an intense interest in amassing a collection of things such as coins or stamps, an activity that doesn't seem all that unusual except for its all-consuming nature. Even on the high-functioning end, people with autism and Asperger's tend to be most interested in things outside of human relationships, such as computers, science, or maths.

High-functioning adults with autism can be extreme cognitive knowers. In his book *Born on a Blue Day*, Daniel Tammet writes beautifully about how he has become progressively better at navigating the social world.

> I could see more clearly than ever before how my "difference" affected my day-to-day life, especially my interaction with other people. I had eventually come to understand that friendship was a delicate, gradual process that mustn't be rushed or seized upon, but allowed and encouraged to take its course over time. I pictured it as a butterfly, simultaneously beautiful and fragile, that, once afloat, belonged to the air and any attempt to grab at it would only destroy it. I recalled how in the past at school I had lost potential friendships because, lacking social instinct, I had tried too hard and made completely the wrong impression . . . I also now had a database of widely varied experiences that I could reference in all manner of future situations. [Tammet, 2007, pp. 142–143]

Tammet is also a maths savant.

About ten per cent of those with autism and Asperger's have an exceptional ability that stands in sharp contrast to their general functioning. In most cases, these skills only seem remarkable in comparison to the person's general disability—for example, a severely autistic person who cannot dress himself or speak but can play the piano or draw. Much rarer are the *savants*, those with talents that would be extraordinary for anyone. Savants are talented in music (perfect pitch and the ability to play a complex tune after hearing it once), calendar calling (the ability to name the day of the week for any date, past or future), maths (lightning-fast calculations), and art (accurate drawing or sculpting, often from memory). While amazing memory is common among savants, a few remember nearly everything they have ever heard, seen, or read.

From the carnival sideshows of the past to the Discovery channels of today, savants draw a crowd. Audiences are awestruck seeing a fellow human multiply 37 x 37 x 37 x 37 in less than a minute, recite pi to 22,514 decimal places, instantly tell you the day of the week of your first birthday, or draw the likeness of a horse after one glance. In fact, these are simple tasks requiring remarkably little computing power. Tiny computer programmes, downloaded free, and run on ancient computers, can provide pi, to a million decimal places, or call any date. A two-dollar calculator will compute 37^4 as fast as you can press the keys; and a ten-dollar digital camera will picture any horse in an instant.

But humans did not evolve with computers or calculators, digital cameras, or voice recorders; all are products of the twentieth century. It was not that long ago that all music was played, all songs were sung, all stories were told; and the only record was memory. Someone had to remember when to plant and harvest, when migrating birds would leave and return, how long it took to walk to the sea. I suspect that most wandering minstrels and hermit prophets were extremely shy; the seer, the crone, the woodsman, the wizard, the wise man perhaps preferred living alone, away from others. And maybe there used to be a place in the community for some emotionally distant odd folk who could provide an eccentric point of view.

The autistic spectrum is very wide and getting wider. It seems that anyone with a single-minded focus and eccentric appearance is suspect; some have placed Albert Einstein and Bill Gates on the high functioning end. But although Einstein was absorbed in his work above all else, he took a great interest in people, corresponding with Freud in elegant prose about the tragedy of the human condition. And we have seen that Gates is an astute judge of others, understands his customers, has intense long-standing friendships, and can adjust his nerdiness to fit the situation. Both seem to exemplify flexibility and balance: the ability to shift between the intense focus of the autistic undisturbed by the need for human contact and unconcerned with what other think; and the capacity for concern and understanding and deep and lasting human connection.

A good part of the autistic spectrum, it seems to me, represents the wonder of human diversity and not disease. Shall we place the prophet and the psychotic on the schizophrenic spectrum because they both hear the voice of god? The cold-blooded criminal and the heroic fireman on the psychopathic spectrum because they are both fearless in the face of danger? The child molester and the teacher on the offender spectrum because they both like the company of children. To give a diagnosis to all seems both a grand oversimplification and an implicit demand for conformity. Would we prefer a world in which John the Baptist was treated for his schizophrenia; Martin Luther for his oppositional–defiant disorder; Lincoln for his depression; Martin Luther King for his anxiety disorder; Einstein for his Asperger's?

Part of what draws us to the autistic experience is uncomprehending awe, perhaps tinged with a bit of envy, of a person who has no interest in other people. Most of the time our minds are filled with thoughts of other people: how to get closer, how to get further away, how to be loved, how to love, how to keep from being hurt, guilt about hurting. But who does not just want to be left alone when it feels that people are too much to bear; and who at some time does not also feel the dread of being left totally alone, unable to connect at all?

Low reactive and outgoing

Over twenty per cent of babies have notably low-reactive temperaments. They are not frightened by novelty, but rather enjoy new experiences and intensity. They tend to go on to become uninhibited, sociable children and adults, often with a sense of adventure. We know much less about the development of uninhibited babies than inhibited ones. They are the prototypical easy babies—friendly, laid-back, outgoing, fun, and responsive. Low-reactive children rarely cause much difficulty, so they are rarely seen by psychotherapists.

It is thought that a few of them go on to become delinquent adolescents and antisocial adults. That makes sense: uninhibited children do not scare easily. Their less reactive amygdala makes loud shiny toys, snakes, and roller coasters less scary; makes driving too fast, experimenting with drugs, and threats of punishment less scary as well. Unafraid, some become adventurers—mountain climbers, test pilots, and astronauts—and rescuers—firemen and ambulance Emergency Medical Technicians. There isn't much that low-reactive outgoing people cannot do—except perhaps tolerate boredom.

Because situations that are exciting to most people can seem dull to them, so some low-reactive people seek excitement in activities most people consider dangerous. My patient Jim, a therapist himself, dressed in conservative suits and seemed to his colleagues to be calm, even mild-mannered. Jim had grown up in a rough neighbourhood. He was bright, liked school, so was often picked on. Jim was athletic and decided to learn to fight, leaving the neighbourhood to get martial arts instruction. In time, Jim gained the respect of his neighbourhood. Now, as an adult, every once in a while, Jim sneaked off to a working-class bar and found himself in a fight. Sometimes he picked it, and sometimes he stepped in to protect the underdog. He always ended up on top. Jim said to me, "The trick is to stay calm when everyone else is blind with fear or rage. Then it's really easy." He described how he could look at an attacker's face and know when he was about to throw a punch; read his body language and know the direction of the punch, what part of his body would then be exposed; and how he, Jim, could then easily step aside and launch a devastating counterattack while noting the look of shocked surprise on his opponent's face and on the faces in the gathered crowd. Jim sounded like Clint Eastwood in *The Unforgiven*.

Jim worked successfully with the most difficult cases, patients other therapists refused to treat or had given up on: "incurable" schizophrenics; angry, impulsive patients who threatened their former therapists; depressed and frightened patients who had been abused by their former therapists. Jim remained calm in his office, as he did in the bar, observing, predicting, but here not countering, instead offering whatever words he felt in whatever tone he felt would be most soothing and helpful in furthering his patient's growth and self-understanding.

Jim is an emotional knower. A low reactive, uninhibited, highly sociable person, he is capable of feeling what others feel, without being flooded by their emotions. He is also, by the way, highly intelligent, a thoughtful scholar in the field of psychiatry. But he told me he would often say to his students, "Don't let thinking about research and theory get in the way of being with your patients."

Jim is brilliant and can call on his cognitive abilities, but low reactive emotional knowers do not need to cognitively understand relationships in order to feel deeply connected. The world-famous neurologist and author Oliver Sacks (1998) beautifully describes the direct unfettered emotional knowing of severely retarded people. Rebecca, a child-like nineteen-year-old didn't have the intelligence to "find her way around the block" (p. 178) or "open a door with a key" (p. 178). But Rebecca "was capable of warm, deep, even passionate attachments" (p. 178). When her grandmother died, she told Sacks, "I'm crying for me, not for her . . . She's gone to her Long Home . . . I'm so cold. It's not cold outside, it's winter inside. Cold as death . . . She was a part of me. Part of me died with her" (p. 182). Rebecca loved the theatre and Sachs observed that when she performed, "she became a complete person, poised, fluent, with style, in each role" (p. 185). Rebecca never felt frightened or overwhelmed by human contact and could connect deeply to Sacks.

Most people are somewhere in the middle

Since a responsive environment can enable a genetically high-reactive inhibited baby to grow into an outgoing and adventurous child, there is no simple psychological test for temperament in adulthood. The only precise measure of inborn temperament in adulthood is an MRI assessment of amygdala activity in response to novel *vs.* familiar faces. For now, that is not a practical procedure. It is important to remember that most people—over sixty per cent—

fall in a midrange and are not notably affected by their temperament. If you are temperamentally extreme, you probably know it by now. If you like meeting new people and travelling to exotic places, seek thrills and high adventure; if you like doing things that scare most people like rock climbing or sky diving; if you take risks in gambling or investment without feeling anxious, you are most likely low-reactive. If you are more of a stay-at-home type and prefer the company of old friends; if you are not particularly interested in travelling to new places and trying new things; if you invest conservatively and do not gamble or take risks; if you prefer a pleasant walk to a high-speed roller coaster ride, you are most likely high-reactive. If you really cannot tell what you are because neither profile fits, you probably fall in the middle.

All manner of mind reading

A theory of mind, knowing that other people are motivated by intentions and beliefs that are not the same as your own, is an important achievement that is accomplished by different people in different ways. Each one of us has laboured in childhood to construct an understanding of those who were important to us, to formulate theories of mind, which we then use as templates to read other minds. Each particular approach is influenced by several factors: our temperament or sensitivity, the availability and sensitivity of our caretakers, the stresses and traumas of early life, and our cognitive capacities to make sense of it all.

By the time we reach adulthood, each of us has developed a characteristic style of knowing the social world. Each style can be placed along a line running between the cognitive and the emotional. While some people achieve balance, most tilt moderately in one direction or the other. Emotional knowers tilt towards making judgements based on their feelings; cognitive knowers tilt towards using their intellect to read others. For some people, as we have seen in this chapter, the tilt can be extreme.

Notes

1.   This, too, is a theory (see Kuhn, 1996).

2. This is probably a rephrasing of the Greek philosopher Terentius, "Homo sum: humani nil a me alienum puto". I am a human being, so nothing human is alien to me.

3. In the late 1960s, neurogenesis was discovered in the olfactory bulb, which houses the neurons responsible for processing the sense of smell. Later, researchers found that the hippocampus also replaced its neurons. The hippocampus receives partially processed sensory input from the sensory systems of the PNS and processes it into tiny morsels digestible by the memory storage areas of the cerebral cortex. Neurons in the olfactory bulb were replaced almost monthly. In the hippocampus, brain cells were lost and restored at a much slower rate. Over the course of a lifetime, all of the neurons in our hippocampus are replaced 2–3 times.

4. Smell works somewhat differently.

5. The hippocampus is also enlarged in autistic children Similar data have been demonstrated for London taxi-cab drivers who must memorize the complex roadway system of the city (Maguire et al., 2000, 2003). If the larger size of the autistic hippocampal formation was evidence of use-dependent enlargement, one might expect enhanced spatial or episodic memory function in autism.

6. Unlike other neuropsychiatric disorders, such as schizophrenia, in which research seems to indicate damage or insufficient development in particular brain regions, in autism and other and fear-based disorders a part of the brain is larger than in normal people.

7. Institute for the Study of the Neurologically Typical (1998–2002), http://isnt.autistics.org/index.html.

CHAPTER FOUR

Trauma: how events shape the brain and the mind

On the morning of September 11, 2001, I dropped my twelve-year-old son Peter at the Hudson River Middle School, four blocks north of the World Trade Center. We have lived in lower Manhattan for almost forty years. Across West Street from our home, a path extends along the Hudson where during quiet times you can feel the old river town. Cruise ships, boats, and barges pass; car repair shops, former factories, and bars line the waterfront. Southwest in New York harbour, a stout green statue—once a lighthouse—holds a torch aloft.

Less than a half-hour walk to the North is Chelsea and midtown; to the south, Soho, Chinatown, Tribeca, and Wall Street. Over low tenements and townhouses, the spire of the Empire State building comes into view. The Twin Towers were once visible from every direction, so omnipresent they faded into the background of clouds and sky. We shopped in their basement malls and every year or so found reason to celebrate at Windows on the World on the 107th floor of the North Tower. As I write this, I am looking above my desk at a photograph of my wife and me kissing there in front of the Windows on our thirtieth anniversary—summer 2001.

On most days, Peter rollerbladed to school along the river and I walked to work, but that day I took the car to carry my golf clubs to the driving range that extends out on one of the old Chelsea piers and dropped Peter off on the way. About ten of us, stealing time on the way to work, were practising, when someone shouted that a plane had hit the Trade Center. Stepping only a few feet forward on to the pier we could see smoke rising from a small hole high on a tower. There were murmurings about private planes and careless pilots, and we resumed hitting golf balls. Then the second plane hit, and the world shattered, sirens and horns blared, street clogged with police cars, ambulances, and fire engines. I jumped in my car, dodged through traffic on side streets, and drove on sidewalks as far as I could. Abandoning the car, I ran to my wife in her office who, like many, still did not know.

The two of us ran down toward the towers through crowds of people—many crying, some covered with soot and ash—running the other way. We didn't stop to ask questions. I did not think about what I saw. Only later, in memory, did I see the terror on their faces. I did not think about anything but finding our son. Later, my wife told me that at some point along the way she looked up and saw no towers. Horror-struck, she said nothing. About halfway down, a lucky call got through the clogged system: Peter was safe at a friend's house nearby. We met him there. The friend's mother had gone to the school, gathered up the kids who wanted to leave with her, and taken them to her home. On their way, the first tower collapsed and they ran from the rolling cloud of dust and debris. Peter feared the Third World War had begun. He wondered if we were alive, if he was all alone. Only years later did he tell us that he had seen bodies falling from the towers through the windows of his school.

Warplanes flew overhead and the sound of sirens was constant. Lower Manhattan was soon under military occupation, cut off from the rest of the world. Only residents and those with an approved purpose could enter. Relatives and friends of the missing walked the streets, posting photographs and messages in faint hope of getting news. For months, fading images hung on lampposts and buildings, smiling young faces now memorials to the dead.

On September 12, Peter and a friend started collecting supplies from drugstores and groceries to deliver to rescuers at the site. My wife and I offered assistance to the shocked and grieving. In the weeks that followed, we lived in the smoke and smell of disaster. My mother's parents, seven of her brothers and sisters, and many other close relatives, had been cremated in Nazi ovens as had most of my wife's family. The smells and the ash on our windowsills made that history live again in our minds. We debated whether to walk twenty minutes south to visit the funeral pyre. Would it make things worse? How could it? When is reality more frightening than fantasy?

About a week after 9/11 we walked down along the river reflecting grey clouds in a dark sky. We turned east on Chambers Street in front of Peter's school, then south on Washington Street and found a place among other mourners standing silent before six stories of smouldering embers and molten steel. From high on tall cranes, fairground spotlights lit lacy remnants of the towers white against darkness. Great machines with hooked buckets dumped debris into waiting trucks. Grime-streaked firemen with lances gently probed for personal effects and human remains.

Every day I remember. How could I not? I walk the same streets by the river, hear sirens, see aeroplanes and no towers. To not remember would be like looking at a picture of my father and not remembering his life and death and who he is to me. Freud wrote, "The shadow of the object falls on the ego", meaning what you lose becomes part of who you are. The events of 9/11 shaped my mind. I was deeply affected, but apparently not traumatized; although that's something I will never know for certain, because trauma sometimes leaves hidden wounds that only later—due to ageing or illness or other stresses—are revealed. The same is true for my wife and son. Unlike so many others we did not suffer injury or loss of a loved one. But we saw horror, feared for our lives, and lived for weeks with the smell of death. Some who experienced less are still injured now, while others who suffered much more have gone on with their lives, as did we.

It stays with you forever

From the vigilante ex-Marine in *Taxi Driver* (Scorsese, 1976) to the repressed former prisoner-of-war high school principal in *The*

Simpsons, the psychologically wounded Vietnam veteran has become a staple of popular entertainment. Whether comic or tragic, all seem frozen in time: they are never fully in the present, never far from the war, and the wrong word or image can trigger flashbacks—a vivid reliving of their horrors. In a similar vein, the abused child is depicted as permanently scarred and incapable of escape from her past. Post traumatic stress disorder (PTSD)—only first gaining medical recognition in 1980—is now one of the most commonly diagnosed forms of psychiatric disorder. While it is clear that tragic events affect the way we understand the world, it is also clear that some are affected much more deeply than others; and that some recover while others do not.

In medicine, trauma is defined as a wound resulting from excessive force applied to the body—bleeding tissue, torn skin, broken bones. Freud took the term from medicine and applied it to the mind: a mental wound due to excessive force applied to the mind—unremitting fear, shock, panic, horror. Trauma is inevitable. No one escapes injury. Children commonly experience trauma when they are hospitalized for injures or illness or when their parents die, leave, divorce, become ill or depressed, or are chronically self-absorbed. Many children are traumatized by abuse and neglect. Children and adults suffer the trauma of accidents, crime, war, and disaster.

Both the body and mind are built to handle trauma. If they were not, we would all be crippled or dead. Most wounds heal well, leaving only an imperceptible scar. Some leave nasty scars; some permanently maim; and sometimes small scars, mental and physical, cause suffering far greater than one might expect. Even minor trauma poorly tended, like an infected wound, can cause permanent damage and pain.

Running exuberantly, a child falls hard. Hurt and humiliated, he sobs uncontrollably. The parent can have different responses: the parent cares for the child, soothing him tenderly; the parent distractedly cares for the child; the parent shouts, "Keep crying and I'll give you something to cry about"; the parent strikes the child. Each response will have a different effect on the healing process. Properly treated, a wound heals and the injured acquires faith in others and security in himself. Badly treated, a wound festers, leaving the injured frightened and vulnerable.

It is impossible to know how well a psychological wound has healed. A Holocaust survivor whom I interviewed had done exceedingly well in his new life after the war. He was happy with his family and successful in his business. But, though he loved baseball, he only watched it on TV. The idea of standing in a line at Shea Stadium to see his beloved Mets terrified him; it brought back the memories of being at Auschwitz and standing in line to learn if he would live or die. Near the end of his life, he became incapacitated, and that, too, brought back all the horror of being trapped and waiting in fear of death. Sadly, the happiness of his most recent fifty years faded in his mind.

Wounds usually heal but do not make you stronger. Stress can make you stronger. Stress is a response to anything that upsets balance or equilibrium. The natural reaction to stress is an attempt to restore equilibrium. Stress is part of daily life and being completely without stress, as when meditating or in a state of flow, is the exception rather than the rule. Intense and prolonged stress taxes the system and, if unrelieved, produces trauma. Minor chronic stressors, tasks that never go quite smoothly, like a long commute or getting your child off to school, are usually resolved without lasting effect, unless you are near your breaking point. If you figure out some way to make those tasks less stressful—a way to relax during your commute, a game to motivate your child—something will be gained and you will less susceptible to other stressors.

Stress can be good or bad. Good exercise stresses the body, causing muscle and bone to increase in strength and flexibility and neuronal connections to become faster and more efficient. As a result, activities that had been stressful are no longer stressful, and a new and less vulnerable state of equilibrium is established. But if it is done incorrectly, exercise can injure the body, debilitate, and weaken. Athletes are aware of the line between pushing hard and pushing too hard. In some sports, injuries are expected, and time to recover is part of the game. A pitcher needs three or four days between starts to rest his arm because it has suffered trauma— muscles and tendons have been bruised and torn and need time to heal. A boxer may take months to heal after a fight. If insufficient time is given, trauma accrues, scars form, and injuries become irreversible and debilitating. Yet at some point in every healing process, the injured part must be stressed again in order to grow stronger.

The mind needs to be stressed to grow. Study stresses the mind, for some more than others. But study can be pleasurable—stress and enjoyment are not opposites and can go hand in hand. Some people love to exercise; some love to study. A good teacher or coach tries to find ways to make study and practice fun. If something is fun, it does not feel like stress, even though the body and mind are being pushed to adapt and grow. Enjoying a stressful activity may even help protect against trauma by increasing the release of endorphins, which, in addition to blocking pain, also reduce inflammation and prevent injury. Some people push themselves to test their limits and ride the thin line between stress and trauma. In the athletic arena competitive runners, for example, may find that they have suffered tears and fractures without knowing it. In the psychological arena, dedicated helping professionals—social workers who work with difficult clients in understaffed clinics for example—may find themselves sleeping poorly, overeating or drinking, without realizing that they are suffering from work-related trauma or "burnout".

Stress, like fear, is managed by the amygdala. Both stress and fear are warning signals of danger: fear is a red light signalling *stop, danger*; stress is like a yellow light signalling *caution, danger may lie ahead*. In response to stress and danger, the amygdala signals the adrenal glands to release numerous hormones, including adrenalin and cortisol, into the bloodstream. Adrenalin increases heart rate and blood pressure. Cortisol, sometimes referred to as the stress hormone, clearly demonstrates that you can have too much of a good thing. Cortisol is a powerful steroid, reducing inflammation and preventing muscle damage; it inhibits insulin, thereby increasing energy-producing glucose (a sugar); it pumps up the immune system to fight infection in the event of injury; and upon entering the brain it becomes a neurotransmitter, heightening attention by stimulating the amygdala and enhancing memory by stimulating the hippocampus. But cortisol is toxic, and too much of it for too long causes the neurons it stimulates to tire and eventually literally burn out and cease to function. Muscles begin to ache and eventually weaken; insulin suppression may lead to diabetes; a weakened immune system opens the door to infection; attention falters and memory fades. In this way, prolonged and intense stress becomes traumatic to body and mind.

What is stressful for one person may not be for another. Coming upon a spider is not stressful to an arachnologist, nor is height to a mountain climber. Even the most common and natural-seeming fears can be transformed into pleasures by the human mind. One person's best response to a yellow light is slowing down and another's is stepping on the accelerator. Even at the most basic level, cognition—the work of the cortex—influences the individual's response to stress and trauma and shapes their ultimate impact (Figure 1).

Inhibiting the fear response can be can be an important aid in reading other minds. As you may recall from the first chapter, the medial prefrontal cortex is a mind-reading centre. Recent research

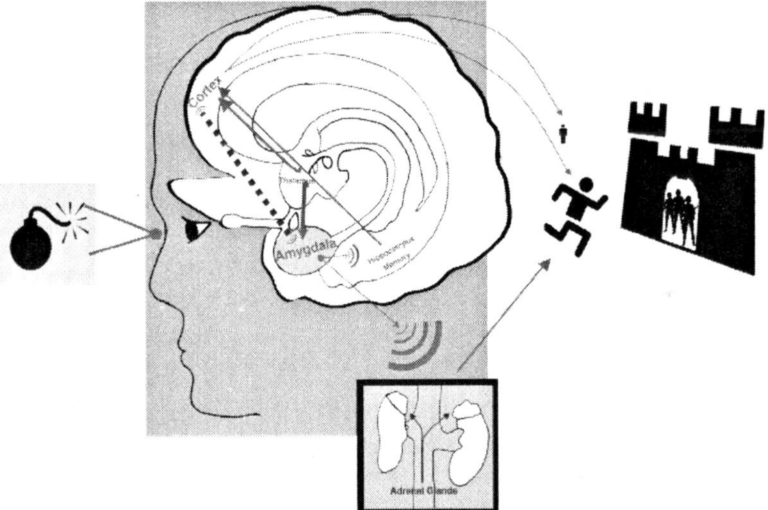

Figure 1. How we respond to potentially traumatic situations. Danger is perceived. The thalamus sends the signal to the cortex and the amygdala. The path to the amygdala is shorter and thicker and the signal gets there first. The amygdala signals the adrenal glands above the kidneys to put the body in a state of alert arousal. It also signals the hippocampus to call forth relevant memories and the cortex to think hard about what to do. The cortex then decides whether to signal the amygdala to calm down or to continue on alert. It also decides what the body should do—in this case, run! By this time, the person is consciously involved in the process. The people in the castle on the right represent the safety of community. How that community responds to the fearful runner will determine in part whether or not the frightening event becomes a trauma. (Figure art by Jules August.)

has shown that people with more of a specific receptor (5-HT$_2$A) in this region are less afraid of both angry and fearful faces (Fisher et al., 2009). The ability to not react instinctively with fear to others who are angry or afraid can be extremely helpful. It allows a more reasoned assessment of a situation and engagement with frightened or angry others when appropriate. Having more of these fear-inhibiting receptors is partly genetic but is largely a product of learning. Experienced psychotherapists, for example, have learnt when not to be afraid of someone who scares most people away. Perhaps the more we think about and understand other minds the less afraid of them we become. Psychoanalysts might call this identification.

Don't hit the dog

Some important discoveries are made by accident. Alexander Fleming noticed that bacteria didn't grow in some mouldy Petri dishes. Instead of throwing out the dishes, he examined the green mould; it turned out to be penicillin, the first antibiotic. Smallpox vaccine, insulin, LSD, the PAP smear, America, X-rays, Thorazine, Velcro, and Viagra are but a few of the discoveries made by someone looking for something else. Isaac Asimov reportedly said, "The most exciting words a scientist can say is not 'Eureka' but 'that's funny.'" Most scientists look closely at data that is relevant to testing their theory. Great scientists pay attention to everything.

In the 1890s Ivan Pavlov, a Russian physiologist, was measuring dog spit when he accidentally discovered something that was there for all to see. Pavlov was studying the digestive system, especially how it flexibly adapts to the particular food being eaten; how, for example, much more saliva was produced when dry bread rather than meat was fed to a dog. He noticed that his dogs got excited and began to salivate when they heard his footsteps, well before any food was near their mouths. All dog owners know this and use the association between food and sounds to teach dogs all manner of things, but in the previous 15,000 years or more of dog–human relations, no one had thought to develop a theory to explain it. Pavlov spent his next thirty-plus years experimenting and theorizing about learning by association and, though he received the 1904 Nobel Prize in medicine for his work on digestion, his great legacy

is his theory of learning, now called classical or Pavlovian conditioning.

Pavlovian conditioning provides a way of understanding the
impact of trauma. Pavlov showed that if you ring a bell[1] and then
give a dog a treat, after a few repetitions the dog will salivate at the
sound of the bell. You know how your dog gets excited when you
walk towards where the dog food is stored. You know how easily
dogs learn associations. You also probably know how difficult it is
to unlearn a response once it is established. If your dog barks when
the doorbell rings, it's nearly impossible to get Buster to stop.

Painful associations are learned much more quickly than pleasurable associations and are even more difficult to unlearn. Pavlov
rang a bell and then shocked the dog. Often in just one pairing, the
dog cowered frozen in fear at the sound of the bell. A previously
meaningless sound becomes terrifying. If you have ever known a
dog that has been abused, you know that when you raise your hand
to pet it, the dog will flinch or may even try to bite you. Dogs will
continue to flinch their entire lives, no matter how much good care
they receive. Humans, like their canine companions, condition to
painful events quickly and with great tenacity.

Pavlov also studied the process of unlearning, breaking the
connection between a natural response—salivating in expectation
of food, cowering in fear of shock—and the learnt or conditioned
stimulus—the bell. He claimed that if you keep ringing the bell and
never again feed or shock the dog, the connection would be
unlearned. He called the process extinction, a very unfortunate use
of the word. Extinction implies that the connection is unlearned,
fades away, disappears, becomes extinct. It doesn't happen that
way. It may look as if the connections disappear, but they never do.
Positive connections may fade but painful connections stay powerful forever. Pavlov knew it. He saw dogs stop responding to the
sound of the bell with fear for a few hours only to become fearful
again later that day; and not only were they afraid of the bell, they
became fearful of other sounds as well. Today we would say the
dogs were traumatized. Pavlov noted what happened but he did
not have a theory to explain it, and it dogged him to near the end
of his life. Finally, in 1927, he wrote that extinction was not a fading
away, it was an inhibition. Something new was learnt in order to
suppress something old.

Unfortunately, as is often the case, subtleties got lost in translation. Generations of psychologists, following John Watson, the first American behaviourist, acted as if extinction was a simple process of fading away. Even today, many behaviour therapists fail to appreciate the complexity of the mind and are baffled when phobias return and war veterans remain traumatized years away from the battlefield. Despite what is written in the psychology textbooks, Pavlov was not a behaviourist. He struggled to understand the interactions between the body, the brain, heredity, and the environment. He viewed the individual as "a highly complex system consisting of an almost infinite series of parts connected both with one another and, as a total complex . . . with the surrounding world, with which it is in a state of equilibrium" (Pavlov, 1904).

From an evolutionary perspective, it makes sense that painful, frightening associations should never go away. If there is something frightening out there in the environment, who is to say when you might not stumble upon it again? If something hurt you in the past, who is to say it will not hurt you in the future? In dangerous circumstances, it is adaptive to become sensitized to potential danger. But if the environment changes to a safer one, the previously adaptive response continues to persist even though it is no longer needed. This is a good example of how adaptation and psychological well-being can be at odds.

The central premise of evolutionary theory can be summarized in one sentence: *A characteristic (phenotype) that increases the chance of survival is more likely to be reproduced.* Learning to avoid a dangerous situation through a single experience is an adaptational bonanza. In a dangerous environment, the more fearful/careful an individual, the more likely he will live to reproduce; and the brain is wired to make us more fearful with each fright. However, if the environment becomes less dangerous, there is little reproductive advantage to becoming less fearful. Better safe than sorry seems to be the evolutionary mantra.

That is why painful punishment has such lasting effect and is a terrible tool for teaching except in a very few instances. Neuroscience shows that individuals differ constitutionally in their sensitivity to trauma, but no one is immune; even the most biologically laid-back, non-reactive among us can be made highly vulnerable by repeated trauma; and the biologically sensitive can be made less vulnerable by successfully coping with tolerable stress. Painful punishment has a reverberating traumatic impact, making the individual more frightened in general and more sensitive to subsequent trauma. Pavlov's dogs became frightened not only of the bell but also of the other sounds, the cage, and Pavlov. One bad experience, one trauma, changed the dogs' view of the world; all perceptions were now filtered through fear.

Though punishment induces fear, it is not effective at stopping pleasurable behaviour. Think about a male dog who is indiscreet and indiscriminate in his sexual behaviour—he attempts to mount other dogs, your neighbour's leg, and a number of other things without regard to gender, species, or receptivity. Severely punishing that behaviour will not get the dog to stop. Rather, he will continue in a frightened and furtive manner, always on the lookout for a potential punisher. Similarly, people who have been punished for their childhood masturbation and sexual exploration do not stop their sexual behaviour; they become furtive and guilty. Punishment may even spur on excessive and premature sexual behaviour. The same is true for eating. When a person lives in fear of being prevented from getting something to eat she particularly desires, she may try to get it whenever she can. If punishment, threat, and danger stopped people from eating and procreating, humans would have been extinct aeons ago.

From a neurocognitive evolutionary perspective, punishment as a teaching tool has only one adaptive use: teaching the organism to avoid danger. If a child is about to walk into traffic or on to a minefield, frightening the child creates a mini-trauma, putting him on guard for the future. Even then, it is important that the punishment is keyed to the child's temperament and delivered so that the child associates fear with the situation and not with the teacher. Naturally, in times and places where danger abounds, punishment is more frequent and people live more fearful lives. But since each trauma is more sensitizing, fear may become constant and eventually too much to bear.

Inescapable intense stimulation eventually leads to emotional shut down and passivity in all animals. Dissociation, shutting down emotionally, and feeling cut off from the world are now recognized as common responses to trauma. Pavlov saw tremendous variability in how soon the shut-down point is reached and assumed basic genetic differences, but decades of research have failed to confirm any one single cause—genetic or psychological—that makes one person easily overwhelmed and another imperturbable; temperament, security of attachment, and childhood stresses and traumas all play a role.

Like many human traits, from height to intelligence, sensitivity probably falls on a bell-curve, with more than two-thirds of us being normal enough to get by in the usual range of environments. Genetics and environment both shape sensitivity. The technical term is phenotypic plasticity. Take two identical pine nuts, plant one in a fertile meadow and it will grow a hundred feet tall shaped like a Christmas tree; plant the other on a windy mountaintop and it will grow short and gnarled like a bonsai. Take identical twins with high-reactive inhibited temperaments, one grows up in a chaotic disconnected family and becomes a shy socially awkward cognitive knower; the other grows up in a calm related family and becomes a socially confident balanced knower.

Hug the monkey

Though only humans have language and theory, many other mammals live in communities and depend on social cognition for survival. Pack animals, like wolves for example, signal each other about prey and danger. Only our primate cousins, however, have prolonged mother–child relationships and family structures similar to our own. Next to humans, rhesus monkeys are the most populous and widespread primates on the planet. Like humans, they are remarkably adaptive, eating almost anything and living comfortably in parched deserts, temperate and tropical forests, and cold mountain climes. Our biological kin, they share about 94% of our DNA. Like humans, rhesus monkeys live in complex multi-layered societies. They are noisy and playful, and have intense and sometimes difficult relationships. When in distress they can become withdrawn and abusive, and readily turn to drugs or alcohol for solace when it is offered. These human-like traits have made them a favourite subject for psychological research.

Stephen Suomi, Chief of the Laboratory of Comparative Ethology at the National Institutes of Health, studies rhesus monkey psychology. He is particularly interested in psychological repair: what allows some individuals to overcome adversity? A few years ago, I visited Dr Suomi's lab in Bethesda, Maryland. As I neared my destination, a high prison-like chain link fence appeared on my left. No buildings were visible and I imagined some secret government agency within. Then I saw monkeys: monkeys sitting, running, playing, and swinging incongruously from maple trees. This was Suomi's lab, rhesus monkeys living freely on five acres of prime suburban real estate.

Suomi was a student of Harry Harlow at the University of Wisconsin in the early 1970s. Harlow set out to study love. Rhesus monkeys were his subjects. Some of his conclusions, then controversial, are now taken for granted: the nature of the earliest attachment relationship influences not only future relationships but our relationship with ourselves and the world; touch is the most important way of establishing a secure relationship; abuse distorts bonding, but in some ways makes it stronger; peer relationships can be profoundly healing. Some of his conclusions remain controversial: males can rear infants as competently as females;[2] even the most severe wounds resulting from early abuse and neglect can—with determination—be healed.

Harlow is most famous for his experiments showing the importance of soothing touch. Newborn monkeys were placed with two artificial mothers, crude mother monkey dolls. One was wrapped in wire mesh; the other was wrapped in soft terrycloth. The wire mum had a functioning milk-producing nipple; the cloth mum did not. The baby monkeys clung to the wire mum only as long as necessary to drink their normal fill of milk. They spent far more time—all their time when not feeding or exploring—clinging to, climbing on, and hugging the cloth mum. If frightened while exploring, the babies ran to the cloth mum for comfort. Love is built on touch, not food. The baby monkeys related to their cloth mums as if they were real monkey mothers; they became fiercely attached to them and got upset if anything about them changed.

Abusing baby monkeys

Less well known today are Harlow's experiments in abuse and trauma. (Though at the time, student outrage at Harlow's methods helped start the animal rights movement.) In the same way that Jonas Salk infected rhesus monkeys with polio in order to find a cure, Harlow hoped to traumatize his monkeys into depression and then find a cure. In one particularly diabolical experiment, blasts of cold air or blunted spikes would unpredictably burst from the mum doll, hurling the clinging baby across the cage. As soon as possible, the babies scampered back to their crazy mothers—iron maidens, Harlow called them—and clung harder and longer, rarely leaving to explore their world. Babies not only attached to their abusive mothers, they attached more desperately.

Harlow became obsessed with figuring out ways to inflict more and different types of damage. Babies were taken from their mothers repeatedly and for increasing lengths of time; babies were raised in isolation; some were raised by playmates; others were not allowed playmates. To varying degrees, all of these poor tormented monkeys developed psychological symptoms, symptoms that that Harlow thought looked like the symptoms of human depression: hand wringing, self-clasping, crying, looks of despair. They had little interest in play or exploration; most were socially inept, masturbated frequently, and had no interest in intercourse; some were unpredictably aggressive.

Unlike humans, however, most could recover something approaching a normal social life if they were given the opportunity to spend time with other monkeys. However terribly traumatized, they never lost the possibility of connection. In order to study the effect of trauma on mothering, uninterested females were forced to mate by being strapped to what Harlow called his "rape rack". Even these devil-doll raised, sadistically-raped monkeys could not completely turn away from their baby's pleas; mothering was therapeutic and even those who were initially abusive became better mothers with each subsequent child (Harlow, Harlow, Dodsworth, & Arling, 1966). Harlow and his students were completely surprised. Finding connection for the first time in their lives, some of these mothers became more playfully engaged with their infants than normal wild monkeys. The healing effect of mothering extended to other aspects of their lives; they became more socially appropriate and sexually active.

Here's where Stephan Suomi comes in. Suomi was Harlow's graduate student in the late 1960s when Harlow devised the pit. Its technical name in scientific papers was "vertical chamber apparatus", though everyone in the lab called it the pit, dungeon, or well. It was a tall, V-shaped, metal container with barely enough room at the bottom to move about. The sloping walls made climbing impossible. Isolation was not total; the sounds of monkeys and people in the lab could be heard and fleeting images could be glimpsed above. It was like being imprisoned in a deep well in the middle of the town square.

Suomi's doctoral thesis and first papers reported the results (McKinney, Suomi, & Harlow, 1971): the pit produced greater and more consistent damage more quickly than ever before. Even hardy normal monkeys emerged in fear and despair; and when combined with other torments the damage seemed permanent, not subject to natural social healing. Yet the monkeys did not detach. Listless and frightened, they still tried to connect, but they behaved so oddly that they were shunned.

Searching for a cure

The pit of despair experiments seemed to traumatize the experimenters. It was as if they finally realized how detached they had been; initially investigators, they had unwittingly become torturers unable to accept that their monkey subjects could not reveal the secrets of human depression. One student took a hammer to the hated apparatus. Suomi's work took a new direction; he determined to find a way to cure the damaged monkeys. The monkeys were not hopeless but they were socially inept, and when introduced into normal monkey society, they were attacked and ended up huddling in a corner in much the same way a shy, awkward child entering a new school gets picked on and ends up sitting alone. Monkey troops are socially complex, highly competitive organizations, and the newcomer who does not know the rules either withdraws or gets killed.

Building on his observation of the baby healing the mother, Suomi raised "therapist monkeys" designed for the task. They were raised by cloth dolls and spent time with playmates that had been similarly raised. They were younger than the patient monkeys and had not yet developed competitive aggression (McKinney, Suomi, & Harlow, 1972). When therapist monkeys were introduced to traumatized patients, who typically sat immobile, huddled in a corner, they immediately approached and hugged. At first unresponsive, within two weeks the patients started hugging back. The therapists then initiated play. Slowly the patients responded. Within two months, the doll-raised, pit-traumatized monkeys were well. They could not be distinguished from normal monkeys.

Many human therapists feel they, too, have been designed for the task. I often ask students in my social work classes how many of them have a depressed parent, and a sea of arms rise in the air. Having some success in engaging and enlivening a troubled parent, especially when other family members only seem to provoke or withdraw, is often formative for future therapists. Years ago, I directed a therapeutic community for schizophrenic patients at the New Haven Veterans Administration Hospital. Many of us were young and enthusiastic, true believers in psychological healing, working in a world not yet dominated by biological psychiatry and medication. Some of the older psychiatrists used to joke that inexperienced therapists were much better with these difficult patients because we didn't yet realize that cure was impossible.

When I met Stephen Suomi, it was more than three decades after his work with Harlow. He no longer keeps monkeys in cages. He observes them both in his Maryland lab, where they live unencumbered but from time to time become his experimental subjects, and also in the Cayo Santiago sanctuary, a thirty-eight acre island just off the coast of Puerto Rico. There, several thousand monkeys live without fear of predators or hunger. Suomi studies gene–environment interaction, but his goal is still cure. If we can understand what makes the same gene express itself differently, harmfully in one case and helpfully in another, it may be possible to intervene to prevent the harm.

Suomi explained that Rhesus monkeys live in socially complex communities of between twenty to two hundred monkeys. Each troop consists of a number of female-led multi-generational families. Females stay with their troop for life. Upon reaching puberty, males leave their troop, join free ranging gangs, and have to compete to gain membership to another troop. Competition is fierce and about half the males do not survive adolescence. "It's a rough world out there for adolescent monkeys," he said.

There is tremendous variation in how males establish themselves in new troops. Some try to fight their way in. They pick the dominant monkeys and challenge them to fight. If they are successful, they are in great shape, entering the new troop with high status. But it is a risky strategy and many do not make it. Others take a more conservative strategy, befriending the lower ranking members of the troop to gain admittance, and then slowly trying to work their way up in the troop's hierarchy. For the conservative monkeys, eventual status is determined more by social competence, the ability to make alliances, than by physical strength. This strategy has its own disadvantages. In lean times, low ranking males are the last to get food, and in inclement weather the last to get shelter. There is no one best strategy. The aggressive strategy is perhaps best in difficult times and the conservative strategy best in good times.

Rhesus monkeys have distinctive personalities, ranging from sociable to shy, and from meek to extremely aggressive. About twenty per cent of them are unusually fearful and shy. They could be described as anxious or inhibited, but in informal discussion Suomi—perhaps betraying 1960s nostalgia—calls them "uptight monkeys", and normal monkeys are "laid back". In new playroom situations, with toys, swings, and ladders, laid-back monkeys have a great time and "explore like crazy". Uptight monkeys might not play at all. They sit alone or sometimes hang on to a friend. An uptight monkey in a playroom looks like a shy adolescent at a dance, "sitting on the outside looking in".

This comparison was a rare slip for Suomi. In his professional writing he, unlike Harlow, does not make connections between monkeys and people. We live in a different political climate, he explained. You have to be careful not to imply that people are anything like monkeys; and the idea that you could identify troubled children very early and do something about it disturbs a lot of people. You have to stay away from controversy if you do not want to risk losing funding. He noted that he was a federal employee, and the monkeys were living on government land. So he left it to me to draw comparisons.

Suomi's uptight monkeys look a lot like Kagan's high-reactive, inhibited children; and the similarities begin early. Uptight monkeys have difficulty separating from their mothers, are difficult to soothe, explore less, and have trouble making friends. Like inhibition in children, the uptight trait is inherited; and scientists have identified the specific gene in the rhesus monkey that that causes uptight behaviour. The gene makes the monkeys more fearful of novelty. Except in familiar situations, uptight monkeys have higher than average cortisol levels and are in a constant state of stress. If they are left in the new playroom for hours or brought back day after day, they will eventually calm down and look normal; but even a small change will stress them out again. If the stress is too pervasive, as in times of famine or drought, when moving is frequent or competition between troops is intense, high cortisol levels will stunt growth, suppress the immune system, and leave the uptight baby monkeys vulnerable to illness and early death.

Uptight monkeys are heavy drinkers. Though there are reports of wild monkeys eating fermented fruit to get high, alcohol is generally not available. However, when Suomi and his associates held a monkey "happy hour", providing sweet drinks with and without alcohol, most monkeys drank enough of the 14-proof cocktail on the first day to be mildly impaired—above the legal limit for driving. On subsequent days, the drinking of normal laid-back monkeys varied: sometimes they would drink more; often they would drink less. The uptight monkeys consistently drank nearly twice as much as the others. Unlike their peers who quickly relaxed at the monkey bar, the uptight monkeys looked consistently stressed, and Suomi reports that they seemed to be self-medicating.

About seven months after giving birth, mother monkeys go off to find a mate. They go off into the woods for hours or days at a time. For most baby monkeys the initial separation from the mother is a growth experience; this is not so for uptight monkeys. Like someone in mourning, they pine away. Lethargic and uninterested in life, their sleep is troubled and they eat poorly. Some die. It does not get better with subsequent separations; each is a new trauma. This makes birth order a particularly important factor for these needy babies; and this is likely to be true for inhibited humans as well. If she is the first of several siblings, she will be repeatedly traumatized and retreat further into social isolation with each new birth. If she is fortunate to be last born, she may be doted upon by her mother and avoid the trauma of separation.

Uptight male monkeys avoid leaving their troop for as long as possible. They are tolerated by the dominant older female monkeys because they are shy, unassertive wallflowers. When they do finally leave, they either stay on the periphery of the male gangs or go directly to another troop where they gain entry by the conservative strategy of befriending the less dominant males. In nature, when conditions are good and stress low, a few uptight males—probably those who have not been traumatized by excessive maternal separation—are sensitive to social cues and can form good connections and build alliances. They will often enter a new troop with supporters in tow and use their social skills to work their way up the social ladder—like the unpopular nerdy kids who turn up later as successful businessmen or politicians.

The social life of the rhesus clearly shows how relatively small changes in stress level can dramatically alter the impact of genes. It is a good example of phenotypic plasticity. For females, it is even more striking, because, unlike males, they never have the stress of leaving their home troop. In a bountiful environment where there is no competition for food, they are well cared for by their mothers. They develop calm sociable personalities and easily form alliances with other females, and they become wonderfully caring mothers. In the Cayo Santiago stress-free monkey paradise, uptight females are dominant in many troops. In more typically stressful situations, they are fearful, unsociable, and not well liked; and they become uncaring, often abusive mothers. Here we see not only how the same gene is expressed very differently in different environments, but also how that difference is dramatically altered by gender.

Suomi wanted to see if there was a way of inoculating genetically uptight-prone monkeys so that they would not be susceptible to normal stresses. The rhesus develops at about four times our pace; females are usually between three and five when they first get pregnant. Rhesus mothers give birth seasonally; all babies are born at around the same time every year. A mum does not seem to object if her newborn is exchanged for another and continues to mother just as before. Suomi took newborns that were genetically likely to be uptight and placed them with mothers who had been exceptionally engaged and tolerant with their previous babies. As expected, they were devoted, gentle foster parents. Suomi says these mums "buffer the child" against the scary world. The impact of their care was soon apparent. Unlike other babies with the uptight gene, these adopted monkeys were not fearful or shy. They explored confidently and socialized easily. Even though they were outgoing, they retained the social sensitivity typical of uptight monkeys, so were skilled at forming alliances, including alliances with aggressive competitors. As a result, they rose to the top of their groups (Suomi, 1997). Suomi referred to them as supermonkeys.

As an information processor, the mind is somewhat like a camera, taking in, transforming, and recording the events in the world. These receivers of the raw data of reality—film, the amygdala—come in a wide range of sensitivities. The typical chainstore camera comes with film of medium sensitivity and a lens that does not have to be adjusted in order for it to take good-enough pictures in most situations where there is enough light. A specialized camera may have a lens that can open very wide; and, loaded with sensitive film, can record the subtle shadings of night-time. But if that camera is not held steady, the image will blur; and if it is turned towards bright light, the film will be overexposed and the image will disappear in barren whiteness.

Most of us are like the chainstore camera, needing no adjustment to make good enough sense of the social world in most situations. Like the uptight monkey, the inhibited child is sensitively attuned to shadings of mood and change, but, unable to adjust to intense stimulation, is easily shaken and overwhelmed. The buffering caretaker, like the aperture of a good camera, allows in just enough of the world for the child to absorb. If all goes well, the child learns to self-regulate what is taken in but, still equipped with her original sensitivity, can focus on the subtleties of the social world. Suomi concludes that, "a 'risk' factor under some circumstances can be advantageous under others . . . primates live in such a wide variety of environments that no single developmental outcome is going to be optimal in all conditions" (*Facts of Life*, 1999).

Only humans detach

Harlow was not successful in getting his monkeys to act like severely depressed people. They never became completely apathetic and detached. Even those subject to the torment of the pit of despair continued to crave contact with other monkeys. Suomi discovered that under the right conditions a connection could occur and lead to cure.

Detachment is a state found all too frequently in depressed and traumatized human beings. John Bowlby, one of the most influential psychiatrists of the twentieth century and the father of attachment theory, studied hospitalized children who were separated from their mothers. He described a three-stage reaction: protest, despair, and detachment. In protest, the child is obviously distressed, often crying loudly and throwing toys and whatever else he can get his hands on. He rejects anyone who tries to help him. At the same time he looks expectantly towards anything—an opening door, the sound of footsteps—that might signal his mother's return. In despair, the child becomes increasingly hopeless. Other-directed activity decreases and he no longer pleads for his mother's return. Self-soothing stimulation—thumb sucking, rocking, and masturbation—increase.

In detachment, the child may look less troubled. He may accept care, play with toys, and smile again. Detachment may seem like improvement, especially to overworked staff, but it is an illusion. If the child's mother visits, he shows no interest and turns away. If, as is often the case with children in orphanages or foster care, caretakers come and go, the child stops trying to connect to anyone. He may focus his interest on material things like toys, food, or TV and seem placid or even cheerful. He may be open and friendly to everyone and may fool psychologists into thinking he is OK; but it is only a way to get what he wants. Other people no longer matter (Bowlby, 1982). Harlow could only traumatize baby monkeys into states of protest and despair, but he could not get them to detach. When reunited with their mothers, whether real or wire mesh iron maidens, they would run to them and cling chest to chest.

Detachment is a common human condition. Over twenty-five per cent of children detach when briefly separated from their mothers and take some time to reconnect. For about the same percentage of adults, moderate detachment is their usual way of relating. Extreme detachment—where love and connection cease to matter—occurs in two very different kinds of mental illness, severe or psychotic depression and psychopathy or antisocial personality disorder.[3] The severely depressed person feels unlovable—too defective, bad, or toxic to hope that anyone will care. To relieve the pain, suicide—a uniquely human act—is common. The psychopath feels quite the opposite: that he is special and no one else is worthy of love or even life. Other people are coldly manipulated and sometimes tortured or killed for the thrill of it. These are also uniquely human behaviours.

We marvel that our dog is always happy to see us when we come home. Unlike our children or mates, our dog does not hold a grudge from being ignored that morning or from a scolding the day before. If he has been hit too often, he may flinch when you raise your hand or approach with a halting sideways gait, but he will still approach lovingly. We treasure fidelity and loyalty because they are too often absent, even among friends, and we cannot discount betrayal even by those who love us.

Only humans can detach because only humans have a theory of mind. Humans, like rhesus monkeys, are naturally drawn to each other for comfort and protection. Even the shyest baby longs for the care of his mother. If the longing for care is repeatedly disappointed and especially if it is met by pain—whether the pain is inflicted intentionally through abuse or unintentionally through overstimulating the high-reactive child—the child may construct a theory of mind of the other as essentially inhuman. The exact formulation of the theory varies, but most often others are seen as predators only interested in themselves; expressions of concern are interpreted as camouflage for the others' "real" predatory intentions. This is the theory of mind of the psychopath. Survival demands becoming predator rather than prey.

People who are depressed and hopelessly detached have constructed a different theory of mind. In childhood, the uncaring and attacking behaviour of others is interpreted as a response to something abhorrent in one's self. Later, expressions of concern are interpreted as empty platitudes masking the others' "real" contempt. "No one can love me because I am unlovable" is the theory of mind of someone suffering severe depression.

While detachment is a chronic state for some, it is temporary state for many. People may have a tendency to a mental disorder without having the disorder itself. So, someone may have psychopathic tendencies or depressive tendencies and only move into a state of detachment under conditions of severe stress. For some people, the loss of a loved one or a business failure can push them into states of detachment. Under conditions of disaster or war, many more will detach: some may become hopelessly withdrawn and unable to fend for themselves; others may become coldly uncaring about other victims and only concerned with their own survival

One businessman patient had not yet left home for his office in the North Tower when the building was hit. He watched the events unfold on TV. He lost several colleagues, but claimed not to be particularly bothered. "They were only business associates, not close family," he explained. His main concern in the months after the attack was getting a good deal on a new office as rents came down; he also stocked up on survival equipment and supplies and purchased a weekend home away from the city. It was months before he could see that his response was not purely rational but that it was also his way of warding off his guilt for having been so lucky to survive when so many people he knew had died.

Depression. It is not difficult to recognize that someone is severely depressed, but it often difficult to know when a depressed person is in a state of detachment. Someone who is depressed looks preoccupied and sad, lacks energy, and takes little pleasure in life. Those who know him are aware of his suffering, his self-recriminations, and hopelessness. A depressed person's constant expressions of despair may make his loved ones feel similarly despairing and helpless. But it is important to recognize that as long as someone is complaining, he is connecting. Complaints are an expression of hope. When a severely depressed person stops complaining, there may be cause for greater concern; it may be a sign of detachment and loss of hope. Feeling another person's detachment is frightening. There is something so eerie about being in the presence of someone who is not connected to other human beings that most of us push the feeling aside. Some emotional knowers remain sensitive to the feeling of disconnection, but most of the rest of us can improve our recognition of detachment by cognitively knowing the signs. When a severely depressed person shows sudden improvement—seems peaceful and no longer complains—it is often a sign that the he has decided to kill himself.

The psychopath. In terms of protecting yourself and those you care about, recognizing psychopathy is an important mind-reading skill. The popular image of the psychopath is the serial killer, someone like Jeffrey Dahmer or the fictional character Hannibal Lecter. While most serial killers are psychopaths, very few psychopaths are serial killers. Psychopaths—like Dahmer and Lecter—are often charming, engaging, and intelligent, and totally without empathy, conscience, or remorse, but most do not end up in trouble with the law. Some are successful con artists and hustlers. A surprising number thrive in the cut-throat, competitive, impersonal business world of today, according to Dr Robert Hare, professor at the

University of British Columbia, the world's leading expert on psychopaths. Dr Hare estimates about one in a hundred people are psychopaths and many more have psychopathic tendencies to varying degrees (Babiak & Hare, 2006). Hare believes that many corporate scandals, including WorldCom and Enron, were caused by psychopathic CEOs and executives. A 2005 study compared the personality profiles of thirty-nine chief executives of leading British companies with those of criminals and psychiatric patients diagnosed with psychopathy. The executives were about as exploitative and lacking in empathy as the criminals and diagnosed psychopaths, and more superficially charming, egocentric, insincere, and manipulative (Board & Fritzon, 2005).

Psychopaths are not easy to spot, since they are adept at camouflaging their predatory intentions and seducing their victims into their trap. Like adventurers and rescuers, psychopaths take great risk and show little fear; a low-reactive temperament seems to be a prerequisite for them as well. A traumatically abusive childhood is common among violent psychopaths and seems to be at the root of their detachment; many non-violent psychopaths did not suffer abuse, but rather persistent insecurity and neglect; some psychopaths seem to have had a normal childhood. Once again there is a complex interplay of genetic and environmental factors that scientists are only beginning to unravel.

People are often drawn to psychopaths for the same reason they are drawn to adventurers—their self-confidence and willingness to take risks in pursuit of profit and excitement. Wishing to be relieved of their guilt and inertia, depressed people are particularly vulnerable to the psychopath's seductions. If you have ever been conned or found yourself in the middle of a shady deal, be especially wary—you know you are vulnerable. I cannot stress enough that if you have a gut feeling that someone is uncaring, sleazy, creepy, cold-blooded, or dangerous, go with your gut and get away. The few who have survived encounters with serial killers—who others thought normal, even charming—didn't get in their car or ran the other way because their gut told them to. Almost anyone can be duped in a brief encounter, but almost anyone can learn the warning signs: if someone you know seems superficially charming to everyone, lies without remorse, thinks he is so special ordinary rules do not apply, and does not seem troubled by upsetting events or other people's pain, either stay away or seek a professional consultation to help you evaluate the situation.

The severely depressed person and the psychopath illustrate the human capacity to create troubling and inflexible theories of mind. Trauma and chronic severe stress tend to fix the mind in rigid patterns. But theories of mind can also rapidly shift. It is hard to imagine any set of circumstances that would transform your loyal dog into your foe. Yet betrayal can turn friends to enemies in an instant, and you are more likely to be murdered by someone who once loved you than by someone you do not know. Hate is love turned angry, as many who have been through a divorce can attest. The hated spouse is transformed from lover to tormentor, and the past is remembered in new and less pleasant ways.

Because enemies tend to maintain distance, the transformation of foe to friend is less frequent, but it does happen—feuds are settled, couples reconcile, enemy nations become allies. I think minds can change more quickly than most people want to know. We like the idea of stability, of consistency and continuity of our selves and those we know. We tend to see revelation and transformation as belonging to the biblical past. But our theory of mind can change rapidly—altering our view not only of another person, but also of our entire life.

What do you expect?

The cognitive science revolution is young, and the human lifespan long; studies tracing the effect of the earliest relationships on adult personality are just beginning to bear fruit. We do know that gentle engaged parenting can lead a constitutionally inhibited child to become sociable rather than shy. We do not yet know if those children will, like the rhesus, become especially socially adept leaders. Scientists cannot experimentally manipulate people's lives as they do monkeys, but they can measure the effect of what are commonly called experiments of nature—chance circumstances that seem as if they were designed to test a theory.

While scientists cannot arbitrarily take a child from one family and place it with another, adoption provides us with many such experiments of nature. In 2003, psychologists at the Anna Freud

Centre in London reported on sixty-one abused and neglected children observed from the time they were adopted by new families. At the time of adoption, the children ranged in age from four to eight and had suffered numerous separations, some having been in as many as eighteen different foster homes. By any measure, these children had been severely traumatized and were at high risk for having difficult relationships and perhaps even on their way to detachment.

For over three decades, attachment theory has dominated the study of child development. John Bowlby proposed that attachment evolved to protect children from predators by keeping them close to their parents. In a dangerous world, natural selection should favour the survival of closely attached infants. The Anna Freud group was investigating a central tenet of attachment theory: that based on relationships with caretakers, the child builds an internal "working model" of the social world, which becomes the pattern for future relationships. They wondered if a new relationship could alter a model established by years of trauma.

Three types of attachment have been identified based on observing children's response in an unfamiliar setting to a parent's leaving and returning. (The experiment is known as the "strange situation".) The *securely attached* child explores the new environment when his parent is present, gets upset when his parent leaves, but calms quickly, and is happy when his parent returns. The *insecure–ambivalent* child is clingy and anxious in the strange situation, and gets upset when left, but seems stuck between anger and neediness upon the parent's return. He might run to mum only to push away when picked up, yet cry if put down. The *insecure–avoidant* child shows little emotion, blithely explores and seems not to care when the parent leaves or returns. A small percentage of children, many who have been neglected and abused, may also become *disorganized*. When left, they may freeze or engage in odd behaviours like hand flapping or head banging. Cortisol levels rise sharply, indicating high stress. The disorganized behaviour lasts for varying periods before the child reacts in a more usual way.

One of the most powerful findings of thirty years of attachment research is the strong relationship between the attachment status of a mother and that of her child. That is, if a mother feels secure in her relationship to her own mother, there is a great likelihood that her child will feel secure with her. (The same is true for father to only a slightly lesser degree.) This finding is based almost entirely on the observation of children and their biological parents who share genes and a long-term relationship.

The London researchers asked if having a securely attached adoptive could mother reverse years of abuse and neglect. This is an important question. Many potential adoptive parents are reluctant to accept a traumatized older child, fearing that real connection and love may never occur. Amazingly, within three months of adoption, the children with secure mothers felt significantly more secure themselves (Steele, Hodges, Kaniuk, Hillman, & Henderson, 2003). They were also less aggressive. The jury is still out on how these changes will hold up in the long term, but the initial results are hopeful. But there is ample evidence from other reports that determined, caring parenting can bring a child back even from the pit of detachment (*This American Life*, 2006).

A person's style of attachment is not as stable as psychologists once imagined. In the course of development, people can change. Trauma and loss can undermine security; healing relationships can build it. Recently, researchers have named a new group, "earned-secure" (Roisman, 2002). These individuals have suffered the kind of painful parenting—perhaps abuse or neglect—that usually leads to insecure and even disorganized attachments; and though they may carry a residue of sadness, as adults they are secure in their attachments and can have intimate romantic relationships. A defining characteristic of the earned-secure is their ability to weave a narrative of their early experience, to tell a coherent story of their painful past that can be communicated to others. In that way, they are similar to the survivors of horrific adult trauma who find meaning and a way back to connection by telling their story. It is more than just saying what happened. Some survivors compulsively talk about their trauma, but gain no relief in the retelling. Others do not tell the story at all.

Usually, earned-secures in their childhood had the consistent support of caring adults that helped them overcome difficult family circumstances. They can then enter adulthood feeling secure. In the next chapter, you will meet James, who had such a childhood. Less frequently, someone may enter adulthood insecurely attached and find a relationship that changes their view of the world. A recent study (Szecsody, 2008) shows that psychoanalysis can lead to earned security.

Attachment and reading minds

One way to think about attachment is that each attachment reflects a particular theory of mind. The secure person assumes that others can be trusted to act reasonably, that caretakers can be depended upon, and will not withdraw or disappear without warning. The secure adult[4] assumes the same about herself; that she can depend on herself and care for others. She knows there are people who cannot be trusted, but believes it is possible to tell who they are. The secure person is the perhaps the most likely to be a balanced knower, feeling confident in both her thinking and emotional perception. The secure person is more likely to read others accurately though perhaps over-optimistically, tending to see the best in people. It may be that the earned-secure have the most accurate view of the social world.

The avoidant person assumes that caretakers cannot be depended upon, that others are selfish and cannot be trusted, and that they may withdraw without warning. The avoidant adult rarely asks for help, and rarely offers it. Needing another is seen as weakness; those who offer help are seen as duplicitous. The avoidant person tends to read others through a lens of distrust and may use either cognitive or emotional data, choosing whichever confirms his suspicions.

The ambivalent person feels that others have the capacity to satisfy her needs but withhold it to manipulate or torment, often feeling the torment is justified. The ambivalent person vacillates between feeling angry with others for withholding care and feeling bad about herself and undeserving of help. The experience of ambivalent adults is characterized by anxiety and worry, fearing that others will not give them what they need or will ruin what they have. They show obvious distress in an attempt to elicit care, which, if offered, is then often rejected. The ambivalent person is most likely to vacillate in her judgements and may go back and forth between reading emotionally and reading cognitively, unable to integrate the two. Others are likely to be either judged harshly or idealized.

Your attachment style

Attachment style in adulthood is generally assessed using a similarly complex and difficult to score procedure, the Adult Attachment

Interview—but researchers at the University of Southern California found you can fairly accurately determine your attachment classification by answering one simple question (Hazan & Shaver, 1987). Which of the following describes you:

A. I am somewhat uncomfortable being close to others; I find it difficult to trust them completely, difficult to allow myself to depend on them. I am nervous when anyone gets too close, and often, others want me to be more intimate than I feel comfortable being.

B. I find it relatively easy to get close to others and am comfortable depending on them and having them depend on me. I don't worry about being abandoned or about someone getting too close to me.

C. I find that others are reluctant to get as close as I would like. I often worry that my partner doesn't really love me or won't want to stay with me. I want to get very close to my partner, and this sometimes scares people away.

If you answered B, you are secure. If you answered C, you are insecure–ambivalent. If you answered A, you are insecure–avoidant.

You do not need to take a complicated psychological test to determine your attachment category but these, like all categories, are over-simplifications.[5] Even toddlers make distinctions; many are attached differently to mother and to father, for example. Most people's theory of how others will respond to their needs is nuanced; not everyone is seen as the same. Yet one of the truisms of human psychology is that under stress, people's characteristic attitudes and ways of relating are amplified, and nuance fades. The strange situation experiment was designed to be stressful in order to elicit the child's most characteristic attachment behaviour. Pushing beyond stress, traumatic events threaten our survival and the survival of those we love, calling forth our infant-self dread of being alone, and triggering our most basic reactions to separation. Those reactions in turn affect our success in coping with those events.

The healing power of narrative resides not in the telling of the story, but in the feeling of connection and care that comes with being valued and understood. People who experience trauma tell their stories in different ways. The more securely attached will tell the story to reach out as the child reaches out for a hug, in expectation of touching and being touched, of sharing and being cared for. The ambivalently attached will tell the story as a cry of anger and accusation with little expectation that anyone will understand or care; it may be told repetitiously in order to inflict the teller's helpless pain on the listener. The avoidantly attached may try not to tell the story, or may tell it in a flat and unemotional way. Children of ambivalently attached Holocaust survivors often report feeling dumbfounded, helpless, and guilty in the face of a parent's repeated descriptions of the horror, while those with avoidant parents often hear nothing about it at all.

America's outrage over the bombing of the World Trade Center, the immediacy of the televised imagery, the palpable tragedy of the victims, along with its location at the centre of one of the largest concentrations of academic institutions in the world will make it the most examined traumatic event in history. The data collection and analysis will go on for generations. The victims, their children, and their grandchildren are already being studied, and unprecedented levels of mental health care have been made available to them.

We live in a strange time. On the one hand, there is a heightened expectation that distressing events will probably traumatize and cause longstanding mental illness. On the other hand, there is a diminished faith in the healing power of love and human connection. Despite ever increasing scientific evidence that relationships can change the structure of the brain, prevailing popular theory, given massive support by the pharmaceutical industry and subscribed to by many physicians, is that people can cause psychological damage but only drugs can really heal.

Even among mental heath professionals who value psychotherapy, it is increasingly assumed that people are fragile and require immediate intervention to prevent trauma from becoming a disease, post traumatic stress disorder (PTSD). My son and his friends complained that in the weeks after 9/11, they could not turn a corner at school with being stopped by a counsellor, psychologist, or social worker offering help. They were disturbed by flood of condolences and the well-meaning assumption that they had been damaged, and they feared it might be a self-fulfilling prophesy.

Blink author Malcolm Gladwell, in the *New Yorker* article, "Getting over it", incisively illustrates that between the post-Second World War period and post-Vietnam period there was been a dramatic shift in our culture's view of resilience, the ability of an individual to survive adversity. The Second World War veteran was expected to overcome the mental wounds of war and live a good life; the Vietnam Veteran was expected to nurse permanent wounds and live a life limited by PTSD.

The diagnosis PTSD was invented to explain the Vietnam veteran's suffering, but it placed the pathology within the veteran and not in the culture that sent him off to fight a meaningless and unwinable war. Trauma's impact is influenced by the beliefs of community that treats the victim. The Second World War veteran was treated as a hero; the Vietnam veteran was too often treated as a cripple or a fool. Now a trauma industry has developed, and the diagnosis PTSD is liberally applied to justify treatment of dubious worth. It has even been suggested that watching something distressing on TV can cause PTSD.

Scientific research does not justify these developments. The post 9/11 studies have shown that while many suffered PTSD, many did not. Based on door-to-door survey in October 2001, the New York City Health Department estimated nearly forty per cent of people living near the site had symptoms of post traumatic stress disorder. Another particularly interesting study found that highly secure people not only showed relatively healthy adjustment in the month following the attacks, but many in fact showed psychological improvement over their pre-9/11 state: that

> highly secure people were not only able to show better adjustment than others in the face of the tragedy but that they were able to use the experience as a means for exhibiting other forms of personal growth or strength. [Fraley, Fazzari, Bonanno, & Dekel, 2006]

There is growing evidence for what psychologists now call "post traumatic growth" (Linley & Joseph, 2004). Many such individuals seem to be focused on caring for others during the traumatic event and continue to offer assistance afterward. It is usually assumed that the stronger and less affected are the ones who offer help. More and more research shows that volunteering to help others improves the volunteers' self-esteem and satisfaction with life (Van Willigen, 2000).

My son's American white middle-class sense of security was shattered in an instant—and it only took a little longer for him to go from boy to man. Helping others helped him to feel like he could take care of himself. He has continued to try to understand the larger world and the lives and minds of people who suffer trauma nearly every day. He has continued to volunteer and help others when he can. He often too, with blinkers on, retreats into the comfort of his life—but it will never be the same.

Perhaps Nietzsche's tired platitude, "That which does not kill you makes you stronger", can now be amended: "If it doesn't hurt you too badly, and you are securely attached and have the support to take action, it may make you stronger".

Notes

1. Pavlov actually used a variety of stimuli and it is unclear whether he ever used a bell, but the bell has become the accepted general term.

2. "If the researches completed and proposed make a contribution, I shall be grateful; but I have also given full thought to possible practical applications. The socioeconomic demands of the present and the threatened socioeconomic demands of the future have led the American woman to displace, or threaten to displace, the American man in science and industry. If this process continues, the problem of proper child-rearing practices faces us with startling clarity. It is cheering in view of this trend to realize that the American male is physically endowed with all the really essential equipment to compete with the American female on equal terms in one essential activity: the rearing of infants. We now know that women in the working classes are not needed in the home because of their primary mammalian capabilities; and it is possible that in the foreseeable future neonatal nursing will not be regarded as a necessity, but as a luxury—to use Veblen's term— a form of conspicuous consumption limited perhaps to the upper classes. But whatever course history may take, it is comforting to know that we are now in contact with the nature of love." [Harlow,1958]

3. The psychiatric diagnosis antisocial personality disorder includes psychopathy along with others, but most researchers think it is an overly broad category.

4. The adult attachment categories are different for no apparent reason: secure–autonomous, dismissing, and preoccupied.

5. The relationship between different measures of adult attachment is complex and has generated considerable literature. See, for example, Bartholomew and Shaver (1998).

CHAPTER FIVE

Ways of understanding

Evolution has given each of us two ways of understanding the world—the cognitive and the emotional. Roughly speaking, these two approaches conform to the traditional distinction between head and heart, logic and gut, thinking and feeling. Everyone, to some extent, uses both cognitive abilities and emotional reactions to formulate theories about other minds. Over-reliance on either approach can lead to flawed theories of mind and mind-misreads. Ideally, we would naturally use a balance of the two approaches, shifting the balance as the situation demands, maybe, for example, relying more on emotion with friends and family and more on cognition at work. Yet everyone knows that there are difficult family situations when it is good to be as thought-ful and clearheaded as possible; and there are work situations where it is better to rely on your gut.

Being a balanced knower does not mean being inflexibly tied to equally weighing emotion and clear-headed thought. It means being able to use the data available to formulate your best guess, your best theory of what's going on and what you should do. That means not ignoring upsetting information or dismissing odd and uncanny feelings. It also means being able to discard false or misleading information, whether in the form of dry statistics or sly seductions.

No one ever achieves perfect balance, though some, like Bill Gates, come closer than most. From what we know, Gates made the best of his good fortune: an even temperament and sharp mind, a loving and supportive family, a good education, and freedom from trauma. Fortunately, others with more difficult lives can achieve balance as well.

Finding balance

James began his therapy by telling me about a warm summer evening in Harlem when he was pulled over by the police. A bag of cocaine was stashed under his seat. His worst nightmare was coming true. James had never wanted to work for drug dealers. He hated them as he hated what drugs had done to his mother; but for him, like so many poor black teens, a job in the drug trade seemed like the only option. He got no money from his parents and needed to buy clothes and books, and mum's medicine. Soon he would be graduating from high school and was planning to enlist in the Navy.

James is 6'3" with the build of a sumo wrestler. Though mild-mannered, he can put on the don't-mess-with-me look of a night-club bouncer. A good observer, conscientious and reserved, he was trusted to carry drugs from one dealer to another. He had always been careful and stayed away from trouble. He wasn't a user himself. Now with the red lights of the cop car pulsing from behind, his heart raced. Anxious, near panic, almost frozen, he held the steering wheel tight and thought, "I'm going to jail. Please don't get killed."

Through the driver-side mirror, James saw the police officer approaching, his gun drawn, held stiffly low in a two-handed grip. James noted he was alone, looked young and scared. Motioning with his pistol to a spot on the ground, the officer shouted, "Get out of the car." James released the steering wheel and turned as slowly as he could bear toward the car door, making sure to keep his still-cupped hands in plain sight. Only when he could see the officer's face and the officer could see his, did he drop his left hand to pull the handle and step out of the car. As he stepped out, he hunched his shoulders and cast his gaze downward, trying to look smaller; he raised his hands higher and clasped them, fingers entwined, behind his head, turned and placed his forehead against the roof of his car. He was following commands never spoken, commands he imagined the officer would issue if the young man were not too scared to think. James pictured Amadou Diallo, shot forty-one times with his wallet clenched in his hand, a wallet the police claimed they thought was a gun. James was determined to give the anxious officer no more reason to fear him, no excuse to shoot him in the back. By now, a small crowd had gathered, its presence breaking the officer's frightened focus. The officer demanded James's licence and registration. James replied clearly and respectfully, "They're in my wallet in my back pocket. Please take them."

The officer seemed to shudder at the thought of taking a hand off his pistol and jamming it into James's back pocket. He shouted again, "Licence and registration." James repeated his reply. Two more times the same words were exchanged. As the crowd grew larger, giggles and catcalls grew louder. James prayed that no one would jump to his defence.

Unlike the nervous burglar in the first chapter, who confessed when the officer called stop, or Brett Koh in the second, who had no plan, James's thinking and judgement was not blocked by his anxiety. On the contrary, his anxiety was a signal to him of the seriousness of the situation, a signal to focus intently on what was going on in the mind of the police officer. James was afraid of dying. He experienced the fear intensely but was able to contain it with his thoughts. He thought carefully and formulated a plan based on his read of the officer and his surroundings. Thinking and feeling counterbalanced each other. Intense emotion spurred on complex thinking; complex thinking kept intense emotion in check.

If the officer had been more experienced, perhaps he would have handcuffed James or called for backup. If he were mean, he might have tried to provoke James with contemptuous words or by prodding him with his nightstick. Instead, he asked James where he lived. James gave him the address of his aunt a few blocks away. The officer told him to go home. James got in his car and drove away.

James, like Bill Gates, is a balanced knower, using both thought and emotion to read other minds more accurately. Unlike Bill Gates, James did not have the advantages of a stable family and economic privilege, yet he was able to successfully navigate though life despite his difficult childhood. James's mother struggled with heroin addiction and alcoholism. She and his father often fought violently until James was eight and his father disappeared from the scene. James remembers seeing nodding addicts in his apartment house hallway; finding one he knew dead on the street; seeing relatives ravished by AIDS; feeling surrounded by chaos and despair. James also remembers an uncle, a gentle gay man who sometimes cared for him. He took him on long walks and bus rides to other parts of the city, to movies, museums, baseball games. And he remembers a "white lady social worker" who would visit every month without fail. These visits were imposed by the bureau of child welfare as a condition for his mother to retain custody so that James would not be placed in foster care. On the day before each visit, he remembers his mum frantically straightening up the apartment and herself. The social worker always brought something for James, a game, a comic book; they talked and did homework together, and they played for a while. She got him a subscription to the *Weekly Reader*. James beams as he remembers. He thinks the fact that she was a white lady and his uncle was gay have helped him feel comfortable with people different from himself.

James is a survivor. Psychologists call it resilience: that is, he was able to cope with stressful situations and learn from them, and each time the likelihood that stress would become trauma was reduced. Two things are common among resilient children: they tend to be temperamentally laid back, and they often have at least one secure attachment. As an adult, James defines easy going. A big man with broad smile and a soothing manner, it is easy to imagine him a placid, smiley Buddha baby. He wasn't fussy and seldom cried; he was OK being often alone. He felt secure in his connection to his uncle and his social worker. They were consistently nurturing and warm; and though they were not with him often, they were with him predictably, and he could hold them in his mind.

Security is a state of mind

Feeling securely connected and cared for is a state of mind. One person can live in luxury with a constant loving companion, have caring friends, the adulation of crowds, and still feel insecure and alone. Another can walk alone in a dark forest and feel held by nature and loved by god. Some children require little to feel cared for, occasional attention, the sense of another's presence. Others need to be held almost constantly, enveloped by a second, thicker skin.

James needed little to feel connected. To my surprise, I discovered he was securely attached to his mother. One way we assess adult attachment is by analysing memories—it doesn't matter if they are happy or sad, painful or pleasant; what counts is their depth and coherence. If someone can paint a realistic picture of his childhood mother, it is a sign of secure attachment—in James's case a secure attachment to a troubled human being. He compassionately described his mother's struggles with addiction and her abusive relationship with his father. James imagined his mother's mind and constructed theories to explain her life: she took drugs to soothe her sadness; she accepted abuse because she desperately needed a man. Most telling was his understanding of what it meant that each month before the social worker's visit she pulled herself out of her sloth and fog, cleaned up and dressed up: she loved him and didn't want to lose him. James's discovery of his mother's love was a product of his constructing a theory of her mind; and the joy of that discovery led to him to become an explorer and reader of other minds.

Creating a parent

The mother James described was his creation. Of course, he had a real mother. But she never spoke to him about her mind, her motivation for doing what she did. He could have understood her in a very different way. Had he had a more reactive temperament, he might have felt overwhelmed and unprotected by her. Maybe his uncle helped James understand his mother. Often an older sibling or relative will help a child understand his parent's mind. One patient recalls at age seven running to his room crying after one of his mother's angry outbursts. His older sister came to him and said, "You know mum's crazy." He recalls a huge feeling of relief. He had been searching for an understanding his mother's unpredictable behaviour. Now he did not have to blame himself. As he grew older and learned more about what crazy meant, he became more sympathetic to his mother's plight.

We are always creating and recreating our understanding of the minds of the important people in our lives. Some of us are given a great deal of material with which to fashion our creation, some hardly any at all. But we do know that children will even construct an image and a theory of mind of parents they have never seen—parents who died or were never part of their lives. Our understanding of our parents usually changes as we mature, sometimes in the context of a real relationship with them and sometimes not. If a person's understanding does not change, it means there is a problem, a reason for being stuck. That our parents seem smarter as we grow older is another piece of folk psychology that is sometimes true. Some people are too stuck in anger or hurt to re-examine and change their understanding of their parent's mind; others are afraid of discovering something they do not want to see.

Ideals as alternative parents

Our feeling of connection and security in the world most often depends on our relationships to the parents or caretakers we create in our minds. Our feeling of security can shift as our understanding of those relationships change. In some cases, a person's sense of security comes not from their attachment to a parent, or even a person, but rather to an ideal. Deeply creative people may be more attached to an ideal embodied in their creations than to other people. Some are notably indifferent (Phillip Roth) or even cruel (Picasso) to former friends and lovers for the sake of their art. Einstein referred his life outside of physics as "the merely personal".

Master spy novelist John Le Carré had a dismal childhood. His father was a con artist, impostor, poseur, politician, and philanderer who was completely indifferent to the needs of his children. Le Carré and his brother were often used as props in various scams. When he was five, his father was sent to prison for a year and his mother abandoned the family; he was told she was dead and did not see her again until he was twenty-one. During his father's imprisonment and many times after—whenever it suited his father—the boys were cared for by their paternal grandparents. They were stodgy, strict, and religious, and demanded at least the appearance of upright behaviour; and Le Carré kept secret from them all he knew of his father's dissolute life. When with his father, he was cared for by one of the many "lovelies" drawn to the high life of casinos and fancy sports cars.

The two boys were sent to boarding schools where their father—pretending great wealth—conspicuously visited in Rolls Royces and Bentleys. Le Carré's father conned people out of millions, but always spent more than he had; in 1954, bankrupt, he owed the equivalent of forty million dollars, and the boys were left to make excuses for tuition bills unpaid. The contrast between his father's debauchery and his grandparents' rigid morality, Le Carré said,

> instilled in me a condition of subterfuge. The catastrophes in our family were so great and the disproportion between the domestic situation and the orthodoxy of my educated program was so great that I seemed to go about in disguise. [Bragg, 1983]

Like my patient, James, Le Carré tried to formulate a theory of his parents' minds, but he had little to work with. He remembers nothing of his childhood mother. In interviews he says little about her except she was probably sensible to leave and that he could never understand why she didn't take her children with her. Le Carré has laboured all his life to understand his father's lying mind. After college, he entered the British Intelligence service and was working in Germany as spy when he wrote his first novel. "If you're growing up in a chaotic world without reason, your instinct is to become a performer and control the circumstances around you," he explains (Wootton, 2002).

Le Carré speaks about his father frequently and has used him as the model for more than one of his characters. "For years, I tried to block my father out of my life. After he died, I became aware that was not possible," he says (Wilson-Smith, 1999). But Le Carré still does not feel he understands his father. The unremitting, unapologetic, self-destructive, and especially uncaring nature of his treachery seems incomprehensible. After he became rich, he offered to take care of his father, if he agreed not to "work". His father was enraged and proceeded to try to use his association with a now famous son to bilk money from a film studio. "You can't come to terms with a phenomenon like that. *It goes on living in you forever*," Le Carré said sadly (*Fresh Air*, 1989, my emphasis from the listening).

Le Carré's passion is exposing the liar, even if it is himself. His ideal is revealing the truth. When asked if as a child he knew his father was fraud, he quickly answered, "I just assumed everybody was . . . I just thought that's what grownups were" (*ibid.*) Leading inevitably to his adult self,

> Nothing that I write is authentic. It is the stuff of dreams, not reality. Yet I am treated by the media as though I wrote espionage handbooks. I am regarded as a sage . . . And to a point I am flattered that my fabulations are taken so seriously. Yet I also despise myself in the fake role of guru, since it bears no relation to who I am or what I do. Artists, in my experience, have very little centre. They fake. They are not the real thing. They are spies. I am no exception. [Taken from remarks made by John Le Carré to the Knof Sales Force, 12 August, 1996]

Le Carré is uncompromising in denouncing the self-serving hypocrisies of government institutions and the pretence of class. Offered the possibility of a knighthood, he refused, later saying, "I hate the idea that you have some sort of invisible academy that will oversee England. I won't be a part of it" (Wilson-Smith, 1999). Unable to form a satisfactory theory of his father's mind, he recreates all forms of deception in the minds of his characters, making their minds an open book to all who care to read.

For some, faith is their most important connection. Buddha's mother died when he was seven days old. His father was a King and, like many children of wealthy parents, Buddha was cared for by servants. During the spring celebration, his nursemaids sneaked off to take part in the festivities, leaving the baby Buddha unattended. When they returned, they found him relaxed in deep meditation. He later described it as his first ecstatic experience. Buddha went on to preach the virtue of detachment as the only way to avoid the pain of unfulfilled desire and inevitable loss. His life exemplified his teaching. At twenty-nine, he renounced his princely wealth and abandoned his wife and newborn son to live the life of a wandering monk. Yet while Buddha's detachment from personal relationships provided freedom from the fleeting illusions of material existence, his goal was access to the eternal embrace of nirvana and infinite connections to all. In his wanderings, he touched all he met with kindness. He was attached to no one person but to all people.

Jesus, too, renounced personal relationships in order to minister to all, and he preached that devotion to God came before devotion to family. Still now, some deeply religious individuals abandon human attachments in order to strengthen their connection to their faith. The lives of many troubled people have been transformed by a deep attachment to their faith, which brings them greater security and contentment than they ever hoped to find in their personal relationships.

Making the most of your style

As we go through life, each of us develops a characteristic approach to constructing a theory of mind. Each can be placed on a continuum of ways of knowing, from extreme cognitive knowers who reject feelings completely, to extreme emotional knowers who rarely bother to reflect at all. Though these extremes are rare, so is the totally balanced knower. Most people lean towards the cognitive or emotional and shift the balance depending on the particular situation. The flexibility to shift depends in part on one's sense of security.

A person's style of knowing is largely, but far from completely, dependent on inborn temperament or amygdala reactivity. Emotionally reactive shy children tend to become cognitive knowers. Emotionally less reactive children tend to become emotional knowers. Cognitive knowers have learnt ways to inhibit their emotional reactivity. It is possible, even as an adult, to learn new ways of inhibiting emotional reactivity and become a more cognitive knower, as well as to unlearn cognitive inhibitions and become a more emotional knower. Sometimes a therapist's help is necessary, but life events and relationships can cause the balance to shift; and even a small shift in the balance can be a tipping point in one's life.

Cognitive knowers

Mike is a sales manager in telecommunications. He has an MBA and is a genius with numbers, but some mistakes he has made in hiring his sales force may stand in the way of promotion. In one case, Mike felt something troubling about a young man he was interviewing, but he couldn't put his finger on what bothered him, except that he felt uncomfortable about the way the young man bragged about winning some local golf tournaments. Mike's gut nagged at him for a few days, but the young man had an ivy-league education and a 3.9 GPA, so, rather than listen to his instincts, he suppressed his doubts and hired him. Eight months later, after his employee filed a series of suspiciously high expense vouchers, company auditors launched an investigation of the young man. When he was found to have padded his expenses to the tune of eight thousand dollars, Mike had to dismiss him—but the story does not end there.

About a year later, Mike ran into an old colleague who belonged to one of the country clubs where the young man said he had won a golf tournament. Mike mentioned his name to the colleague and asked if it sounded familiar. Yes, the colleague said, it did, "That fellow played in our annual tournament a few years back."

"He won it," Mike said.

The colleague shook his head, "No he didn't; he came in third or fourth."

Mike is a cognitive knower. He focuses on the facts. There is nothing wrong with having an impressive resumé, but sometimes that's not enough. People can pad resumés and cheat their way to a high GPA. If the facts told everything, there would be no need for an interview. But Mike didn't trust his gut. That is typical for a cognitive knower, to dismiss feelings as untrustworthy. In doing so, Mike neglected important data, information that his emotional brain was clambering to provide. Mike had collected cognitive data but did not collect emotional data.

Had Mike been aware of his own style of knowing, he could have saved himself and his company much grief. As soon as a cognitive knower becomes aware of his approach, he can learn an important lesson: don't deny discomfort. When cognitive knowers get a "buzz of emotion" it makes them uncomfortable and they tend to do what Mike did—dismiss the feeling as untrustworthy. If you know you are a cognitive knower, even before you learn to be able to decipher and trust your emotions, you can use your discomfort as a signal that something else may be going on, and then call for some help. Prior to hiring the young man, Mike might have called his old colleague at the country club, or asked an associate with better emotional antennae to do a second interview.

Emotional knowers

One successful venture capital firm I worked with has a special consultant. They call him the "gut-man". He is a retired Wall Street executive, well loved by all who know him, who has a reputation for remarkable people skills—he is an uncannily accurate emotional knower. After the usual due diligence, examination of business plans, and the like, before finalizing an investment in a company, the venture capital firm calls in the gut-man. He takes the CEO of the prospective company out to dinner to converse about life and things in general. If gut-man comes away feeling uneasy, the deal is off.

Understanding your deficits in data collection and using trust-worthy friends or associates to help fill in the gaps is important for emotional as well as cognitive knowers. Carol started a real estate brokerage when her youngest child left for college. The company had grown fast, but now was standing still. Carol always felt over-whelmed. She had to do everything herself. She had not been able to find people she could rely on. She had started with a partner, a friend, but it soon became apparent that her partner was not inter-ested in working hard and learning the business. Soon, Carol lost a business partner and friend.

Carol used her heart but not her head in selecting employees. She chose people she knew from the playground or PTA. She hired them because she liked them, but she often misjudged their compe-tence or motivation. She hired "nice" people and her office was warm and friendly, but there was no one with whom to share the burden and no one to count on in a crunch.

Carol collects emotional data but not cognitive data. She tends to judge people with her heart. She makes emotional connections easily and is a good judge of character. The people she likes are well meaning and decent. This in itself would not be a problem, and, in fact, Carol's life was relatively untroubled until she started a busi-ness. Like most emotional knowers, Carol tends to disregard the data that doesn't fit with her feeling for someone. If Carol heard gossip that a close friend drank too much or was in credit trouble, she tended to dismiss it and even eventually forget it. If the facts became undeniable, Carol was understanding of her friend's flaws and went out of her way to help.

Also, like most emotional knowers, Carol was unaware of how her own needs coloured her judgement. She was drawn to people who were dependent, who wanted to be taken care of, who needed her. She enjoyed the caretaker role and was super-mum and super-friend. Her business partner was recently divorced, and Carol had helped nurse her though it all. In their new business, her friend had expected Carol to carry the ball. Readily available data indicating that her friend tended to be passive and dependent when stressed was ignored by Carol when her friend suggested the partnership.

When hiring, Carol didn't do much investigating beyond what her gut told her. If she had a good feeing about someone, she rarely checked references or enquired about gaps in resumés. For her employees, she chose "nice" but dependent individuals without much motivation. Had Carol been aware of her style and her deficits in data gathering, she might have been able to implement an important lesson for emotional knowers: listen very carefully. Being so focused on their own feelings makes it difficult for emotional knowers not only to read the minds of others but often to hear their words as well. Emotional knowers tend to hear what they want to hear. Had Carol listened very carefully, and looked at resumés very carefully, she might have had the data to make more informed judgements. But lacking practice in the cognitive approach, Carol probably should have asked for help. When the situation allows, it is often useful for emotional knowers to enlist a spouse, friend, or colleague to act as a reality checker, someone with a cooler cognitive approach who is willing to challenge their gut impression of an interview or conversation.

The role of temperament

Temperament plays an important role in how we understand the social world. Uninhibited people tend to misjudge optimistically. Assuming others share their enthusiasm, they don't stop to reflect and pay attention to negative signals. Inhibited people tend to misjudge pessimistically. Assuming others share their apprehension, they are vigilant for signs of criticism and blind to signs of praise.

Ariel is a psychology professor who feels chronically disappointed because her innovative research doesn't get the recognition it deserves. She writes too few papers and publishes in less prestigious journals. In graduate school, she never sought out a mentor but succeeded in writing an original thesis with remarkably little support or advice. While writing her first paper, she showed her work to close friends. They praised her work, but were unfamiliar with her field of research and offered no constructive advice. She submitted the paper to a major journal and it was rejected. She then showed it to another graduate student in her field, who was harshly critical.

Ariel now asks no one for help with her papers. Instead, she engages in endless re-writes, trying to anticipate any possible criticism. She sends her papers to less prestigious journals where she is sure they will be accepted. Ariel knows that her creativity and productivity are inhibited by her fear of rejection.

Ariel is aware that there are older, well-established colleagues she could ask for help, tenured professors who might not be competitive and might even be supportive, but she is afraid to find out. She ran into one such professor at a conference recently. He smiled at her across the room, and, emboldened, she approached him. But when it became clear that he did not know her name, Ariel became flustered and, feeling very hurt, made excuses, and fled to her room. Had Ariel asked anyone about the professor, or had they spent any time chatting, she would have discovered that he was famous for his absent-mindedness—he couldn't remember anyone's name—and for his friendliness..

Ariel's mind-reading problems stem from her shy and inhibited temperament. She is easily overwhelmed by intense feelings, both negative and positive. She cries not only at funerals and weddings, but also while watching sitcoms on TV. It takes her a long time to make friends and she keeps her distance from people she doesn't know. She was comfortable showing her work to close friends, but they could not give her the feedback she needed. When her first paper was rejected, she approached someone who had the capacity to help, but Ariel did not know her well enough to know how she would react. Ariel, like most inhibited individuals, is easily hurt, and she was shaken, traumatized, by the experience of rejection and criticism. She is now too anxious to approach professors who could help her because she is both afraid that she might be criticized and feels overwhelmed by the idea that someone powerful and famous might take an interest in her.

By becoming aware of her temperament, she can understand the intensity of her reactions. In the same way that inhibited infants overreact to a noisy toy, Ariel overreacts to social stimuli. Knowing you are highly reactive is sometimes enough to reduce anxiety. Like a mother who soothes her child by saying, "It's OK, that noisy toy is really not scary," you soothe yourself with an internal mantra—"It's really not as intense as you think it is." When Ariel finally learns to subtract her own intensity from her perception of others, she will be able read other minds more accurately.

Carol, Ariel, and Mike all suffer from mind-reading difficulties, but each one's difficulty has a different cause. Successfully overcoming their particular problems and learning new approaches depends on appreciating these differences. It is a law of medicine that any symptom can have various underlying causes. Headaches, for example, can be caused by tension, poor posture, allergies, hormone shifts, a hangover, a concussion, a brain tumour, and more. The successful treatment of the symptom, the headache, will depend on understanding and treating its underlying cause. No doubt, aspirin and other painkillers can alleviate headaches in many cases, but unless the underlying process is changed, headaches are likely to recur, and in some cases get worse.

Mind-reading difficulties, like other psychological symptoms, can also come and go depending on circumstances. Life changes, loss, and marital tension are some of the circumstances that can exacerbate problems in social perception. Talking to an understanding listener is the equivalent of taking an aspirin for the mind. Whether with a therapist, teacher, friend, or clergyperson, a conversation with a reflective listener can often help solve a minor mind-reading problem, one brought on by stress or abrupt change; but unless the underlying process is changed, if the problem is serious, the symptom will return, sometimes worse than before.

With Carol and Mike, their mind-reading problems stem from their characteristic approaches to understanding the social world, their style of knowing. For Ariel, her difficulties arose from her characteristic response to anxiety and other intense emotions, or her temperament. Each of us falls on a continuum with respect to both of these characteristics, style of knowing and temperament, and from these traits stem both our weaknesses and strengths.

Good mind reading does not require a perfectly balanced style of knowing or an always-even temperament. If nature and nurture have provided these gifts, you have a head start. But whatever a person's style and temperament, being aware of them helps avoid misjudgements and allows the development of new approaches to social understanding that, with practice, can become second nature.

Even people with extreme styles and temperaments can navigate their social world well, though they are more prone to disruption if something unexpected occurs. Twenty years ago, if someone who generally got along well enough unexpectedly found himself in trouble with his social environment, psychotherapists would look primarily for psychological sources of this impaired mind-reading ability. Is the person feeling guilty for his success? Has he suffered a recent loss? Now there is an additional important factor to consider, as another of my patients, Nicholas, discovered a few years ago.

Nicholas is an extreme example in both in style (emotional) and temperament (low-reactive). In fact, it was his even and unflappable temperament that gave him sufficient control to enjoy the advantages of an extreme emotional style. Good instincts made art dealer Nicholas a quick study, and acute gut-level reactions gave him a good feel for other people's tolerance levels, for what they would and would not put up with. This latter attribute was particularly useful to the exuberantly freewheeling, high-spending Nicholas in his business dealings. Buying and selling major artwork requires access to big capital. No one was better at sensing when a creditor's patience was close to exhaustion, and no one was better at mollifying an aggrieved party with a well-timed loan payment— at least, no one was better until the summer of 2003, when Nicholas's emotional acuity suddenly deserted him and disaster ensued.

Like the characters in the Kurosawa film *Rashomon*, everyone who witnessed the spectacle of Nicholas's financial collapse that summer had a different perspective. To his wife, Bethany, Nicholas had been "cute" one time too often; in the middle of a debt restructuring negotiation, Nicholas had decamped to Spain on a two-week art-buying spree. From his partners' perspective, Nicholas's hubris had done him in—he was so sure the bank would approve a new loan, he had spent most of it by the time he learnt the loan was denied. Nicholas himself saw his collapse as a tale of magic lost. Mysteriously, his "touch"—his feel for people—had vanished, leading him to push his bank one loan too far. "I should have known better," he told me, during our first meeting.

Like everyone else who knew Nicholas, I also had an opinion about his downfall, one that incorporated rather than contradicted those of his friends and family. Almost immediately after the introduction of antidepressants in the 1950s, it became apparent that they can cause mania and psychosis, even occasionally in people who have no history of these disorders. More recently, the popular press has been full of reports about the link between adolescent suicide and antidepressants. But in all the furore over this horrific side effect, another important but subtle effect has been overlooked: antidepressants can blunt emotion and narrow affective experience. And it has recently become clear that SSRIs—drugs like Prozac and Zoloft—profoundly affect that brain structure so central to mindreading, the amygdala (Rhodes et al., 2007).

The day Nicholas visited my office for the first time, I asked him if there had been any significant changes in his life in the months prior to his bankruptcy.

He thought for a moment, then said, "No, not unless you count going on Prozac six months ago."

Changing the wiring of the brain

Nicholas is temperamentally unflappable, optimistic, and unafraid. He rarely felt anxiety in social situations. When he did, he intuitively felt that something was wrong. He might be pushing someone too far, or making too many demands. When Nicholas felt anxious, he knew it was time to stop whatever he was doing, turn on the charm, and take a close look at how he was affecting others. In other words, anxiety was a signal for him to switch from an emotional to a cognitive style of social interaction. Without his usual anxiety as a signal, Nicholas went from pushing people nearly to the edge to pushing them over the edge.

Suddenly Nicholas's usual good-enough approach to reading minds wasn't working. Nicholas was never clinically depressed. He had the usual ups and downs, but, like so many people today, he took antidepressants essentially as a performance enhancer. He had read that Prozac could make people feel "better than well" (Kramer, 1998). Prozac made him feel more energetic, but it also made him less sensitive and perceptive. Its effects were subtle, so that he was not even aware of what was happening until it was too late: Prozac had changed something basic in the wiring of the mind-reading circuits of his brain.

Antidepressants had the effect of changing the sensitivity of Nicholas' amygdala. Already a risk taker and excitement seeker by temperament, on Prozac he completely lost his ability to read social danger. The damage was "functional"—that is there was no lesion or scarring of brain tissue, and it was reversible—a few months after discontinuing the medication, his social judgement returned. Nicholas was lucky. Scientists cannot yet predict the long-term consequences of drugs that change the brain. We know some psychiatric medications—antipsychotics—can cause permanent damage. For many, the benefits outweigh the risks. However, it is important to recognize that antidepressant medications are powerful drugs that directly affect the wiring of the brain. People who take them may unwittingly be taking part in a long-term experiment whose outcome is far from certain.

For some patients I have seen, patients who are temperamentally shy like Ariel, antidepressants can dampen an overactive amygdala, diminish social anxiety, and, thereby, enhance mind-reading skills. In fact, too often people are given the diagnosis of depression based on complaints of social isolation or loneliness. While antidepressants may help temporarily—unless the patient uses her time on medication to learn social and mind-reading skills—the social anxiety may return when the medication is discontinued.

Simply knowing you are a cognitive or emotional knower can quickly help move your style closer to balanced and put you more in tune with the minds around you. When cognitive knower Mike pays attention to his discomfort, he becomes a more emotional knower. When emotional knower Carol listens very carefully, she becomes a more cognitive knower; both shift closer to the centre. The brain never stops changing. Leaning to read minds more accurately, becoming a more balanced knower, builds neural pathways establishing clearer and faster connections between the neocortex and the amygdala. The feelings of your heart and your gut become more accessible and more under the control of your thinking brain, and your thinking becomes less detached from emotion.

The power of emotion to affect thought and thought to affect emotion is remarkable. Biology is important, but it is not destiny. In Chapter Three, we looked at Jerome Kagan's research showing that many constitutionally shy children become sociable adolescents and adults. Inhibited adults, like shy children, can also use their imagination to their advantage, especially if someone important supports them. A shy young man I knew fell in love with a daring young woman. On an early summer evening together they went to the county fair. On the way to the livestock exhibits they passed a giant roller coaster. She excitedly pulled him to the front of the line, saying how much she loved the thrill of the first car. He couldn't tell her he had never been on a rollercoaster before. He felt silly to be afraid, but he was worried he would faint or vomit or scream. Then he remembered a documentary about the first astronauts. The acceleration of a rocket was many times that of the fastest roller coaster, one astronaut had said. The young man vividly imagined he was an astronaut readying himself for lift-off. Holding the young woman's hand, he led her on board. They have been married for many years, and he loves to take the kids on roller coasters.

Finding balance in the brain, the body, and the mind

Balance is important both in body and in mind. A balanced start and the ability to regain balance are central to athletic performance. People with a poor sense of balance are often afraid to move lest they fall. Being well-balanced feels secure; being unbalanced feels dangerous. The scales of justice must be balanced in order for the evidence to be fairly weighed. It is common for metaphors of mind to parallel descriptions of physical experience. Freud famously wrote, "The I is first and foremost the body-I", that is, our psychological sense of self is patterned on our sense of our body. Many contemporary neuroscientists have gone further and embraced a model of the mind called embodied cognition. This theory proposes that all forms of thinking originate in sensations from the body— thoughts are feelings first. Following this, we might conjecture that justice is depicted as blind because our core sense of balance—and fairness—comes not from our eyes but from our gut; and that we deeply know that our most important sense is not vision but introception, our perception of how our body feels.

The part of the brain responsible for introception, the insula, or insular cortex, has come into sharp focus of late. It is a complex structure buried deep in the brain between the parietal and temporal lobes. Because it is so hidden under folds of cortex, it could not be studied with the older methodologies of probes and electrodes, and its full significance has only recently become apparent as neuroimaging has become more refined. It is now clear that it plays a major role in the CEN, and may in fact be the centre of self-awareness and consciousness. The insula gathers information from receptors for touch, heat, cold, pain, taste, itch, rhythm, pitch, heart rate, sexual arousal, and orgasm. It detects hunger and other cravings. It tells us when we need to breathe and when our bladder is full. In addition to integrating internal sensations with the other senses to produce a representation of our body, it is responsible for homeostasis, keeping our bodily functions stable in changing environments. It. regulates heart rate, blood pressure, blood glucose, and more. The insula is thickly connected with other parts of the CEN, in particular the amygdala and medial prefrontal cortex. The question, "How do you feel," is answered largely by your insula, as is the question, "How do I survive during wartime?" (Paulus et al., 2009): "Keep your balance," is its answer.

Under conditions of threat, the experienced soldier has the same initial amygdala reaction as a novice, and though his body is in the same physiological state of arousal, he does not feel the same fear; he does not become unbalanced. Instead, his insula becomes more active and the arousal is turned towards focusing attention both on the external and internal perceptions. The insula's connection with the body provides a visceral sense of stability that makes it possible to feel steady in the face of uncertainty. Emotions are moderated, not suppressed, and become signals about the environment that can be examined. In that way, the soldier can be attuned to danger without being overwhelmed by fear. People who do well in extreme high stress situations do not block emotional knowledge. Gut reactions, and back of the head perceptions are closely attended to and so, in fact, seem become more vivid.

In gathering disparate sensory data—feelings of touch and heat and fullness, and the like—the insula creates a reflection of the internal world as it stands in relation to the outside world, an awareness of a boundaried self. The insula not only gathers information about bodily states, in its balance-maintaining homeostatic role it anticipates how the body will react and how the individual will feel in a future environment that is perceived or imagined (*ibid.*). This felt experience of moving forward in space and time may lie at the root of consciousness. The anticipatory response primes the body for quicker, more effective action. Looking out of the window at a snowy day can prompt a shiver as the insula prepares to take action to maintain body temperature. In the same way, as a soldier enters a dangerous environment, the insula gathers introceptive data—gut reactions, funny feelings, stress, anxiety, etc.—and primes the body to attend to and react quickly to potential threats. An Army study reported that troops who were good at spotting hidden bombs in simulations tended to think of themselves as predators, not prey (Cary, 2009). Whether you are a soldier approaching danger, or a young man awaiting a roller coaster, anticipating a successful action makes it more likely to happen.

CHAPTER SIX

Bad feelings

"¿Cómo estás?" "Comment ça va?" "Wie geht's?" "How are you?" is uttered in greetings billions of times a day throughout the world. "Fine," is the predictable reply. *Do ask, don't tell* is the rule. You are not expected to really answer the question; and if you did, what would you say? "How are you feeling?" is not usually a question about emotion but about health. If you mentioned your cold yesterday, your co-worker might ask, "How are you feeling today?" The same question asked in earnest about your emotional state often leads to awkward fumbling and a vague reply. Therapists' questions about feelings are often answered, "I think I feel this," or "I guess I feel that," or "How should I know what I feel?" To feel, to touch, to sense, and to experience emotion are at the core of our existence. Is it not then odd that we so often do not know what we feel?

Hungry, horny, or scared?

Sara's husband Bill is working late at the office again. It's Friday night. The kids are out. Sara curls up on the couch in front of the

TV. Flipping through the channels, she finds an old James Bond movie. "Sean Connery really was sexy . . . I wish there was more excitement in my life. . . . married sex isn't what it used to be . . . maybe when Bill gets home . . . why is he working late again . . . is something going on," she muses as she reaches for her favourite cookies. Is Sara hungry, horny, or scared?

Emotions and feelings are synonyms. Emotions are feelings, bodily sensations. But what distinguishes one feeling from another? Fear from excitement? Hunger from fatigue? The heart beats faster in both joy and anger. The eyes are downcast in both sadness and shame. Does each emotion have its own body signature, its own unique combination of physical signals? Or are all emotions aroused and energized by the body, named and given meaning by the mind? In one of the most important experiments in the history of psychology, Stanley Schacter of Columbia and Jerome Singer of Penn State, set out to answer this question (Schachter & Singer, 1962). With offers of credit or money, they recruited 184 college students to take part in what was described as a vitamin study. The students were told they would receive a vitamin injection before having their vision tested. Unbeknown to the students, instead of receiving an injection of vitamins, they were injected with either adrenalin or water.

Adrenalin, as discussed in Chapter Four, pours into your blood-stream when the amygdala senses danger. It arouses the body to run or fight. Heart rate, blood pressure, and breathing rate climb, increasing the supply of energy-giving oxygen. Your stomach knots and your mouth becomes dry, as blood flows away from the digestive system to where it is most needed. Dilated pupils make your eyes more sensitive to subtle movements. You sweat in preparation for action. Adrenalin injections produce the same effects. The students were ready for danger. They experienced all the feelings of fear, but there was nothing to be afraid of.

Half of the 184 students in the experiment received adrenalin injections and half received water injections. While waiting to receive their adrenalin injection and again while receiving it, some of the students were told that the "vitamins" might produce side effects including sweating, shaking, and rapid heartbeat; the others were told the drug was mild and should cause no discomfort.[1]

After the injection, each student was taken to a waiting room and introduced to another "student". In fact, the other student was a professional actor, a paid collaborator of the experimenter. When the student and actor were alone together, the actor feigned great emotion. With half the student subjects, the actor pretended to be wildly happy, giddy, and euphoric about the experiment. With the other half, the actor pretended to be unhappy, despondent, and angry.

It is a little confusing with so many groups, so I'll go to the main point. Ninety-two students had received adrenalin, so were feeling the very same sensations in their bodies that are felt in fear. Forty-six of these subjects had a *clear explanation*: They were experiencing a side effect of the vitamin injection. The other forty-six had *no explanation* of why they were feeling what they were feeling.

Clear explanation subjects were not influenced by the actor. They cognitively understood they were feeling a physical reaction and did not experience strong emotion.

No explanation subjects were influenced by the actor. No explanation subjects placed with the angry actor became angry. No explanation subjects placed with the euphoric actor became euphoric. *The very same body sensations produced entirely different emotions, depending on the social environment.* The social environment provided a ready explanation for the inexplicable arousal.

Recall there were ninety-two additional subjects who received a water injection. They were not told anything about the effects of the injection because there were no effects. Interestingly, the water-injected subjects also experienced the emotion of the actor, not as often or as intensely as no explanation adrenalin-injected subjects, but more than the clear explanation adrenalin subjects.[2] In all likelihood the water-injected subjects were feeling some arousal due to anxiety—simply getting an injection makes most people anxious—and that arousal was cognitively transformed into mild elation or anger by the social environment.

In later experiments (Mezzacappa, Katkin, & Palmer, 1999), subjects who were injected with adrenalin without knowing its effects, but who were not manipulated towards an emotion, tended to feel more negative, and they reported more negative memories than those who were injected with water. Their memories were affected without them knowing why. Unexplained, unexpected arousal is usually experienced negatively as apprehension and anxiety and is naturally associated with fear.

It is common to be in a state of inexplicable uncomfortable arousal. If it is not too intense, people try to ignore it. The self-conscious fumbling that often follows being asked, "How do you feel?" is a consequence of being forced to focus on those feelings and label them. Stressed, irritated, overwhelmed, uneasy, anxious, and on edge are some of the ways the state is often described. In this state, people often overreact. For example, a parent who is on edge may scream at a child who didn't pick up her toys. Paradoxically, feeling tired or down is often a response to the stress of unexplained chronic fear arousal.

A recent study shows that most people, when they experience emotion triggered by an unconscious perception, will scan the environment in search of its cause and will readily accept any semi-reasonable sounding explanation rather than rely on their unconscious gut reaction. *Consciously available information suppresses unconscious knowledge.* The authors of the study conclude almost grudgingly that their findings seem "to be in line with the Freudian mechanism of active repression of unconscious information by consciousness" (Jolij & Lamme, 2006). If you are feeling anxious or angry without knowing why, your messy child can provide a reasonable explanation. If you are angry because your gut is telling you something that you don't want to know—your husband is drinking again, for example—you may welcome having your child give you a reason for your anger.

The brain continues to react to the unconsciously processed information—particularly if it is frightening—despite attempts to ignore its signals (de Gelder, Morris, & Dolan, 2005). This can lead to lead to lingering feelings of unease or uncertainty about a judgement or decision. In *Blink,* Malcolm Gladwell tells how the Getty Museum paid nearly $10 million for a forgery of an ancient Greek statue because experts on the board of directors made a decision based on available information rather their gut reactions. Supported by questionable documentation and limited scientific testing, they concluded the statue was authentic. Some felt uneasy about the statue; others knew in their hearts that something was wrong. One art historian even felt revulsion at the sight of the statue, but neither he nor the others could say exactly what was causing their reactions. If the statue were authentic, it would have been a significant addition to the museum's collection, and the desire for this tipped the balance in favour of cognition over emotion.

Anxiety—the chameleon emotion

The words fear and anxiety are often used interchangeably: "I'm afraid that if I really look closely, I'll find out that he had an affair" and "I'm anxious that if I really look closely, I'll find out that he had an affair" mean the same thing. In psychology, a distinction is sometimes made. Fear is a response to real danger and anxiety is a response to imagined danger. If there is a fire in your house, you feel fear. If you think you might have left the stove on, you feel anxiety. You feel fear when you see a bear; you feel anxiety while walking in the woods imagining a bear. The bodily effects of fear and anxiety are the same: the same palpitations, the same sweats, the same shortened breaths. They feel the same, and it is often difficult to know which you are experiencing. Why do you have that knot in your stomach when you think about your husband staying late at the office? Is it anxiety based on your irrational insecurities, or fear based on your realistic perceptions, or both?

In many cases, determining whether something is realistically dangerous is a matter of judgement. Should you be afraid to drive a motorcycle, ride a horse, pet a pit bull, parachute from a plane? Should you fear beef because of mad cow disease, tuna because of mercury, packaged greens because of E. coli, or butter because of cholesterol? The list of foods alone that some people fear and others do not could go on forever. It is possible to make rational decisions about these matters, but people often do not. The best seller *Freakonomics* offers dramatic examples of people unnecessarily fearing certain things and not fearing things about which they should have concern. For example, the risk of your child being killed by a gun is about a thousand times less than her dying in a swimming pool; yet most parents feel more comfortable with their child having a play date at the home of a neighbour with a swimming pool than at the home of one who owns a gun.

In the rural suburbs of New York City, sightings of bears are a frequent topic of worried conversation. Yet in most of the United

States bears present no real danger. The chance of being injured by a bear while in the woods is about one in ten million. By comparison, the chance of being injured in a car accident is about one in one hundred. The bear in the woods is an adult version of the bogeyman in the basement. Many times, people prefer to believe they are feeling rational fear rather than anxiety. Anxiety seems inescapable because it comes from one's own mind. Fear has an object, something that can be avoided. It feels better to believe you don't want to walk alone in the woods because there are bears than to admit you still feel a child's dread of being abandoned and devoured.

Mislabelling anxiety as fear affects people's lives in all sorts of troubling ways. Phobias are unreasonable fears fuelled by unrecognized anxiety. Common phobias restrict both vocational and recreational activities. Fear of public speaking, by some estimates, affects over 85% of the population. Fear of flying affects about 25%. Some phobias, such as fear of going to the doctor, clearly increase risk. Others can increase risk in more subtle ways. September 11 shook America deeply, shattering our illusions of invulnerability and specialness, and threatening to force us to examine our relationships with the rest of the world and to look hard at things we did not want to see. Rather than looking inward to examine the sources of our anxiety, we looked only outward for the sources of our fear, with the encouragement of our leaders. The response of many was to become irrationally fearful. Of course, there were real enemies to fear, but our fear of terrorists was, and continues to be, far out of proportion to any real threat. Anxiety fuels our fears. A few weeks after the attack, a survey showed people thought there was nearly a fifty per cent chance of any given individual being injured in a terrorist attack over the course of the next year (Lerner, Gonzalez, Small, & Fischhoff, 2003). Many people avoided flying and drove long distances instead. In October, November, and December of 2001, there was around a three per cent increase both in miles driven and in fatal traffic accidents (Gigerenzer, 2004). It is estimated that about 350 people died who would not have died if they had flown as usual—350 people who would not have died if they had understood their anxiety and not turned it into fear.

Anxiety can fuel any emotion. While Sara is home watching TV, she feels unexplained anxiety. Maybe she is anxious being alone. Maybe she knows something about her husband she does not want to know. Maybe she is worried about her kids. Who knows? Seeing young Sean Connery, she feels sexually aroused. Having her favourite cookies nearby, she feels hungry. Hungry and horny are common transformations of anxiety.

Most parents respond to their babies by mirroring them in an exaggerated, playful, almost cartoonish manner. For instance, when an infant looks sad or distressed, the parent will mirror the look, but with clown-like frown. By exaggerating the baby's expression, parents are saying, "I understand what you are feeling, but it is not what I am feeling. Don't worry. I'll take care of it." Part of the reason children love cartoons is that they make difficult emotions playful.

Sometimes, when a baby is displaying a difficult-to-soothe or troubling emotion, parents mislabel the emotion. Some parents mislabel inconsistently, leading the child to mistrust emotion and develop a cognitive style of knowing. Others mislabel difficult emotions consistently, responding to distress or anger as if it were hunger and nearly always trying to get their fussy baby to eat. You can imagine how this might lead to an adult who tends to experience his or her distress as hunger. Similarly, some parents respond to distressing emotions by stimulating their baby in an excited way, bouncing the baby up and down, throwing the baby in the air, placing the baby in an automatic rocker. Such babies become adults who soothe their distressing emotions with excitement.

Anxiety is the chameleon of emotions. It feels just like fear, the emotion whose ancient evolutionary function is to arouse the individual to deal with danger and to learn to avoid future danger. In the absence of a clear danger, or in the presence of a danger we prefer not to see—an unfaithful spouse, an uncomplimentary boss, a competitive friend—we look for explanations of our arousal in something that seems easier to handle—hunger, sexual excitement, the pressing need for new shoes. In organizations—work, school, the military—inappropriate sexual behaviour, overeating, and impulsive shopping all increase with the level of unexplained tension in an organization. I think part of the appeal of watching shows like *ER* and *CSI* is in vicariously enjoying the relief of transforming anxiety into sexual excitement while at the same time feeling wisely distant from the dangers of that transformation.

Transforming anxiety into excitement is not always a bad thing. It can make us foolish, but it can also make us brave. People who plunge into situations in order to overcome their fears are sometimes called "counterphobic". This again is the unfortunate pathologizing of diversity. It is often more adaptive to deal with fears by facing them than by giving in to them. We have seen that temperamentally shy people can learn to be outgoing by successfully forcing themselves into social situations. In fact, those temperamentally shy children who become outgoing and sociable are the ones whose mothers have encouraged them to be adventurous even when they are anxious. Most successful therapies for phobia involve slowly facing the fear. The key to confronting fear is to have a strategy that will lead to success, or at worst a graceful exit, and not trauma.

The impact of facing a social fear and having a positive experience can be remarkable. Daniel Tammet's descriptions of facing his fear are poignant. At sixteen, he developed an intense crush on a new student in his school. Tall, confident, and sociable, he was quite the opposite of Daniel. Daniel helped him with his homework and trailed him around. Getting little response, he handed him a note confessing his feelings. The new student waited for Daniel after school. He handed back the note and said gently that he could not be the person he wanted him to be. We can only imagine Daniel's relief at not being taunted or abused, a much more common experience for shy, awkward adolescents. Daniel Tammet had the good fortune and, I would suspect, the emotional knowledge then and in the future to choose people who would treat him kindly when he took great risks. His remarkable progress demonstrates that this is a good lesson for us all.

Anxiety is also the MSG, the flavour enhancer, of emotion. It can enhance whatever else we feel. Its synergy with fear, as we have seen, is particularly striking, since they are similar but for the matter of judgement. Actors enlist their anxiety to feel and express all emotions more intensely; a bit of stage fright is a good thing. Public speakers, lawyers, and other performers who take beta-blockers—drugs that reduce the physical experience of anxiety—sometimes complain that their performances are flat. The anxiety of the unfamiliar and the risky can intensify sexual excitement, but excessive anxiety can impair sexual function. Psychologists talk about the optimal level of anxiety for learning: too little and there is no motivation; too much and focus is lost. Negative feelings, like anger and sadness, are also intensified by anxiety. Anxiety makes physical pain more painful and intensifies the pain of depression. Someone who is anxious and depressed may become agitated rather than listless and is more likely to commit suicide.

Anxiety about knowing

Reading minds is often fraught with anxiety. Do we really want to know what another person is thinking? When knowing what is on someone's mind could lead to an awkward or uncomfortable situation, anxiety may distort or inhibit our perception. If you let yourself know what is on another person's mind, would you really be afraid? Think of all the married people who have been shocked by the discovery of a spouse's infidelity, yet at the same time felt they knew it all along. As children, we wanted to know that our parents loved us and understood our feelings and desires well enough, but we didn't want to know too much about their thoughts when they were angry, preoccupied, or frustrated. When such knowledge is forced upon a child, it feels overwhelming. To read minds, you need to get past childhood anxiety about knowing too much, and begin uncovering the secrets of the adult world.

Unless they are with intimate companions, most people do not want their minds read and try to keep their thoughts hidden in various ways. Even in intimate relationships people try to keep some thoughts hidden. Perhaps the most insidious technique for hiding a thought involves raising and manipulating the anxiety of the potential mind reader. For instance, if Bill were having an affair, he might complain to Sara that work is almost too difficult to bear; he is afraid of having a heart attack; he might lose his job; expenses need to be closely watched. He accuses Sarah of overspending. Sara now feels even more anxious, and attributes all of her anxiety to her concern for Bill's health and their financial worries. She may blame herself and, if anxious enough, feel too frozen to think straight. In the classic 1944 movie *Gaslight*, a charming but sadistically deceitful husband attempts to drive his naïvely adoring young wife crazy by convincing her that she is imagining the frightening events he is secretly causing. When she becomes insane, he plans to steal her inheritance. Any suspicion on the wife's part is pronounced a sign of further mental instability by the husband. Gaslighting now refers to this extreme form of mind manipulation. Unscrupulous political leaders use a similar tactic. They raise the citizens' level of anxiety by amplifying existing fears and making up new ones. Everything is blamed on a conveniently alien enemy. Any suspicion is labelled unpatriotic weakness or treason.

Sometimes people unwittingly make us feel anxious and crazy. Certain character types—sometimes called borderline personalities—subtly and without conscious intent manipulate us to feel their helpless pain. To read minds well you must learn to tolerate the anxiety of social interaction, to question readily offered explanations of your unexplained feelings, to delay, at least sometimes, the ever-popular methods of relieving social tension—sex, eating, drinking, drugs, and shopping—and to entertain the possibility that your anxiety and other emotions reflect something important about the person you are with.

Shame

If fear and anxiety are the primal emotions, then shame and its cousins, embarrassment and humiliation, are the most painful. People kill to save face. Sometimes they kill others; sometimes they kill themselves. Unlike fear, shame seems inescapable. Shame reflects someone's worth. You have been judged and found wanting. You are inadequate. There is nothing to escape from; it is you. You want to sink into a hole and disappear. Suicide eliminates the self. Murder eliminates the judge.

Truman Capote describes Perry Smith, lonely, unloved, legs painfully deformed by a car accident, as a damaged man possessed by visions of grandeur. Breaking into the Clutters' home with his sidekick Dick, expecting to find thirty thousand dollars, instead he finds next to nothing and is reduced to crawling under a bed for a silver dollar. Capote spent countless hours interviewing Smith. Smith says to Capote,

> Mr. Clutter asked me—and these were his last words—wanted to know how his wife was, if she was all right, and I said she was fine, she was ready to go to sleep, and I told him it wasn't long till morning, and how in the morning somebody would find them, and then

all of it, me and Dick and all, would seem like something they dreamed. I wasn't kidding him. I didn't want to harm the man. I thought he was a very nice gentleman. Soft-spoken. I thought so right up to the moment I cut his throat . . . I knelt down beside Mr. Clutter, and the pain of kneeling—I thought of that goddamn dollar. Silver dollar. The shame. Disgust. And *they'd* told me never to come back to Kansas. But I didn't realize what I'd done till I heard the sound. Like somebody drowning. Screaming under water. [Capote, 1965]

Thankfully, most people never experience shame so intense. Yet many people lead their lives in fear of being judged; sulking, irritated, ready to snap angrily at anyone whose accidental glance or offhand comment may be mistaken for criticism. Even more people restrict their activities to avoid feeling ashamed. It is commonplace to avoid speaking, dancing, or singing in public for fear of humiliation. Often, people will not admit it, instead claiming lack of interest or skill. The same is true of reading minds. People do not try because they are afraid to be embarrassed if they are wrong. Even more inhibiting is the fear of being shamed by what you see— what does that person really think of me? Do I really want to know?

Guilt and shame are not the same, though they often go together. Guilt is feeling bad for something you have done. Shame is feeling bad for who you are. If you break a friend's expensive antique platter, you might feel guilty, but you replace the platter or take your friend out to dinner. If you betray a friend and your betrayal breaks a friend's heart, you will feel ashamed. The feeling of shame does not go away quickly. It can be covered up by bravado and lies, but under cover it fades even more slowly. You might cry in shame and beg for forgiveness. But betrayal is difficult to forgive and your presence is a constant reminder. Guilt can be overcome through forgiveness, penance, reparation, punishment. Someone found guilty of a crime might be forgiven, or he might be required to do community service, or make payment to the victim, or serve time. Shame must be borne until memory fades. Some cultures and some individuals view every bad act as reflective of a bad soul. The Puritans punished even minor crimes by public shaming. People who are prone to feeling ashamed similarly believe that any minor transgression reflects a moral defect.

The origins of shame

Imagine this experience: you are walking and talking with a friend in a museum. You are both looking at the art. You are talking animatedly when you turn to your friend and discover she is not there and has not been there for a while. What did you feel? At least a bit embarrassed or ashamed? You can probably feel your startled silence, your flushing face, as you remember. Imagine now that when you turn, not only is your friend not there, but you have been talking to a complete stranger. Your embarrassment is undoubtedly greater, more so if the stranger gives you an odd look, but it is quickly relieved if the stranger smiles and joins you in laughter.

Why does such a seemingly benign interaction leave us feeling ashamed? It is the prototypical shame experience: expecting to be heard and instead meeting silence or, even worse, disapproval. The feeling of shame is heightened if you are excitedly expecting praise. What is more mortifying than giving your all to a performance and being greeted by silence? As early as two months, babies become upset when adults do not respond. The "still face experiment", developed by Ed Tronick and his Harvard associates in 1978, in a multitude of variations, has become a staple of developmental psychology research (Tronick, Als, Adamson, Wise, & Brazelton, 1978). You can try it yourself at home if you have or can borrow a two- to six-month-old infant. Place the baby in the baby carrier or car seat on a table or a counter so the two of you can interact comfortably face to face. Engage playfully for two to three minutes, smiling, talking, and making faces. Then stop. Remain stone-faced and mute, if you can stand it, for two minutes. Then start behaving normally again. During the still-faced period, most babies will stop smiling, fidget with their hands and clothes, and turn away. If you measure heart rate it will be high, indicating arousal and stress. Some babies will cry at a still face, but more will cry when normality resumes. Most babies will remain fussy for a while. I do not recommend that you do this more than once or twice, since your baby will probably get upset, but he or she will quickly recover, and you will face clearly the impact of parental inattention.

Your child runs up to you and excitedly displays his latest drawing, but you are preoccupied, don't really look, and mumble in a monotone, "It's really nice." Everyone spaces out occasionally, lost in thought, staring into space, still-faced. Severely depressed parents do it more often. The children of depressed mothers are more likely to be sad and angry children, depressed and suicidal adults, and filled with shame. Babies develop different strategies to enliven their caretakers. Tronick describes one five-month-old's reaction to his still-faced mum: "He looked at his mother and laughed briefly. After this brief tense laugh, he paused, looked at her soberly, and then laughed again, loud and long, throwing his head back as he did so" (*ibid.*, p. 12). Unable to restrain herself, mum broke into laughter.

Comedians and other entertainers often have depressed parents.[3] Many things that we as adults feel are shameful—drooling, spitting-up, farting, soiling, being awkward and fumbling, using the wrong word—were not at all shameful when we were babies. Comedy can make us feel like delightful babies again. A good part of comedy is saying or doing humiliating things and provoking laugher instead of silence or disgust. In a similar way, lovers take pleasure in each other's bodies, nuzzling up, tasting, smelling, sucking, and taking in odours and fluids that, were they a stranger's, would be disgusting. In erotically charged states, disgust is not overcome; rather, it does not exist, hearkening back again to a time before shame.

Disgust is primal, one of the most basic and universal emotions. Excrement, vomit, bad breath, sweat-soaked towels, nasal mucous, half-eaten food, spit, sweat, rotten meat, maggots, scabs, and rats are some of the things people of all cultures find disgusting. When an animal eats something rotten, spoiled, bad tasting, it is disgusted. Think about biting into a hamburger and discovering it is rotten, crawling with maggots. What happens to your face? Did you wrinkle your nose, squinch your eyes, and open your mouth, feel a little nauseated? Almost all mammals show a similar expression when rejecting something unpalatable. For some scavenger mammals, our dogs for example, almost nothing is disgusting. Maybe that's why dogs are so accepting. But if you can find something your dog takes into its mouth but will not swallow, its facial expression will show disgust. People also show the same reaction when morally offended. Think of reactions to child-abusing priests and prostitute-soliciting politicians. "That's disgusting," is commonly uttered when people disapprove of a sexual behaviour. It is as if they were trying to spit out and get rid of both the offence and the offender. Spitting on someone is an extreme expression of rejection—contempt.

Contempt is an escalation of disgust. It is disgust combined with anger. When one animal looks disgustedly or contemptuously at another, it is giving a warning that if it continues doing whatever it is doing, it will be spit out, rejected. Social psychologists call this a threat of social exclusion. Threats of social exclusion are powerful inhibitors. Individuals so threatened usually stop what they are doing, look downcast, and hang their head in shame. These are signs of submission, pleas for reconnection. Blushing, another common expression of shame, is in other contexts a sign of sexual arousal, and is probably an ancestral signal of sexual surrender.

When people are shamed, they hurt; they feel pain, often intensely. Tears are often shed in humiliation. There is evidence that the same parts of the brain (the anterior cingulate cortex, in particular) that signal physical pain also signal the pain of embarrassment and shame. Well before weapons and words, nature provided primates a method for inflicting pain from a distance: the look. Disgusted frowns, contemptuous glares, inflict pain and communicate: stop what you are doing, get back here now or never come back again. Of course, submission is not the only recourse for the individual threatened by the look. Fleeing or fighting are built-in responses to pain. When painfully shamed, some individuals flee and seek solace in the company of others. In primate groups, a monkey that has been shunned sometimes goes off to another group, or may even try to form a new group of its own. In humans, family fissures and feuds are based on similar reactions. Other shamed individuals counterattack. Violence, intimate violence in particular, is most often a reaction to feeling shamed. It is dangerous to shame someone who cannot submit and has nowhere else to turn.

Shame develops and is experienced at three levels: feeling excitement unreflected, feeling disgust, and feeling contemptible. At around twelve to eighteen months, shame takes centre stage. Children undertake two exceptionally important performances, walking and using the toilet. Too often, their excitement about their accomplishments is met with silence and disgust. Alan Schore, a psychologist at UCLA, has written extensively about the debilitating impact of excessive shame (Schore, 1994). Toddlers' running around and fearlessly exploring the world need to be controlled. Danger is everywhere. Schore estimates that mothers say "no" to their toddlers about once every nine minutes! Sometimes the no is spoken, and sometimes it is given with a look. Almost everyone remembers their mother's disapproving expression.

Like the look of an adult threatening a moral offender with banishment, the mother's look contains elements of disgust, sometimes even contempt, but it is usually tempered with a glimmer of a smile, and followed by joy and praise when the child stops and listens. For the dependent child, much more than the adult, untempered looks of disgust and contempt, and their verbal equivalents, are powerful inhibitors, threatening separation, causing terrible pain. They stop children dead in their tracks, and, if too intense or frequent, plunge the recipient into a black hole of shame. This is what adults abused as children mean when they say, as they frequently do, "The looks and the yelling were worse than the beating." Non-injurious hitting, as strange as this may sound, involves touching and, as such, carries at least a glimmer of connection. "You disgust me, you make me sick," and similar expressions threaten abandonment, and by labelling the poor child unpalatable lead to the chronic question, "Who could ever love me?"

Most parents quickly get past their feelings of disgust about wiping up and changing diapers. Often men, having had no previous experience with babies, anticipate great difficulty only to be relieved when instead they feel an intimate connection. But some parents never quite get over feeling disgusted by their baby's excrement, and others feel it return in force when their child displays creativity by smearing faeces on the playroom wall or, when engaged in the toilet training battle, becomes constipated and has "accidents". It is not an accident that feeling ashamed and feeling shitty often go hand-in-hand.

You are not being judged

Debra deeply loved her new boyfriend, Eric, and felt deeply loved in return. She knew he was smart, talented, and sensitive, and cared for her, but was upset that her friends didn't feel the same way. In truth, they thought he was a pompous ass, always pontificating, opinionated about everything. He thought he knew it all and never seemed to listen. On first meeting him, her friends were frankly awed. He was handsome, almost too well dressed, a successful producer who knew the rich and famous; but they quickly tired of his ceaseless name-dropping. Debra kept telling her friends, "He's not like that with me. You should give him a chance." But it never seemed to work. They found him not only irritating, but also cold.

Fear of being shamed or humiliated makes it nearly impossible to read minds. Everyone becomes a judge. In its extreme and chronic form, for someone like Eric, a narcissistic personality, life is dominated by the need to be admired and praised. Constant adulation is required to counter deep inner feelings of shame. Any hint of disapproval or lack of interest can lead to despair and anger at the offending judge. Narcissists do not seem to care about others' thoughts or feelings. It is not that they are incapable of reading minds, but it usually feels too risky. What if they see they are being judged? It is safer not to try, safer not even to listen to what others have to say. Yet if a narcissist feels really safe in a relationship, he or she can become remarkably relatable. If the narcissist is lucky enough to be an emotional knower, she or he can sometimes make quick gut judgements about who can be trusted to not be critical. That was the case with Eric and Debra. When they met, she saw that he was frightened and vulnerable; he saw that she was caring, uncritical, and admiring. Theirs is not an uncommon relationship: with the difficult self-centred performer, usually a man, and his understanding lover. The difficult performer may be an actor, artist, scientist, lawyer, almost anything; but being admired for his performance is key. His lover's role is to admire his performance and protect him from the potentially shaming criticisms of others by warding it off or countering it with praise. If the lover's admiration falters, or a criticism penetrates, the narcissist can become cruel. Eric was frightened of Debra's friends; frightened that they might undermine Debra's uncritical admiration, frightened they might reveal his shame. To them he was haughty and cold.

A frightened emotional knower cannot read other minds, for fear of feeling judged or feeling ashamed. A frightened cognitive knower has the advantage of tools that can operate from a distance. When someone needs constant admiration, you should look for signs of sensitivity to shame. In extreme cases, an offhand remark or a mild criticism can lead the person to pull angrily away. Reading the mind of the narcissist requires patience and non-critical empathy. Therapists have learnt from generations of disappointing failures that weeks or even months must go by before it is OK to say anything to a narcissistic patient that he does not already know (Kohut, 1971). Until the narcissist feels comfortably secure, being told something new is experienced as a criticism.

The brown dog of depression

If you paint, you know that if you mix too many colours together, the resulting colour is muddy, and dull. If you keep adding colours, it will turn an ever darker brown. Eventually, the mess will look almost black, but still dull, not a clear sharp black. The same is true of emotions. Echoing Winston Churchill, many refer to depression as the "black dog", all-too-familiar, and always hanging around. I know that dog and I think it's a dull muddy brown. Every depression is a complex mix of emotion that can include loss, anxiety, rage, shame, guilt, pride, and hope. Depression is the ailment of our age. Even stock markets and economies get depressed.

Sidney Blatt, a psychologist at Yale, is one of the few researchers to study different types of depression. He has identified two broad groups, dependent and self-critical, each with different core emotions.[4] The core emotions of dependent depression are loneliness, helplessness, and fear of being left without care; those prone to dependent depression feel a great need to be loved and protected. The core emotions of self-critical depression are shame, and guilt; those prone to self-critical depression need constant recognition and praise. You might recognize Debra as someone prone to dependent depression and her boyfriend Eric as someone prone to self-critical depression. That means if either were to get depressed, each one's depression would take a different form, and each would need something different to feel better.

When I teach, one of my favourite words is heterogeneity, which means difference and diversity. No matter how you define a group of humans, if you look closely enough, you will find heterogeneity. Group people by age, sex, ethnicity, even genetic similarity, you will still find within that group a wonderful and astounding diversity. This is just as true if you group people by psychiatric diagnosis. *DSM-IV*, the bible of psychiatric diagnosis, gives a list of symptoms including sadness, emptiness, guilt, worthlessness, tiredness, over- or under-sleeping, weight loss or gain, listlessness, or agitation. If you have a certain number for a certain time, then you are depressed. I agree, you are depressed; you feel really bad. But what depression means for you might be very different than what it means for me. And though we each might feel bad in our own way, bad feelings tend to clump together. Psychiatric research shows that over half of all people diagnosed with depression could also be diagnosed with anxiety disorder. Don't be too impressed by the fact that antidepressants work for different types of depression. That doesn't mean that all depressions have the same cause. Aspirin works for headaches caused by colds, allergies, a bad day at the office, or a knock on the head. A basic principal of medicine is that behind every symptom lies a heterogeneity of causes.

What all depressions do share is that muddy dull mix lacking clarity; a complex, overwhelming, and often conflicting blend of emotions that all feel like too much. Emotional fog is the result. In the middle of the muddy mix, depressed people have difficulty reading their own minds. Friends often have a much better idea of what is going on, what event, loss, or disappointment might have triggered the depression, and often know what emotions lie behind the still face. Friends often sense improvement before the depressed person feels it. A standard psychiatrist's question in the weeks following a prescription is, "Have your friends noticed any change?" Cognitive and emotional knowers relating to the same depressed friend may read different things. The emotional knower may feel anger from their friend, even when the friend is not aware of it. A cognitive knower may figure out that their friend's depression began soon after failing to get a promotion at work. Both may be right. The friend's depression may contain shame and sadness about not getting the promotion as well as deep anger towards the boss who took it away.

Depression affects the mind-reading abilities of cognitive and emotional knowers differently. Depression attenuates all emotion. For emotional knowers, who rely on their gut feelings, depression makes it difficult to understand the people around them. Family and friends will, in turn, feel misunderstood. As a result, the depressed emotional knower feels increasingly isolated and alone. For cognitive knowers, who have little emotional knowledge to begin with, depression can have a particularly curious effect. They become compulsive data collectors in the hope that gathering reams of information will tell them what their gut cannot. But in the muddle of depression, nothing ever becomes clear. Depressed cognitive knowers can become indecisive to the point of agitation. For all, depression interferes with mind-reading ability. Research shows it both diminishes the ability to read emotions from faces as well as to formulate a nuanced theory of the other's mind (Lee, 2003). This depressive blindness to others' thoughts and feelings may be at the root of the social isolation common to all forms of depression.

Paranoia is the default position

When we do not know what is going on, we are prone to feel fearful; when we do not understand another person, we are prone to feel paranoid. The basic function of the brain is to protect the organism from danger, to keep it away from that which may cause it harm. Fear is primary and it forever remains the fall-back emotion. In the absence of social connection, paranoia becomes the default position. Not being able to connect to or understand others leads to fear and distrust. Prisoners in solitary confinement, subjects in sensory deprivation, the lonely elderly, the chronically isolated and depressed—with rare exception—will all become paranoid. We evolved as prey and our basic emotional wiring is more like the hunted than the hunter. We unconsciously perceive fearful faces much more readily than pleasant faces; and when presented with conflicting information our emotional reaction is fear. Researchers showed subjects pictures of people smiling. At the same time they flashed images of frightening faces out of awareness so they were not consciously noticed but were unconsciously perceived. The subjects felt fear (de Gelder, Morris, & Dolan, 2005).

Dogs are predators as well as scavengers. They will hunt when they need to and nothing hunts them, so there is little to fear. Think of a dog startled awake. Contrast that with a startled deer. Most dogs—not abused dogs or genetically damaged "purebreds"—will orientate towards the sound and, if they do not immediately recognize the source, go on the attack by barking. Unless you are a skilled tracker, you have probably never seen a sleeping deer; deer startle and run at the slightest sound. You won't have much trouble finding a sleeping dog. Evolutionarily, humans are more like deer than dogs. The development of weapons made us predators, predators with the hearts of prey. Light sleepers, ready to run: maybe that is why so many Americans feel the need to cling to their guns at night.

Homo homini lupus—Man is a wolf to man, a popular Roman proverb—may be a slight on wolves. Certainly, through recorded history, humans have taken nearly every opportunity to prey on one another. Lies and deceit are often used in pursuit of human prey. Against such manoeuvres, reading minds is the defence. Yet our extraordinary capacity for lying and deceit appears completely unmatched by our ability to detect lies. It is to this difficulty in understanding lies that we shall now turn.

Notes

1. Some were also misinformed about the effects.
2. People who take medication for ADD need to be aware of this effect. Timing is crucial. If the meds, which cause arousal, kick in when you're doing your homework it may become suddenly interesting. If they kick in when you're cleaning, you may spend hours arranging the cupboard.
3. Bringing laughter is a great gift, yet, as we know, even being a successful entertainer does not always eliminate depression and suicidal shame. It is so sad when the cycle of depression remains uninterrupted, because it is can usually be changed. It is not difficult to diagnosis and treat depression in pregnancy, often with simple understanding and support. Of course, most children of depressed parents do well enough, perhaps because there are other important people in their lives.
4. The technical terms for dependent and self-critical are "anaclitic" and "introjective" (Blatt, 1998).

CHAPTER SEVEN

Look me in the eye

In the movie *Exodus*, a 1960 epic about the founding of Israel, a young and handsome Paul Newman plays the Jewish resistance leader, Ari Ben Canaan. In this scene, Canaan is undercover, passing as a British officer. He is talking with Major Caldwell, a pompous anti-Semite played by Peter Lawford.

Lawford: I don't care about the Jews one way or the other.

Newman: But they are troublemakers. No question about it, sir . . .

Lawford: Yes. And half of them are Communists anyway.

Newman: Yes, and the other half pawnbrokers.

Lawford: They look funny, too. I can spot one a mile away.

Newman: Would you mind looking into my eye? It feels like a cinder.

Lawford: Certainly. You know, a lot of them try to hide under Gentile names. But one look at that face, and you just know. With a little experience, you can smell them out—I'm sorry, I can't find a thing.

Newman: Must've been my imagination. Thanks.

I was the only Jewish kid in my elementary school, and among my classmates, there were always a few ready to remind me of that with steady taunts and occasional beatings. I thought I was forever marked by my curly hair, dark eyes, but most especially my give-away big nose.

As a ten-year-old kid, raptly watching Lawford look Newman straight in the eye, I was thrilled. I had heard stories of relatives surviving the holocaust by passing as Christians but I found it hard to imagine. Seeing it on the screen made it seem more real. I could now picture my father and a cousin, who both had Newman's blue eyes, engaged in espionage beyond the borders of my imaginary ghetto, but I still felt stuck in my obvious ethnicity and had to content myself with playing the Sal Mineo role of Jewish resistance fighter in my fantasies. The irony of that ethnic crossover eluded my pre-adolescent mind, and I only recently learned that the film's director, Otto Preminger, was consciously playing with ethnic stereotypes.

Six years later, I visited Montreal for the first time. I was struck by the friendliness that greeted me when I walked into a store. Then I realized everyone assumed that I was French-Canadian. Voilà! I had stumbled upon another ethnicity that fit my looks—I could pass. My new identity was short-lived since I spoke almost no French, but the experience was a freeing revelation. Since then, I've passed as French, Hungarian, Basque, Lebanese, and even English. I don't know if I could get away with Swedish, though some day I may try. Now, forty years after my Montreal epiphany, the study of cultural and ethnic identity is at the centre of my academic life. I sometimes encourage my students to try to pass as someone of other ethnicity or social class. Every year the results are the same: most of them will not try, afraid that their deception will be humiliatingly obvious. But those that try are amazed by how easy it is.[1] Over twenty years of deception research point to this paradox: telling lies is both hard and easy, and the same is true for detecting them.

Easy lies

We can identify and admire the cool liar, the secret agent, the under-cover detective. It doesn't seem to bother most people when leaders lie as long as they believe it is for a good cause. We can even admire good liars who don't help anyone but themselves, like the impostor-hero of *Catch Me if You Can*. Most expect to be lied to, and most people lie, though they generally underestimate how often they themselves lie.

Psychologist Robert S. Feldman and his associates at the University of Massachusetts secretly videotaped 121 students engaging in ten-minute one-on-one conversations with others they were meeting for the first time (Feldman, Forrest, & Happ, 2002). The students had read that the study's purpose was to examine how people interact when they meet someone new. One-third of the students were further told that the researchers were particularly interested in how a person reacts when he meets someone likeable, so they were told to try to be likeable; one-third were told the same about being competent; and the other third were just told to just be themselves. The students then viewed the tapes and were asked to identify any lies they told. Sixty per cent identified at least one, more often two or three lies. (We do not know how many of the 40% who said they did not lie were lying!) Professor Feldman, in an interview (LeTourneau, 2002), said the students were surprised: "When they were watching themselves on videotape, people found themselves lying much more than they thought they had." Most were not aware they had lied until they watched the tape. The lies ranged from saying they liked someone they did not to falsely claiming to be the star of a rock band. Men and women told the same number of lies; but "women were more likely to lie to make the person they were talking to feel good, while men lied most often to make themselves look better," said Feldman.

As expected, students who were trying to appear competent or likeable lied more—averaging over two lies—than students being themselves, but even those students averaged about one lie in ten minutes. We can only imagine how many times people under the real pressure of a job interview lie. Another thing to note is that few people lied just one time; it seems that if you do it once, doing it again is easy.

Lying starts young and children lie much more often than their parents imagine. Researchers observed forty families with young children going about their normal activities in their homes (Wilson, Smith, & Ross, 2003). Each family was observed for six ninety-minute periods. Previous surveys showed that about 20% of parents say their children lie (Stouthamer-Loeber, 1986). Of the eighty children observed, 96% lied at least once—there were only three non-liars. Six lied more than fifteen times in the nine hours of observation. Lies include everything from simple denials ("I didn't do it") and placing blame ("The dog did it") to complex false stories ("I didn't punch him. He fell off the tricycle and hit his head. That's why he's crying"). Lying also increased with age: two-year-olds lied about once every five hours; four-year-olds about every two hours; and six-year-olds about every ninety minutes. Although parents almost universally say that lying is unacceptable, of the 621 lies observed, only twice did the parents directly tell the child not to lie. Parents were more likely to ignore or believe the lie than to address it.

Jean Piaget, perhaps history's most important developmental psychologist, wrote in 1932: "The tendency to lie is a natural tendency, so spontaneous and universal that we take it as an essential part of the child's egocentric thought" (Piaget, 1960, p. 135). By this, he meant that children lie easily and often because they do not think about how their lies might affect others. We now know that egocentricity remains alive in adults, for some more than others, and adolescents can be the most egocentric of all. This is born out by studies that show that college students—average age nineteen— lie about twice as much as other adults—average age thirty-four (DePaulo, Kashy, Kirkendol, Wyer, & Epstein, 1996).

Frank Abagnale Jr idolized his father. A successful owner of a Madison Avenue stationery store, Frank Sr was a politically active social climber—a power broker in local Republican politics. Frank's mother was a bored suburban housewife, full-time mother of four who resented her husband's inattentiveness. When Frank Jr was twelve, she announced her intention to separate. Frank Jr was shocked, but at the same time had the "I should have known something was wrong feeling" of someone trying not to know what he knew.

One of Frank Jr's first scams involved running up huge debts on his father's credit card. He bought merchandise and returned it for cash. When his father received the bill for several thousand dollars, he was nonchalantly forgiving, even tacitly approving of his son's clever deceit. He did not reveal that his business was faltering and that the credit card debt greatly added to his burden. When recently asked if he had any qualms about conning his father, Frank Jr replied, "I was just so young that . . . it was just a matter of doing it and I wasn't really thinking about who was going to pay for it or what was going to happen with it" (*Life Matters*, 2000). But when the business failed, Frank Jr felt terrible guilt while also learning an important con artist's lesson: some people will participate in a cover-up in order to mask their failings and preserve their image; many who are conned do not report the crime because they are embarrassed that they were duped.

While sitting in a tenth grade class, Frank was unexpectedly picked up and brought to court. The divorce was being finalized and the judge asked him to choose whether he wanted to live with his father or mother. "Some stranger suddenly was telling me I had to decide between the two people I loved most in the world," he remembered.[2] He broke into tears—we will never know if they were real—and the judge called a recess; Frank fled and spent the next five years being someone else. While robbing women of their virtue and men of their pride and everyone he could of their money, he inflicted great harm while convincing himself, and now us, it was just a game.

When fate and talent and good looks conspire to provide the improbable opportunity to live out adolescent fantasies, the result is often tragic. Adolescence is a time of vivid imagination when the line between daydream and reality is often blurred. How many teens dream of being a star and how many who too suddenly find themselves living their dream—rock stars, actors, models— never feel real? Adolescence is also a time of shifting identities and aspirations. Many adolescents believe they can be anything. Shall I be a doctor, lawyer, pilot, professor? Frank Abagnale pretended to be all of these, but none of it was real. He felt as if he was playing some great exciting game, like teens today whose lives centre on an Internet fantasy world. Every once in a while he realized he wasn't bilking just big businesses and banks, but also the teller or clerk whose pay cheque was docked because Frank convinced her not to follow procedures, and he would have a pang of guilt—but it quickly passed. Sometimes at night, when there wasn't a beautiful woman beside him, he would cry himself to sleep.

Frank knew he would eventually be discovered, and was probably relieved to be caught before anyone was seriously injured by his exploits. While impersonating a paediatrician, his lack of knowledge almost led to a baby's death from oxygen deprivation. He recalls another instance when he botched the examination of a newborn, "No one is really certain if newborn infants have thoughts or are aware of what is around them. No one but me, that is. That kid knew I was a phony. I could see it in his face" (*ibid.*).

Many compulsive liars want to be caught. They want to end living the lie. They want to know that someone can read their mind and know who they really are. "It is not a glamorous life, it's a very lonely life, because everyone you meet believes you to be somebody you're not . . . and so you really can't get involved with anyone" (*ibid.*).

In "Criminals from a sense of guilt", Freud proposes that sometimes people commit crimes in order to be punished. He wrote about a patient who

> was suffering from an oppressive feeling of guilt, of which he did not know the origin, and after he had committed a misdeed this oppression was mitigated. His sense of guilt was at least attached to something. [Freud, 1916d, p. 332]

Now in his late fifties, Frank is a consultant to the same banking industry he so successfully conned. He spent five years in prison and was released at age twenty-six on the condition that he work for the FBI, and he has worked without pay ever since. Reading his interviews, it seems apparent that Frank is and was a balanced knower. He surely had a gut sense of what he could get away with and with whom. Cognitively he was able to assess people and situations in a flash. It is something he can still do. He's an appealing character because he's not a psychopath and never really was a con man. He was a troubled adolescent who got a chance to live out his adolescent fantasy.

Did you know the word gullible isn't in the dictionary?

It's a favourite kids' joke and it often sends parents running to their Webster's. There are even websites devoted to variations of the joke.[3] We seem to want to believe we do not lie and we want to believe others do not lie as well. What would you think if I were to tell you that based on research, we know that people like you who read books like this one have a well known personality profile:

> You also pride yourself as an independent thinker; and do not accept others' statements without satisfactory proof. But you have found it unwise to be too frank in revealing yourself to others. You have a need for other people to like and admire you, and yet you tend to be critical of yourself. While you have some personality weaknesses, you are generally able to compensate for them. You have considerable unused capacity that you have not turned to your advantage. Disciplined and self-controlled on the outside, you tend to be worrisome and insecure on the inside. At times you have serious doubts as to whether you have made the right decision or done the right thing. You prefer a certain amount of change and variety and become dissatisfied when hemmed in by restrictions and limitations. At times you are extroverted, affable, and sociable, while at other times you are introverted, wary, and reserved. Some of your aspirations tend to be rather unrealistic. Security is one of your major goals in life.

If you are thinking this is a trick, you are right. This description of "you" was part of a classic psychology experiment performed by UCLA professor Bertram R. Forer in 1948 (Forer, 1949). Thirty-nine students were given a personality test. A week later each was presented with the results of the test and asked to rank its accuracy, on a scale from 0 (very poor) to 5 (excellent). Most students thought the test had excellent accuracy, giving it an average score of 4.3. Of the thirty-nine, only five rated it below 4! In fact, Forer's "results" were taken from horoscopes.

"There's a sucker born every minute" is credited to the famous American showman, P. T. Barnum, and the Barnum Effect is the name social psychologists give people's tendency to believe what they're told. In studying the Barnum Effect, psychologists have found people to be more gullible if the messages are mostly positive (MacDonald & Standing, 2002). People prefer positive messages, but will accept negative ones if they are not overwhelmingly negative. Forer's description above is not purely positive. Blatant flattery may raise suspicion.

You might notice that people who use psychics and astrologers rarely remember an incorrect prediction. This is called confirmation bias. People tend to remember what fits and forget what doesn't quite fit. There are dozens of books and articles detailing how psychics, mediums, and the like pull off their trickery. Yet people's wish to be understood, to have their minds read, is so powerful that nearly sixty years of research demonstrating the Barnum Effect in all forms of "psychic" phenomena has done little to diminish people's readiness to be deceived.

Cold reading

Salespeople, psychics, detectives, and interviewers use cold reading to convince people they know much more about them than they actually do. The cold reader starts making a general statement like the ones in the Forer experiment. To a middle-aged man eying a sports car, a sales person might say, "It's really hard to decide what makes most sense. You like having a car that's fun to drive, but you feel you need to be practical." That statement fits just about anyone. The potential customer, feeling understood, may then say more about himself and what he's looking for. A psychic might start, "You look a bit sad." Almost everybody has recurring sad thoughts that they try not to dwell on. Most will feel a sense of connection and say something more about it or be defensive and explain why they're not sad. "No, I'm just tired, I didn't get much sleep last night." The psychic can follow up with, "Working hard?" or "Really, What's up?"

Shotgunning is a variation of cold reading in which the reader rattles off a series of observations, while closely watching for reactions, nods of agreement, sighs, and looks of surprise. Based on those reactions, the reader refines his or her observations. *I see a drug, alcohol problem with someone close, a friend, no a family member, older, a father, a grandfather, an uncle, a cousin* . . . When you read these examples, they may seem unconvincing. It is like watching someone being duped in a movie. You wonder why he doesn't get it. But the words don't convey the emotion of the interchange, the skill of the reader, and the need of the person being read to be understood. Remember from the previous chapter that people in unexplained states of fear-arousal—anxiety, worry, depression—are primed to grab on to any reasonable-sounding explanation of their emotions; and they are the ones most vulnerable to being duped.

Do you want to know the truth?

In most of our personal relationships, unless things are tense and we suspect an affair, we do not think too much about whether we are being lied to. Lies are not on our radar screen. We expect little lies and don't care. If friends call to cancel a dinner date and say their child is ill, but we suspect it's because they're having a fight, how much do we care? If we know our friends are having a hard time, we even try to make the lie easier, and say, "Hope Joey feels better, call if you need anything."

The first people to ever lie to us are our parents and we assume, for good reason, that they are doing it for our benefit. Most of their lies go unnoticed. Mummy has to stop playing Snakes and Ladders to make an important phone call. (Mummy is bored stiff and wants to talk to her friend.) Daddy isn't feeling well (Daddy has a hang-over). There's no more ice cream. (I don't want to get into an argument with you again.) What child really wants to know what goes on when parents retire to the bedroom for a Saturday afternoon "nap". When children discover parents' lies, they often excuse them and even try to help them make the lies more successful. Children of alcoholics, and others whose parents seem needy and fragile, are prone to deny or paper over parents' lies, feeling responsible to care for and soothe their parents. Sometimes called parentified or care-taker children, as adults they often find themselves in relationships with needy, dependent partners and cannot see when they are being taken advantage of, lied to, even abused. Think about how frightening it must be for children to see parents as selfish, uncaring, or mean.[4] Most will go to great lengths to avoid that realization, distorting perception and logic in the process of developing an alternative explanation for their parents' behaviour. Their theory of mind does not allow explanations of a loved one's behaviour based on selfishness, sadism, or malevolence. As a result, when they are adults, it seems impossible to convince them that someone they are attracted to is uncaring, manipulative, or mean. On the positive side, some such individuals, near saintly in their blindness to the dark side of human nature, are drawn to the helping professions, often caring for those most in need, those that others reject.

For children, the first lie is a grand achievement. It demonstrates that we are not transparent to our parents. We have an inner life, a mind that is our own. Authoritarian parents, who harshly try to catch every lie, risk having children who feel they don't have a separate sense of self. Some children, often children who feel very close to their parents, need to go through a prolonged period of lying in order to establish a separate sense of self. Parents in these circumstances may feel dumbfounded, disappointed, even betrayed, and feel like failures. In fact, lying is a natural part of separating and growing up; and for most children persistent lying is a passing phase.

Good lies

We recognize that not all lies are the same. Lying when enemies surround you, as in the Paul Newman example at the beginning of the chapter, is self-protective and the psychological equivalent of camouflage. Other lies are intended to protect people we care about. Imagine driving down a dark country road. You see a car accident ahead. It's just one car, badly smashed, on its roof, parts scattered everywhere. It looks as if the car missed a turn and caroomed off a tree. You run up and, looking inside the car, see a badly injured bleeding figure. Shaking, you turn away and see movement in the grass along the road. Dazed, you walk over and see a small frightened child. You pick him up. He asks, "Is mummy OK?" If you are like most people, you lie. What good would it do to tell the truth? You say, "The doctors will take care of your mummy. Let's go to the hospital." Police, firefighters, and medical personnel encounter similar scenes on a regular basis: a frightened parent of an injured child, a panicked gunshot victim, a sobbing child trapped in a well. Sometimes it is best to lie.

If a dispassionate observer were standing there—perhaps someone with training in human behaviour, such as a police officer or a psychologist—would the lie be apparent? Paul Ekman, a Professor of Psychology at the University of California at San Francisco, has spent his career studying lying and in one of his most important series of experiments, he addressed that question. He enlisted nursing students by telling them that they would need to learn to lie as part of their job (Ekman, 1985). He showed them two videos. The first was a pleasant ocean scene. While they were watching, an interviewer who could not see the screen asked them questions about what they were feeling. The students had been instructed to answer the questions as openly as possible. They then watched another video, the most gruesome video Ekman could devise. In a scene worthy of a teen slasher movie, the video showed a badly disfigured burn victim undergoing an especially bloody amputation. Previous studies had shown that amputations and burns elicit intense negative emotions. The students had been instructed to conceal their true feelings from the interviewer and to act as if they were watching pretty flowers in the park. The student nurses were videotaped.

For the past thirty years, Ekman has shown these tapes to all sorts of people and asked them, "Is she lying?" Most people think they can tell. They are wrong. Most people are right about half the time, which is as good as tossing a coin. Despite what they think, they had no idea whether the students were lying or not. This was true for people who are experts, such as judges and lawyers and police officers and psychiatrists, as well as for ordinary folk. It does not matter how confident people are about their lie detection skills, or what their training is, most people cannot tell. A few can tell. Some rare individuals, one in a thousand—an occasional detective, a well trained psychotherapist—stand out as exemplary lie catchers and got it right over 80% of the time. But law officers in general, and therapists in general, did no better than anybody else and got it wrong as often as they got it right.

It may seem like a paradox that evolution has given us a brain with a remarkable capacity to both read minds and yet be so easily deceived, but it is not. Like other primates, the environments in which humans evolved consisted of small communities of related families that helped provide for one another. One individual had no reason to suspect that she would be lied to, or at least not lied to in a way that might cause harm. Humans evolved reading minds of others and believing what they read because there was no reason not to. Even if we have a feeling that someone may not be telling the truth, we tend to ignore it because, as we saw in the previous chapter, consciously available information trumps unconscious perception.

As babies, we were lied to for our own good, to protect us from being overwhelmed by anxiety or fear. "Don't worry, the lion won't hurt you," whispered by the mother to the child as they huddle together hiding in the cave is the evolutionary ancestor of the nurse's lie and every mother who says with no certainty, "It will be OK." Why should we be attuned to detecting lies when we want them to be true?

Who can catch a liar?

In subsequent studies Ekman discovered that US Secret Service agents were better than others at detecting lies (Ekman & O'Sullivan, 1991). About one-third of them, generally the younger ones, scored in the superior range, detecting lies more than 80% of the time. Other researchers discovered that stroke victims who had lost their ability to understand language were also good lie catchers (Ecoff, Ekman, Mage, & Frank, 2000). What do stroke victims, Secret Service agents, and other good lie catchers have in common? They don't just look the person in the eye and listen to their words. They pay attention to cues most people ignore: tone of voice, body language, and subtle facial expressions. Research also suggests that chronically abused children may also be better lie detectors (Bugental, Shennum, Frank, & Ekman, 2000), even though they are not particularly good at reading emotions (Pollak, 2000). "What are you looking at!" is a common reprimand shouted at the child who looks questioningly at the abuser's face. Perhaps abused children, turning away from faces, learn to look for clues of deceit in more predictive body language, but do not learn the subtlety of facial expression as well. Children learn the language of emotion at home. People raised in less expressive families are more sensitive to subtle expressions of emotion than those raised in emotionally demonstrative families.

In a 1999 study, Ekman found that under interview conditions in which questions were posed to suspected liars, some psychologists are also decent lie detectors (Ekman, O'Sullivan, & Frank, 1999). It is a good example of place-dependent learning, acquiring a skill in a particular situation but not being able to apply it outside that situation. Secret Service agents practise spotting deceit from a distance. Psychologists are used to interviewing people up close. Place-dependent learning also explains the stereotype of the socially inept bungling therapist who relates perceptively in the clinical situation.

Demeanour refers to a person's bearing, outward appearance, and general behaviour. "What was the suspect's demeanour?" is a typical police question, and there is good reason to believe that demeanour plays a role in who is arrested and charged with a crime. Teenagers who are respectful and deferential when stopped for a traffic violation are less likely to receive a ticket than those who are defensive and surly. Defendants who show little or no anxiety are less likely to be found guilty than those who fidget, stammer, mumble, and avoid eye contact (Pryor & Buchanan, 1984). An open smile, good eye contact, upright posture, a sure gait, and clear speech are some of the behaviours people see as signs of trust-worthiness. In fact, demeanour has very little to do with deception.

Most people firmly believe that looking away when asked a question is a sign of lying, and looking the questioner in the eye is a sign of honesty. But in fact many liars are good at maintaining a likeable demeanour; lying while looking someone right in the eye is commonplace. And unusual demeanour does not always indicate that someone is lying. Many people get anxious when questioned and show signs of fear. Anxious smiles are often misinterpreted as contempt for the questioner and incorrectly interpreted as a sign of lying. The innocent person's fear of being disbelieved looks just like the guilty person's fear of being caught (Ekman, 2003, p. 67).

When Ekman first tested police officers for their ability to detect lies, the officers judged everyone a liar explaining, "Everyone lies, especially to the police" (Ekman, 1996). This is a particularly troub-ling attitude, since Ekman and others have developed tools that could aid the police in their interrogations. Yet police departments around the country continue to use methods that have been proved worthless in detecting deceit. In fact, many departments pay for courses and videos to train their officers in an approach—the Reid Technique—that is specifically designed to coerce confessions with-out regard to the actual guilt or innocence of the subject (Kassin & Fong, 1999).

These are occupational hazards: police see everyone as liars, con artists see everyone as dupes, pastors see everyone as sinners, and psychotherapists see everyone as troubled. Each person's theory of mind is shaped not only by biology and development, but also the group to which the person belongs. Unfamiliar ethnic groups are less well read, and are less trusted, than familiar ones. Majority group members are much worse at reading the emotional expressions of minorities than the reverse—blacks read whites better than whites read blacks (Elfenbein, Marsh, & Ambady, 2002). Outward appearance determines judgements as well. Attractive people are seen as more trustworthy than unattractive people. Dress matters. When I first worked in a hospital, I soon learnt that if I wore a jacket and tie, I could go anywhere, no questions asked, no matter bleary eyes, unshaven face. When possible, people tend to focus on what puts them at ease. An African-American colleague was surprised late one evening when fellow subway riders seemed unusually relaxed and friendly. White people in general found his demeanour a bit threatening. Yet that night they seemed to be standing closer; some even smiled and offered hellos. Reaching up to scratch his head, he discovered he had been an inadvertent imposter. He was still wearing the yarmulke he had donned for a friend's wedding just before.

The amygdala again

What does neuroscience have to say about why we trust one person and not another? Once again, we look to Queen Square, London (Winston, Strange, O'Doherty, & Dolan, 2002). Subjects were asked to rate faces for degree of trustworthiness. The researchers chose faces that were as neutral as they could find. All were ordinary-looking white men, with bland expressions. Still, some were ranked trustworthy and others were not, although there was no obvious difference between them. The researchers then showed these pictures to other subjects while their brains were being scanned by MRI machines. In one case, they were asked to judge the trustworthiness of the face; in another to estimate their age. Untrustworthy faces set the amygdala ablaze with activity even in those subjects who were only asked to estimate age. In other words, *untrustworthy faces scare us whether we are thinking about it or not.*

What made some faces seem trustworthy and others not? The neuroscientists tried to pick faces with neutral expressions but some emotions were still evident. The results showed that happiness was linked to trust; sadness and anger to distrust. We know that smiles do not scare us—even though perhaps they should because they can so easily be faked. But why do sad and angry faces scare us? Sadness and anger are both found in depression. We are once again forced to confront the fact that some of our most important judgements are based on our most basic, infantile reactions: smiley mummy makes us happy; angry, sad mummy makes us scared. It is fortunate that there was no TV coverage of the Lincoln–Douglas debates and that Honest Abe was never subject to the unguarded close-ups of today. Under the glare of the camera, candidates with signs of depression—Nixon, Dukakis, Gore, Kerry—suffer; we prefer the smiley face even though it sometimes masks a thoughtless mind. It is worth noting that many faces seemed untrustworthy for no apparent reason; researchers are now trying to figure out why.

Hard lies

For the most part, lies are easy to tell and hard to detect—perhaps it is more accurate to say we do not care to detect them. That is because people often are not even aware they are lying and show no signs of deceit. Most lies are harmless; some even meant to make the listener feel better; and many are designed to protect. In most relationships, we want to trust and be trusted.

It's different in politics and war. In competitive and adversarial relationships, we try to read the adversary in order to see what we can get away with; social perception and deception become weapons. If only one party is aware of what's going on, it's a con; if both are aware, it's spy *vs.* spy; if you make it a game, it's poker. In all of these circumstances, the greater a person's capacity to read minds, the greater his capacity to deceive.

In general, people lie less to those they are close to. In a major study of adults (DePaulo & Kashy, 1998), about half of whom were college students, participants told fewer lies to people they interacted with more and (for other than college students) people they knew longer. For everyone, closeness was the most important factor. Lies create distance—the liar must always be on guard not to slip and a good liar must have a good memory. But the study found a more practical factor as well: in closer relationships, lies were more likely to be discovered. People who know us are better at detecting our lies.

Interestingly though, participants felt very close to their mothers and romantic partners yet lied to them as much as to anyone else. In fact, college students lied to their mothers more than to anyone else, over fifty per cent of the time! It seems that people feel a great need to impress both their mothers and their lovers, but for different reasons, one would suspect.[5]

Catching a liar

With practice, it is not that hard to catch a liar. Just two behaviours, raised pitch and fake smiles can distinguish liars from truth tellers 86% of the time, at least in the laboratory (Ekman, O'Sullivan, Friesen, & Scherer, 1991). A true smile, sometimes called the Duchenne smile after the nineteenth century French neurologist who first described it, involves not only the muscles around the lips, but the muscles around the eyes as well. It is hard to fake a true smile. The false smile, sometimes called the Pan American smile in honour of the first airline stewardesses, involves only the muscles around the mouth. The permanent expression of game show hosts and Miss America contestants, this smile is now expected to be shown by retail staff and many service professionals even though it is clearly false. If you observe it in someone who is trying to gain your trust— a stock broker or real estate agent for example—check other sources of information to make sure you are being told the truth.

If someone you are close to flashes you a false smile, you can be pretty sure that something is being covered up. The false smile does not necessarily indicate a significant lie; it indicates anxiety about something being revealed. The secret may be something benign, like a surprise party being planned. However, if the false smile is asymmetrical—one side higher than the other—it is usually a sign of contempt.

Raised pitch is harder to notice, but can be learned with practice. While reading minds by way of raised pitch is somewhat difficult, reading body language is easy. In fact, reading body language comes naturally to most people. The irony is that while people have a natural ability to read body language, we tend not to use skills to detect lies or read minds. How, then, do we know that we have these skills? There is evidence that people use their ability to read body language to assess not minds, but mood. Researchers have found that when judging a baby's mood, we look at body language much more than facial expression, and when judging another adult's mood we look body language as well as facial expression.[6] Why not in assessing people's truthfulness?

For one thing, a person who is misunderstood and falsely accused can look just like an accused guilty person with all the same signs of anxiety. We all know what it feels like to be falsely accused, and who wants to risk doing that to someone? False accusations can end friendships, lead to enduring enmity, and worse. Sometimes we are deceived because we want to be; we readily accept the lies of flattery and concern. Lying and accepting lies are ways of acknowledging our private minds. Most of the time, life is easier if we do not care if we are lied to. Think about what life would be like if we caught every friend and associate in every little lie. A person who points out every little social lie would seem rather odd, like the television detective Monk; and he too might even be diagnosed with Asperger's Syndrome.

People like Monk are driven to point out every contradiction and inconsistency in their surroundings and interactions; they seem unable to tell the important from the unimportant: nothing slides by. These relentless mind readers are annoying to others and are probably exhausting to themselves. Most people do not want to be like Monk, compelled to report everything they notice. What most people do want is the choice of keeping information private or making it known, of revealing or concealing what they are able to detect, of protecting themselves or others from information that may be harmful. The ability to read minds gives us those choices. Being able to read minds gives us opportunities to protect ourselves from imposters and exploiters, and opportunities to enrich our lives with skills that connect us to others.

Notes

1. See *The Color of Water: A Black Man's Tribute to His White Mother* (2006) by James McBride for a great example of a white woman passing as black.
2. It is perhaps not surprising that Abagnale tells his story in slightly different versions in various interviews, but the basic shape is the same. See Pulfer (2003).

3. For a good example of the "gullible joke", see, "Did you Hear 'Gullible' Isn't in the Dictionary? This Time, it Really Isn't", The Watley Review (2006), vol. 4. no. 5. www.watleyreview.com/2006/051606-1.html.
4. Two papers by Fonagy and Target beautifully discuss these issues (Fonagy & Target, 1996, 2000).
5. The researchers conjectured that people lie to their lovers to impress and student lies to their mothers to cover up.
6. In this study, researchers showed computer-generated images of conflicting emotions, a fearful face on an angry body, for example. Observers were then asked to judge the facial expression. Brain scans indicated confusion and the judgements took longer. The results showed judgements of facial emotion were influenced by body language without the person being aware of it (Meeren, van Heijnsbergen, & de Gelder, 2005, p. 16519).

CHAPTER EIGHT

Intimate relationships: reading your family, friends, and lovers

U ntil now, we have discussed reading minds as a skill that helps us survive in a complex social world. Those who excel at it have a competitive advantage over those who do not, in any arena that requires social interaction. In the world of work and commerce and in casual relationships, a skilful mind reader can uncover concealed information and use it for his own benefit, sometimes to the detriment of others. IBM executive Jack Sams didn't want Bill Gates to know IBM was in a weak position. Gathering that information was a win for Gates and a loss for Sams. Sometimes the skilful reader benefits with no cost to the person being read. When James (Chapter Five) read the police officer's inexperience and fear, it enabled him to calm the officer and avoid being arrested or possibly killed. The officer suffered no loss and in fact probably benefited from being helped to act reasonably, not violently. But any benefit to the officer was unintended. James's goal was to help himself.

Intimate relationships are different. Intimate derives from the Latin word meaning "inward, essential, intrinsic; pertaining to the inmost thoughts".[1] While there is considerable cultural and individual variation concerning what is considered intimate, unwanted exposure of anything someone considers intimate makes that person feel ashamed or vulnerable.

Intimate relationships are based on trust and caring. People reveal their intimacies when they believe they will not be harmed by those revelations. In intimate relationships, when one person reads the mind of another and discovers something that had not yet been revealed, it must be handled with great care. We read the minds of those we love for their benefit—to fulfil their desires, to ease their pain.

Intimate relationships vary in direction and depth. A therapist–patient relationship is intimate in only one direction—only the patient's intimacies are revealed—and moves progressively deeper as the therapist learns more. A parent–child relationship starts out unequal but moves to greater mutuality as the child matures; its depth varies in complicated ways over the course of a lifetime. Friendships vary in mutuality and depth. Romantic relationships are ideally mutual and deep.

In all cases, it is the responsibility of anyone holding intimate knowledge of another to cherish it. To reveal it, to use it in self-serving or hurtful ways, betrays the intimacy. Intimate relationships can bring great joy but they can also bring great torment. Those who know us best can hurt us most. All intimate relationships begin in hope; too many end in disappointment. How each participant reads the mind of the other and uses what is learnt is often what makes the difference.

Two heads are sometimes better than one

Intimacy and reading minds go hand-in-hand. We expect to know our intimates' minds and expect them to know ours; the greater the intimacy the greater the knowledge. In our most intimate relationship we want the knowledge to be complete, two minds so open to each other that they become like one. We want nothing to be hidden, no secrets, no lies. Romance adds the erotic. In the bible, to know someone means to be sexually intimate. In romantic relationships our bodies as well as our minds are open to each other and pleasure for one brings pleasure to the other.

In intimate relationships one mind can complement the other. Intimates can use each other as a mirror. As you might ask a friend,

"Do my clothes match?", or "Is there is a poppy seed between my teeth?", you might also ask, "Do my thoughts make sense? Is there something obvious that I'm missing?" The ongoing nature of intimate relationships provides a setting in which the participants can practise mind-reading skills and come to understand each other in ever great depth. Not subject to inevitable blindspots and inhibitions that each of us has about knowing ourselves, our intimates can in some ways know us better that we do. An old friend may understand why you are in a bad mood better than you do. Your spouse may know what you would like to say, even if you are too shy to say it.

In intimate relationships, two heads can be better than one. By reading each other's mind, intimates can help one another overcome distortions and inhibitions; they can use each other's strengths, compensate for each other's weaknesses; and—when good fortune adds passion to intimacy—be at one with the other, and feel whole and satisfied.

Difficulties in intimacy

Sadly, the waters of intimacy are seldom untroubled. Intimate relationships bear the weight of unconscious wishes that can never be completely fulfilled. Openness brings vulnerability and concerns about how the other will react. Will sensitivities be respected? Will confidences be kept? Breaches of trust are inevitable and painful; repair always difficult. Will a real effort be made? Each of us has different sensitivities, but it doesn't take much hurt to close someone's mind, to make him feel wary and put up barriers of emotional distance or even deceit.

Positive transference

People are often unrealistic in what they expect from their intimate relationships. If those expectations are not brought into line with reality, disappointments are unavoidable. Transference—the tendency to view new acquaintances through the lens of significant past relationships—is universal, but what triggers a particular transference is individual. For example, Yoko meets Dave at her new job and has a warm feeling about him. While not attracted to him, she thinks he'll be someone she can rely on. What leads Yoko on first encounter to feel a bit about Dave as she felt about her protective father may be his tone of voice, his manner of speech, the colour of his hair, or any number of other things, alone or in combination. Yoko's transference to Dave, like most transference, is nuanced. Yoko experiences Dave in subtle and unconscious ways as similar to her protective father and likes him for that reason. In this example, she doesn't experience him as her exciting, enthralling, or critical father, although she may experience other men in all those ways.

Positive transferences can help initiate friendships and romantic relationships. Without conscious awareness, people tend to respond to transference expectations (Andersen, Reznik, & Manzella, 1996). Dave—if he can—may try to be protective, and if Yoko's expectations are not unrealistic, a friendship may grow. On the other hand, Yoko may expect entirely too much—protection from her own failings at work for example—and end up feeling hurt and disappointed. Or Dave may dislike the role of protector, and reject Yoko along with her transference expectations, leaving her feeling baffled about why someone she likes doesn't like her.

Charisma

Some people seem like flypaper for positive transferences. Possessing charisma, they are outgoing, charming, self-assured, and calm, and tend to rise to positions of leadership and power. Others feel enhanced and protected in their presence and want to be their friends; but many charismatic people do not make good friends. Homer, the great Greek poet wrote: "To have a great man for an intimate friend seems pleasant to those who have never tried it; those who have, fear it."

Zero acquaintance. Charisma is the one exception to the rule that mind-reading involves a relationship; it can be accurately sensed with a glance. Researchers who have studied this phenomenon named it zero acquaintance (Kenny, Horner, Kashy, & Chu, 1992). With just a quick look across a room, it is easy to tell if someone is outgoing, affable, and self-confident. Perhaps evolution has built the ability to spot potential leaders into our brain. Attributes that make for potential friends and lasting relationships—commitment, honesty, and concern—cannot be assessed in the same way; reading those qualities accurately requires a relationship.

Charisma, like most human qualities, comes in a wide range of intensities. From kids voted "most popular" in high school to well-loved leaders of nations, people with charisma stand out and draw others to them. Most treat charisma as a gift of fortune: like good looks or a quick wit, it can make life a bit easier. Those who become leaders learn to combine charisma with their mind-reading abilities to produce a mental tool of great power.

Charismatic leaders are emotional knowers who read others quickly and accurately. Cognitive information is often discarded because it takes too long to process. They respond to others smoothly and without hesitation. They connect at a gut level and often seem to emanate a feeling of concern. Their admirers are loyal, and many feel like friends. They welcome and encourage that affection, but do not genuinely reciprocate; relationships are easily discarded when inconvenient or no longer useful. Ronald Reagan and Bill Clinton are recent examples of charismatic leaders. While both were loved by many, neither valued close friendships. Invariably those who once imagined themselves friends ended up feeling neglected, discarded, or betrayed. For Reagan and Clinton, achieving their goals was far more important than maintaining friendships. Lest we be judgemental, isn't this what we expect of our leaders: that their commitment to their nation takes precedence over personal relations?

Powerful leaders in business and other fields often have similar traits. A few have been my patients. All came to therapy as a concession to a spouse or a lover who wanted more from the relationship. With the first, I learned the hard way that I could be seduced by charisma into the illusion that I was a valued confidant. This illusion, along with a measure of my self-confidence, was suddenly shattered by the shock of a summary dismissal accompanied by words like, "I feel you are no longer useful." With this client my suggestion that we take some time to consider his decision in light of what had seemed to be a good working relationship was coolly rejected. In retrospect, my dismissal seemed to follow our first glimpse together of some feelings of regret over what he had sacrificed in order to attain his seemingly enviable position.

I subsequently learned to be gently sceptical when other similar patients said anything positive about the therapy. I questioned any assertion of my insight or intelligence and wondered about the need for such flattery. It was usually a relief for them to find I was neither charmed nor seduced, and could see though their manipulations. In response, some of these charmers thought there was a chance I might prove useful.

Negative transference

Sometimes a negative transference may prevent potential friends from ever breaking the ice. Negative transference occurs when something about a new person reminds you of a difficult past relationship. At Yoko's new job, she meets Nancy. Nancy seems stand-offish and unconsciously reminds Yoko of her critical older sister. Nancy responds by being subtly stand-offish and critical. Unless the two of them are brought together, perhaps by a mutual friend who tells them of their shared interests, or by working together in a sustained way, they will most probably reinforce each other's transference distortions and stay distant.

Some people who appear aloof have persistent negative transferences, the most common being a critical parent or older sibling transference. If they are approached with recognition of their sensitivity, they are often eager for connection. In organizational workshops that extend over several days, people are forced to confront their negative transferences and are frequently surprised to see their feelings change towards others they initially did not like.

Research suggests that initial transferences can easily be overcome if approached systematically. Holding someone accountable is one such approach. Simply asking someone to justify his initial reactions towards a new acquaintance to a third person usually eliminates distortions and leads to a realistic appraisal. Just thinking about the details of the initial interaction is often enough to eliminate distortions.

For the most part, friendships once established are not terribly troubled by transferences. As friends get to know each other better, they see each other more realistically. Two people connected by proximity, shared interests, or life circumstances with time to spend together tend to grow closer; friendships tend to self-correct.

Friendships do have their crises. Often they occur when one friend is having a problem. The other friend thinks he understands something about the mind of his troubled friend; something the troubled friend is unable to see himself. The way that understanding is conveyed and received may lead to the two growing closer or moving apart.

Telling friends what we read in their minds

Mary and her best friend Jane have been planning a night out together for weeks. They've both been busy with work and family and eagerly look forward to time together. They agree to talk on Saturday afternoon to decide what to do. Mary calls and asks if Jane has thought about what she wants to do. Jane sounds listless and says, "No, I really don't care. You pick."

Mary feels something must be wrong. Jane is a movie buff and always has some great suggestions. Mary was counting on her. In addition, Jane is picky about what she likes. Mary is now worried that if she chooses something Jane doesn't like, they'll both have a bad time. Mary asks Jane what's up.

She says, "I really don't feel like doing anything. Maybe tonight's not such a good idea."

"What's wrong?" Mary asks.

"Nothing, I'm just feeling blah. I won't be much fun."

Mary knows Jane can get depressed and withdrawn, though she hasn't been that way in a while. But she's concerned and says, "Are you feeling depressed?"

"Yeah, maybe," she answers.

"What's been going on?" Mary wonders aloud.

"I don't know. Sometimes I just get like this," she replies.

"Not for a long time," Mary reflects.

"That's true," Jane admits.

"You know you sounded great on Thursday when we talked."

"Really? It feels like a lot longer," Jane says.

"It always feels that way when you're depressed. You know that."

"I guess you're right," Jane replies, her mood lifting.

"Did anything happen at work on Friday?"

"Just the usual stuff."

"Like what?" Mary presses, "What happened on Friday?"

"The usual meetings, weekly summaries, I presented that proposal," Jane mumbles.

Mary remembered that Jane seemed enthusiastic about the proposal earlier. She knew from their time together in high school that Jane worked hard to get good grades. She relied heavily on her teachers for advice and guidance and basked in their attention. In college—a large state school—she had a hard time adjusting to the huge lectures and the professors' inaccessibility. Jane struggled with feeling depressed her entire fresher's year, but she got particularly withdrawn and despondent after receiving a B on a big marketing project. When Mary talked to her about it, Jane seemed especially upset because she had made an effort to speak to the marketing professor during the semester and he had seemed encouraging. She blamed herself for not listening carefully to the professor and not working harder, and she fell into a self-critical depression that lasted a few weeks. Remembering that time in college, Mary now asks Jane how her boss Sheri responded to her presentation.

"OK. Not great. She wasn't thrilled. She said I should go ahead but didn't seem enthusiastic," Jane answers.

"So you didn't get an A."

Jane almost laughs. Her voice noticeably brighter she says, "No, a definite B."

"Didn't Sherri seem positive before?" asks Mary.

"I thought she was liking it, but I think she was too busy to pay much attention."

"What does she expect when she doesn't tell you what she wants? You could have used some direction."

"I guess."

"I think you're mad at Sherri."

"I think you're right."

"So stop kicking yourself. You have a right to feel angry. Let's meet for a drink and make fun of Sherri."

"Good idea. Then we can see this new murder mystery I was thinking about."

This exchange again illustrates point number one about reading minds: mind-reading requires a relationship. You cannot know someone without interacting with her. Even knowing something meaningful about a person's mind by observing her dress and demeanour means you are relating, relating as an observer; and the person you are observing is communicating something through her dress and demeanour that may be intended to reveal something about herself or to conceal something or even to deceive. Obviously, intimate relationships provide more opportunity for relating and mind-reading; in addition, the participants often want their minds to be read. In Jane's case, she wanted Mary to know what she was thinking even if she wasn't fully aware of it herself. She wanted Mary's help in understanding why she felt so bad; and she needed the help because those bad feelings were inhibiting and distorting her thinking, keeping her in a self-critical funk.

It is common in intimate relationships for one person to want to express complicated and confusing private thoughts that she cannot clearly articulate. She may start with something vague like, "I don't feel like doing anything," or "I feel blah." An interested, sensitive listener will ask questions and pose possible explanations to try to help the other person understand her own mind. If it goes well, together they will arrive at a good explanation, a useful theory that brings clarity to a once confusing state of mind.

Saying the right thing at the right time

Because intimate relationships allow for continuing conversation and a way to test and refine theories, they provide the best opportunity to read and deeply understand another mind. But it's not always easy sailing. Saying something about another person's mind is a delicate undertaking. It is a paradox of intimate relationships that people can feel terribly misunderstood while being understood. You know how futile it is to tell a friend she is going out with the wrong guy again; or drinking too much; or setting herself up to fail a course. People often do not want to face the obvious and do not want to be told what they don't want to see. Therapists have long known that understanding how a person's mind unconsciously causes him problems is only a first step in helping the person change. Just as important is communicating the understanding in a way that can be accepted and put to use.

Jane opened her mind to Mary. If she had wanted to keep Mary away she could have lied and emailed an excuse giving no hint of distress. Instead, she showed obvious signs of unhappiness, which Mary correctly read as a call for help. Together, they understood that Jane's bad feelings—shame about her imperfection, guilt about her anger, anxiety about her boss's reaction—coloured and distorted her perception and inhibited her thinking. Mary's accurate reading of Jane's distress led to a useful conversation, yet it is easy to imagine that their conversation could have taken a different turn.

What if Mary had felt rejected when Jane said, "I really don't feel like doing anything. Maybe tonight's not such a good idea." In order to understand her feeling of rejection, she might search her memory for something she had said that angered Jane. She finds it in their last conversation and says, "I wonder if you are mad at me. You know, it was none of my business to criticize the way Jack (Jane's ex-husband) treats the kids. I'm sorry if I offended you."

Don't jump to conclusions

In this case, Mary misreads Jane's mind. She correctly reads Jane's anger, but the theory she constructs to explain it is based on her own concerns. She assumes Jane's anger is directed at her; but rather than ask Jane about it, she searches her own memory for an explanation. In other words, she jumps to a conclusion. Had she shared her emotional read and said to Jane, "I sense that you are angry. Are you angry with me?" Jane would have had the opportunity to reflect on Mary's reaction and perhaps unravel the true reason for her anger. Instead, Mary's too quick explanation can only divert Jane into thinking about something that was not on her mind and away from understanding her distress.

In intimate relationships, jumping to a conclusion is almost never helpful. Even if the conclusion is correct, it can still make matters worse. Imagine Mary having responded to Jane's mood by saying, "I wonder if you're depressed because your presentation at work didn't go as well as you expected. I'm sure it went fine, but I know you're a perfectionist." Mary's theory is correct but Jane is not ready to hear it. Through the distorting lens of self-critical depression, Mary's well-meaning comment is misinterpreted as a criticism. Jane is already feeling inadequate for not getting it right, not reading Sherri correctly, not doing a perfect presentation. If she accepts

Mary's explanation of her bad mood, she will feel even worse for not having figured it for herself. Since she doesn't want to feel worse, she defensively and angrily rejects Mary's explanation.

Negative mind-reading

Even if Jane were not depressed, she might have responded defensively. In general, people get defensive when another person presumes to know what they are thinking better than they do. Research shows that negative mind reading often elicits anger along with defensiveness and creates distance in a relationship. Negative mind reading makes a person feel she is doing something wrong. For example, telling a friend who cancels a date, "I know you are really not interested in spending time with me." Even if it were true, saying it like that would do no good. Negative mind reading never helps resolve problems between friends or brings them closer. Making a wavering friend feel ashamed or guilty will most probably only drive her further away. Telling a friend, or anyone with whom you are intimate, what you read in her mind can strengthen your connection, but only if it is done without judgement and with care and permission.

The vulnerability of men

When someone is feeling vulnerable, even the mildest everyday form of mind reading, like noticing he is upset, can feel like an attack. Many men think feeling bad is a sign of weakness. They don't admit to their unhappiness or talk about their feelings because they fear others will attack. In many social situations, a man's amygdala is activated when a woman's is not. Men tend to be more physiologically primed for danger.

In social situations, the neurotransmitter oxytocin primes women to feel close. Women display their unhappiness and talk about their feelings because they expect others will be concerned. That's a major reason why women are diagnosed with depression and Borderline Personality Disorder, or BPD, so much more often than men are. (I will discuss BPD in some detail soon.) Many more women than men enter psychotherapy, and women stay in psychotherapy longer.

A 2007 study[2] dispelled the myth that men do not talk as much as women. It found men speak as much as women, but they talk about gadgets, cars, and sports. They don't typically talk about emotions or relationships. In fact, men tend to avoid talking when there is conflict. They fear they will expose their vulnerability, so they clam up. They drink, take drugs, and behave badly in an attempt to cover their feelings and show their strength. Rather than talk, they take action; all too often, it's impulsive, aggressive, and ultimately self-destructive action. Prisons are full of men unable to admit that anything is wrong. In the general population, there are three times as many women diagnosed with BPD as there are men; in prison populations, men are diagnosed BPD more often than women (23 per cent *vs.* 20 per cent) (Singleton, Meltzer, & Gatward, 1997).

Let's briefly imagine Mary and Jane as two men named Mike and Jim and some of the ways their conversation might play out.

1. Jim doesn't show Mike he is upset about Sherri's response to his presentation; or he suggests to Mike they go drinking instead of going to a movie and Mike agrees. In either case he doesn't get any help from Mike. At work, he acts on his angry feelings and does something that gets him into trouble.

2. Jim suggests they skip the movie and go drinking. Based on past experience, Mike thinks that's a sign that Jim is upset and asks if something is wrong. Jim gets defensive and clams up. Later he provokes an argument with Mike.

3. Jim suggests they skip the movie and go drinking. Mike thinks that's a sign that something is wrong, but doesn't say anything about it. Instead he says he really would prefer seeing a movie. Jim suggests a violent slasher movie. Mike says he's not interested in that. He was hoping Jim had picked something good. Jim says he doesn't give a damn. He doesn't want to see a boring movie. Now Mike says, "First you suggest going drinking. Then you pick a slasher flick. Then you get pissed-off when I don't want to do that. Are we back in college? What's up?"

The point I want to make here is that to get a man who is feeling bad to talk, you can't let him act in a way that will divert his attention from those feelings. Mike said no to drinking and a violent film before Jim says anything that indicates he's upset. Many men, like children, are more likely to indicate they are upset though action rather than speech. They are also more likely to get defensive when they are told what they are thinking. If a man is hiding his distress and you want to talk about it, try to limit his actions in a way that doesn't feel unpleasant—take a ride, go for a walk. Wait for him to show his upset, and offer your thoughts about his feelings only after he admits he has them.

Difficult relationships

For some people, intimacy is fraught with difficulty. Relationships seem to start out well, but soon become stormy and end painfully, or move into a state of perpetual crisis. Tanya was a lively, athletic, aspiring artist in her early twenties when I first saw her. She made friends easily, but invariably, after a period of excitement and mutual idealization, her friendships became stormy and deteriorated, leaving Tanya feeling hurt and abandoned. The same pattern held for her romantic relationships as well as for her three previous therapies.

When, near the end of our first meeting, Tanya looked directly into my eyes and said with intensity that she felt she had finally found a therapist who really understood her and could help her, I knew that she had said something similar to each therapist before. Now, she thought each had been incompetent in some obvious way and wondered how she ever believed they could help. I knew I would soon share the fate of my predecessors if I did not tell Tanya what I knew about her mind.

I told Tanya I thought she often felt empty and uncertain about who she was. When someone paid attention to her, she suddenly felt filled with excitement and the conviction that she had finally found a special person who cared about her. But things never worked out as she hoped. At the first sign that the new person was not completely there for her, she felt hurt and got enraged. Sometimes she felt that it was her fault, that there was something wrong with her, and she begged to be forgiven. In the end, it never worked out. I told her that if we were going to work together we would have to try to pay close attention to what was happening between us and pay attention to her unrealistic expectations; and I would like her to try to come and talk about it even when she felt it was no use. Tanya said she felt sad. She was no longer excited, but she agreed that what I said made sense.

Many people have had a friend like Tanya. Tanya's official diagnosis is Borderline Personality Disorder or BPD. It is estimated that two per cent of the population, six million people in the US, have BPD. The defining trait of people with BPD is their tendency to split, which means to experience others either as all good or as all bad. They approach new relationships with intense split transferences. Every person is both a potential rescuer and a potential betrayer. Anyone who seems attentive is immediately viewed as a rescuer. If his interest seems to wane, that person may be instantly transformed into a betrayer. The same person may be alternately viewed as one or the other several times a day.

People were attracted to Tanya by her intensity and directness. She said what she felt, which was at first invariably flattering. Being idealized can feel wonderful, especially if one's daily life is humdrum. Tanya was often idealized in return. In the thrall of mutual idealization, her new friends and lovers thought her quirky, creative, impulsive, and unconventional. After her rages and accusations of betrayal began, they thought her eccentric, untruthful, reckless, and immature.

Let me now say that I think borderline is a terrible term. It is a historical artefact from the 1950s, a time when American psychiatry was extraordinarily rigid and patronizing in its approach to patients. Patients who responded badly to their psychiatrists' authoritarian and disengaged manner—sometimes becoming angry and rebellious and sometimes becoming despairing and self-loathing—were deemed untreatable by proper insight-orientated psychotherapy. Psychiatrists decided that these patients were precariously perched on the border of psychosis and that the stress of real psychotherapy could push them into madness. They were given the label borderline psychotics. Borderline became a derisive term meaning difficult and untreatable.

As we came to understand both the delusions of psychiatry and the minds of these patients, it became clear that they are nowhere near psychosis. Some function poorly, but many do quite well. What these patients share, in addition to their tendency to split, is acute sensitivity to rejection and difficulty controlling emotion. If therapists understand this, carefully attend to their patients' reactions, and accurately read their emotions, therapy works very well and "real" insight-orientated therapy works best of all (Høglend,

Johansson, Marble, Bøgwald, & Amlo, 2007). Unfortunately, we are still stuck with the term borderline and its negative connotations. "Personality disorder" also has negative connotations. Despite my reluctance to use those terms, I will use the conventional acronym BPD to refer both to a person diagnosed with borderline personality disorder and to the disorder. That will help me avoid awkward constructions and create at least some distance from the actual words.

Emotional contagion. Friends and lovers of BPDs typically describe their experience as "like being on an emotional rollercoaster", or "like dealing with Jekyll and Hyde". A patient of mine described falling asleep with a loving wife in his arms and waking up to an enraged madwoman screaming that he was the cause of all her misery. He had no idea what he had done to trigger her change in mood and behaviour since all he had done was sleep. Anything he said to answer an accusation was countered with sharp, hateful recrimination.

She said, "You treat me like a maid. The house is never clean enough for you."

He said, "Really? I don't care if you clean. It's fine if you don't."

She said, "You say that, but I know you don't mean it. I know you're sick of me. Maybe you do want me to live in filth."

He fell silent in a state of hopeless despair.

She said, "Don't try to hide it. I know how angry you are. I can see it in your face."

Was he angry? He wasn't sure.

"Can't you even stand up for yourself? You're such a wimp. You disgust me."

Now he was sure. He was enraged

A BPD's emotional life is filled with hopeless despair and rage. That my patient was now feeling what his wife was feeling is an example of emotional contagion. Emotional contagion is a form of communication. It takes over when experience is too overwhelming to put into words. For BPDs it's a way of letting their companions know how terrible they feel. They are not consciously aware of what they are doing. If my patient asked his wife why she yelled at him each morning, she would say, "I don't know what got into me." She was right.

Often emotional contagion occurs and it is not possible to tell how the bad feeling was transmitted. You find yourself feeling bad in someone's presence and don't know why. Communications may have occurred out of awareness via direct-to-amygdala perceptions. A friend's face suddenly turns sad whenever you look away. His sad face beyond the periphery of your conscious perception is emotionally but not cognitively processed. You feel inexplicably sad.

It is often said that life with a BPD is a constant drama. So it is. A dramatist uses actors to stage scenes that create powerful emotional experiences in his audience in an attempt to communicate something about his understanding of life. A BPD uses his companions as both actors and audience to stage scenes that re-create his own emotional states in them in the hope of communicating something about his experience of life.

Complex emotional states are difficult, if not impossible, to convey with words alone. Our cognitive tools, such as rational thought and language—fairly recent evolutionary acquisitions—often seem weak in comparison to our ancient urges and emotions. The artistic impulse tries to overcome this gap and find ways to communicate the ineffable. Try to describe the emotional state of Lady Macbeth, Blanche Dubois, or Willy Loman. Unless you are poet or novelist, your description will be overly general and could probably apply to a wide range of people. Phrases like "terrible guilt", "panicky desperation", and "abject failure" pale before the complexity of these characters' inner turmoil; but when the dramatist puts these characters into action and interaction with other characters, their mental state becomes vividly real and you can almost feel what they feel.

My patient could see how his wife staged the morning drama to communicate her mental state. He did not understand why she was in such misery each morning, when the evening before had been fine. I told him how I read her mind. I said that I thought that when they both were in bed and he held her in his arms, she felt protected and loved. I wondered if perhaps she blocked out her worries by focusing on the pleasurable feeling of his body close to hers until she fell asleep. In the morning she awoke feeling panicked that he would soon be gone and she would be alone. She hated him for leaving and hated herself for needing him so much. She felt helpless, desperate rage. She wanted him to know how she felt in the hope that he might stay.

He said that sounded right. Weekends were much better except when she thought he was going out. Knowing more about his wife's mind did not change her, but it provided him with a shield that changed the meaning of her sharp words; they were not meant to drive him away but to keep him close. He now tries to hug her tight in the morning when she begins to wake and to tell her that he loves her. The mornings are getting better now, he thinks.

His theory of her mind. It was no mystery to my patient *how* his wife made him feel so bad; the mystery was *why* she was doing it. He had no explanation, no theory of her mind that made sense of her behaviour. Having no explanation added confusion to his anger and despair. He didn't want to believe she hated him, but sometimes he did. He was losing hope. He had started to think about ways of staying at work or even moving out. Had he done those things, it undoubtedly would have made things worse, fuelling her fears of rejection and abandonment.

The theory of his wife's mind I had offered explained the dramatic change in her mood while they slept as well as the meaning of her rages. Not only did that end his confusion, it gave him a tool to examine other interactions, and made him more sensitive to her fears and ways of communicating. He paid closer attention to her other reactions, such as raising her eyebrows or suddenly needing a hug. He realized that she experienced some seemingly little things he did—not turning from the TV when she was speaking, taking a phone call during dinner—as abandonment. Whenever he inexplicably felt bad, he wondered if it was emotional contagion, and asked himself if there might be something she unconsciously wanted him to know

Why it is important to understand BPD and other similar personalities, including our own

BPD is common, and even more people have what psychiatrists call "borderline tendencies", that is, they have some but not all of the symptoms of BPD. The fact is that seeing the world in black and white, having sudden swings of emotion, feeling overly sensitive to rejection and loss, being uncertain about one's identity, and getting inappropriately angry happen to almost everyone on occasion, especially under stress. Remember adolescence. It is often hard for psychiatrists to tell the difference between a normal adolescent and a BPD. Being diagnosed borderline means having many of these symptoms so much more consistently and intensely than other people that life becomes painfully difficult for the sufferer, and sometimes for those around them. Being able to read the BPD's mind can make life less stressful for all concerned. That BPD symptoms are universally experienced—unlike many other symptoms, such as compulsions, hallucinations, and bulimia, to name a few— make that task all that much easier.

It's far from hopeless. If there is any borderline in BPD, it is the borderline with normality; and it is frequently breached. Despite what many mental health professionals say, BPD is not a chronic condition. Researchers at Harvard University have been studying 290 patients who were first hospitalized with a diagnosis of BPD over ten years ago. After two years, 47% were no longer BPD, after six years, 73.5% were no longer BPD, and after ten years, 88% were no longer BPD. There were very few recurrences; only a handful ever became borderline again (Zanarini et al., 2007). The researchers concluded that "the majority of borderline patients experience substantial reductions in their symptoms far sooner than previously known". And the most important factor in getting better was feeling as if someone understood. "Once they feel better understood, they are often able to learn more adaptive ways of handling their many and varied symptoms."

Unfortunately, much of the popular literature and information on the Internet would have you believe that BPDs are dangerous manipulators who snare the innocent in their web and cause terrible pain. The character Alex, played by Glen Close in the 1987 movie *Fatal Attraction*, is often cited as an example.[3] In the movie, Alex seduces Dan (Michael Douglas) into what she seems to promise will be a fun-filled fling over a weekend when his wife and children are away. When Dan is about to return to his family, Alex begins to cling desperately. After Dan insists on getting on with his life, Alex tries to kill herself. When that doesn't get Dan back, she goes on to announce she is pregnant, stalk his family, boil his daughter's pet rabbit, and try to kill his wife.

"Be wary of BPDs. They are difficult and dangerous," popular culture seems to proclaim. Yet to see them as the evil other is in itself a form of splitting. The fact is we are as much attracted to them as seduced by them; and relationships with them are much more likely to end with them damaging themselves than us.

Many of the people I have known have been in an intimate relationship with a person with BPD; and many remember it with bitter-sweet nostalgia as a time of intensity, an experience worth having despite the pain. Their idealizations are total and convincing and make the idealized person feel wonderful. Some can be direct in the expression of their desires; they cut through the restraints of convention, often paying scant attention to the boring demands of adult life, like paying bills or cleaning house. Their concerns are basic and take on a life-or-death intensity: will I be completely loved or totally abandoned? Will I feel shattered or whole? It's all or none. A new friendship can feel like an adolescent infatuation or a mad love affair. I have seen more than a few people who chose only borderline lovers even after one painful break-up after another. The excitement of the early days is intoxicating, and more normal long-term intimacy seems like a trap. For those who wish to stay away from such relationships, the signs are easy to read, though many choose not to look.

Idealizations—amplifying what is desired and ignoring what is not—are the lubricants of new relationships. They enable people to get past awkwardness, inhibitions, and minor irritations. If things go well they will be replaced by a satisfying enough reality and never will be missed. Your new friend doesn't know everything about modern art, but she knows a great deal about it and other things. He may not be totally cool, but he is cool enough and kind. Sometimes idealizations are far enough off the mark to create disappointment but not so far as to feel like a betrayal. He is not nearly the lover you thought he was but you think you can work it out.

The idealizations of people with BPD reflect a desire that is impossible to fulfil; the fulfilment of other desires is not an acceptable substitute. Feeling betrayed is inevitable. What is said, no matter how lavish, is a cover for the impossible desire. She may say your looks are her ideal or you listen like no other—what she feels is that you will take away her pain and make her feel solid and complete. When something makes her see it is not going to happen, she feels led-on and betrayed. Unfortunately, BPDs are often led on and abused by those who hold out the promise of fulfilment. Some BPDs will do almost anything for someone who promises to end the pain and the longing.

The mind of a BPD is not a great mystery: their concerns are so basic and their emotions so intense. For most, relationships with BPDs are unavoidable. For some, they are preferable—life is rarely dull. The depressed man–BPD woman couple is a common match. When it's working, her intensity enlivens him; his limited responsiveness helps keep things in control. When it isn't working, bitter fights full of recrimination ensue, Though turmoil is inevitable in any intimate relationship with a BPD, it may be possible to reduce its intensity and frequency; these same principles can help in connecting to any person who is in distress and emotionally volatile. The key is reducing splitting and then working to heal splits when they occur. A mantra: no one is perfect, no one is worthless. Try to gently help the person to see you and others realistically, not as all good or all bad. Don't accept idealization and be flattered into thinking you can be the rescuer. Heroes inevitably fall. Be clear about your limitations in terms of what you can realistically give and the boundaries of what you can tolerate. Admit your mistakes and your imperfections. Don't encourage descriptions of others that sound like one-dimensional caricatures, whether good or bad. Ask questions and gently probe for more nuanced descriptions of people and situations. Always be aware of sensitivities to rejection and abandonment. When you find yourself on the bad side of a split and are accused of being inadequate, disappointing, or worse—listen and try to understand. If the accusations come in the context of an argument, don't fight back with accusations of your own. That will only lead to escalation. A BPD in the midst of an emotional conflict is re-experiencing a long-ago trauma and is fighting for her life. In states of intense fear, reason doesn't work. Be calm but engaged if possible; if that's not possible, try to negotiate a truce; failing that, it's perhaps best to withdraw.

Strike while the iron is cold has become a common piece of advice to those who work with BPDs and other emotionally volatile people.[4] What this means is, don't try to make a rational point to someone who is irrationally emotional. Whatever you say is likely to be experienced as an attack or criticism. Wait until a period of relative calm, and then remind the person about what happened and offer your observation. This doesn't always work.

Having lived a life of turmoil, many having been abused as children, BPDs often live in a state of anticipation, waiting to be attacked. This state is usually heightened by feelings of guilt, or shame, or hurt following a fight, and a generalized autonomic arousal that may be hidden behind brittle calm. In this state almost anything can be viewed as a criticism, a whisper can sound like a scream. Sometimes it is better to wait for the other person to come to you.

In an fMRI study (Berns et al., 2006), subjects received a mild but clearly painful electrical shock to a foot. Once shocked, they were told they would be shocked again, but there was no shock until after thirty long seconds had passed. While waiting, the subjects' cortical pain circuits went wild. In anticipation of the pain, the insula seemed to be orchestrating a rehearsal of the event to come. The subjects were not particularly frightened—amygdalae were not aroused—but they were very uncomfortable. They couldn't focus on anything else. Neuroscientists call it dread. When given a choice of waiting for the shock or getting it immediately, nearly all chose to get it over with. When given a choice of waiting for the shock or getting an even *more painful* shock right away, nearly a third chose increased pain over waiting in dread. It can feel like torture. Some people should not be forced to wait.

Romantic relationships

In most relationships, unrealistic idealizations are a warning sign of storms to come. No one can be perfectly attentive and caring; no one can fulfil another's every need. When reality doesn't live up to expectations, disappointment and anger are inevitable. Yet when a couple is embarking on a romantic relationship, fantastic idealizations are par for the course. When in love, each lover views the other as perfect and essential, each one feels she has found just the right person, that there could be no other; and each feels he has discovered in the other his one true love. In the blush of new romance, lovers feel they will never part.

Despite what people know rationally about the difficulties of relationships and the prevalence of divorce, people still seek a relationship that will last forever. Most people feel that deciding whom to marry is the most important decision of their life. Given that people want to find a mate with whom to spend a lifetime together, you might expect them to choose carefully. All evidence suggests that they do not.

It is not rational, concluded two Swiss economists who looked at the way people pick partners in the United States and Europe. They were surprised to find: (1) people don't spend much time searching; (2) they focus on factors related to lovability—appearance, warmth, sense of humour—and ignore practicality—reliability, organization, ambition; (3) they don't ask advice; (4) they wildly underestimate the risk of divorce.

Most people find their "one true love" in their own neighbourhood, at school, or at work. Unfortunately, spending more time searching does not make for better marriages. Living together before marriage does not decrease the risk of divorce. Once smitten, information and advice are deemed irrelevant. In many cultures, parents choose their child's mate and love is not a factor. In cultures where young people choose, love is what matters. Parents are rarely asked for advice. Friends and even therapists have little influence. I have seen cases where friends begged a friend to at least pause and reconsider to no avail, and others where therapists warned of difficulties to come without effect.

What is this kind of love?

In ancient Greece, groups of men gathered in the evening to eat, drink, and talk. Some nights were wild with non-stop drinking, naked dancers, and singing. Others were passionate with debates and sharing ideas. They were called symposia, Greek for drinking party. Plato's *Symposium* reports on one such gathering of seven good friends in Athens nearly 2500 years ago. Serious drinking was about to begin when a doctor among them noted they were still hung-over from the night before. He suggested they moderate their drinking and have a serious discussion, and proposed that they start by taking turns talking about love. Men, he said, spoke often about sex, wine, and beauty, but they rarely talked about love. The others agreed.

The first three state the perspectives of their professions: love in literature, law, and medicine. Then it's Aristophanes' turn. He's a well-known comic playwright, as well as an anti-war activist and feminist. He begins by saying that men have never at all understood the power of love. Then he tells a story about how love began. Long ago, he says,

> . . . man was round, his back and sides forming a circle; and he had four hands and four feet, one head with two faces, looking opposite ways, set on a round neck and precisely alike; also four ears, two privy members, and the remainder to correspond. He could walk upright as men now do, backwards or forwards as he pleased, and he could also roll over and over at a great pace, turning on his four hands and four feet, eight in all, like tumblers going over and over with their legs in the air; this was when he wanted to run fast. [Plato, 360 BCE]

There were not two sexes but three: men, women, and a union of the two. These two-faced, eight-limbed creatures were so powerful and arrogant that they dared to challenge the gods. As punishment, Zeus cut them in half and cursed humans to forever remember their original state and perpetually search for their missing half. The pursuit of the whole is called love. Love explains our reaction to finding our missing half: we are overwhelmed with affection and concern, cling desperately to each other and never want to part. Love is more than lust. Love is our greatest benefactor, leading us back to our own nature, and giving us hope for the future, Aristophanes concludes.

It is a wonderful story and a remarkable theory of love, even more so for being true. It was over two thousand years after the *Symposium* before love would be scientifically studied; first by Freud and other psychoanalysts in their consulting rooms, then by developmental psychologists in their nurseries and experimental psychologists in their laboratories, and now by neuroscientists in their MRI machines, which scan the brains of people in love. Together they have confirmed essential aspects of Aristophanes' theory:

1.   Same-sex love is as much a part of our nature as love between men and women.
2.   Love's power is seeking, not finding.
3.   Finding someone to love is in fact a re-finding.
4.   We are looking for ourselves to love.

5.   Love is not sex, and sex is not love.
6.   Love heals our wounds.

Same-sex love. Aristophanes was not justifying same-sex love. He was explaining the origin of love and how it is the same for lovers of men and lovers of women. He and his friends had no notion that the sex of the person you love matters. All had wives and families as well as young male lovers. They flirted with each other and some of them were lovers. I mention this in part because many in the scientific community now agree with Aristophanes' position: Both heterosexuality and homosexuality are natural and both require explanation. To the point of reading minds, it provides a good illustration of how in certain matters of sex, race, and religion, some people cannot accept that another person thinks differently. For example, you say to someone that you believe being gay is as natural as being straight. That person says back to you, "I don't believe you really believe that. You are saying it to justify your sin." His statement is a mind mis-read that asserts "I know your mind better than you do". I have seen gay patients whose parents love them but react in this way. I suspect that for these parents their faith is what keeps them anchored. To question it at all is too frightening.

Love's power is seeking, not finding. To say love's power is seeking, not finding is the same as saying love is a motivational system. A motivational system drives someone to seek something. Hunger is a motivational system. People do what they need to do to get food. When they eat enough food, they are satisfied for a short time, and then hunger starts the process up again. Love drives people to seek someone to love. When someone finds his love, he is sated by the pleasure of the connection. Lovers are not consumed. They continue to provide satisfaction as long as the connection continues.

Love is not sex and sex is not love. Sex is also a motivational system. It drives people to have sex—before culture and contraception—in order to mate and procreate. People are more discriminating about whom they love than about whom they feel sexual attraction to. Many men are attracted to almost anyone. Neuroscientists have traced the pathways of both sexual excitement and romantic love in the brain. Seventeen young men and women who were, "truly, deeply, and madly in love" viewed pictures of their beloved as well as pictures of opposite-sex friends during an MRI brain scan. While viewing their beloved, a characteristic pattern of brain activity emerged. Romantic love affected a wide range of brain structures from the amygdale to the cortex, including structures of memory and social interaction. Areas associated with positive reward were activated in a pattern similar to that triggered by cocaine. It appears that love, like cocaine, does make you high. Of equal interest were the areas that were deactivated. Areas associated with depression, sadness, and fear (the amygdala again) were put on hold. Everything positive was enhanced; everything negative was diminished. We can see why people in love feel as if they are floating in air.

There was no overlap between the brain activity of love and the brain activity of sexual arousal. Previous studies of sexual arousal had shown activity in the area that processes vision (Stoléru et al., 2003). Areas that trigger bodily excitement and fear—the hypothalamus and the amygdala—were also active, more so in men than women (Hamann, Herman, Nolan, & Wallen, 2004). This increased interest in looking. For some men in the study, almost any picture turned them on.

Sex without love is a staple of our culture. Seeing it in the brain is no surprise. Why does love without sex seem an odd or second-class idea? Socrates, later in Plato's *Symposium*, praises creativity as another, higher form of love. Today we seem to disparage Platonic love as either superficial or a cover for an affair. We are expected to leave our same-sex sexless passions behind in adolescence when we go on to the real thing.

Though sex and love in the brain do not overlap, they come close. They also are connected through adjacent structures. It is clearly possible for one to stimulate the other and for fear and anxiety to stimulate both. An old soldier friend told me that sex during war was the best. During the Second World War, he was parachuted behind enemy lines in France to gather information from the villagers. The young women he met were more than happy to see him, he said. Fear and anxiety can raise passion, and the closeness of death loosens inhibitions, providing the solace of intense pleasure amid the horror of war.

War and intensity can also stimulate love. Many soldiers married women with whom they could not exchange words, but with whom they shared intense emotion and, in most cases, passion. Does it matter if love is triggered by great sex or war? Are the ordinary triggers of proximity and appearance somehow better? Once love starts, it seems to continue on its own.

Finding someone to love is in fact a re-finding. We are looking for ourselves to love. The idealizations of romantic love are nothing to be afraid of. They are playful to begin with and will never be disappointed. Maybe when marriage occurred at fourteen, the loving couple completely believed what they said. My patients who marry in their late twenties, thirties, or forties know, "You are the most beautiful woman in the world", is not objectively true. It means you are the most beautiful woman in the world to me and will continue to be forever. More often, they say something like, "You are the most interesting person I have ever known", or "No one makes me laugh like you". The idealizations of love require no comparison with reality. The old woman visiting her failing husband in the nursing home can always say, "You will always be my handsome soldier."

What is idealized in romantic love is the lover's capacity to love. The lover wants to love his beloved with the fierce love of a mother for her baby child. It cannot be done, of course, but that is love's ideal. What we re-find in love is that experience of mother's love when we were so close we felt like one, when she mirrored our movements and anticipated our needs and we moved about together like a mighty beast with four arms and four legs.

Each lover loves himself in the other. Researchers have consistently found that most people look for romantic partners like themselves. They tend to be attracted to others of similar intelligence, good looks, socio-economic status, religion, and athletic ability, among other traits. Using computer graphic techniques, a psychologist at the University of St Andrews in Scotland created photographs that bore essential similarities to the experimental subjects but were of the opposite sex. The subjects did not recognize the similarities but were more attracted to faces of the opposite sex that were shaped like theirs (Penton-Voak, Perrett, & Peirce, 1999). These similarities are transference cues that can trigger the beginning of love. Our romantic partners do not need to be just like us, but we need to see enough of ourselves in the other to feel we have found a part of ourselves.

Opposites do not attract. Researchers have found that choosing a partner for distinct differences of style or character often leads to a quick break-up. Many of these relationships become what the researchers called fatal attractions. The person who was first liked for their difference ended up being hated for it (Felmlee, Flynn, & Bahr, 2004). One exception to this is temperament. People tend to choose romantic partners whose temperaments are like their soothing parent. In that way, partners' temperaments complement each other. Couples in which one partner who is high-reactive, edgy, anxious and high-strung is paired with a partner who is low-reactive, laid-back, and unflappable are common. The high-reactive partner enlivens the laid-back one; and the laid-back one calms his high-reactive partner.

Love heals our wounds. Increasingly, researchers are finding that being in a loving relationship improves physical health. Hugs lower blood pressure. Sex improves the heart. New York University research psychologist Lloyd Silverman has demonstrated that the experience of being at one heals many psychological wounds. In numerous experiments, Silverman flashed images subliminally, that is, so quickly that subjects were not aware they had seen anything. The image in most of Silverman's studies was a line drawing of a mother holding a child and the words, "Mommy and I are one". Silverman found that the image, presented out of awareness, could soothe and sometimes cure.[5]

Silverman's first subjects were hospitalized patients with schizophrenia. He found that their symptoms, including illogical thinking and inappropriate behaviour, declined after subliminally viewing "mommy and I are one". Silverman and his associates conducted over fifty studies and other research groups another fifty more. For a wide range of problems, including shyness, adolescent behaviour problems, phobias, eating problems, and smoking, among others, "mommy and I are one" reduced symptoms. Every day we are learning more about the curative effects of love and there is much left to learn. But if an image flashed in an instant has such power, imagine what a long-lasting romantic relationship can do.

Mind-reading problems in romantic relationships

What triggers falling in love is often obscure. From what we know, it is some combination of cues that makes each person feel the other is like him. In addition, each must feel that the other will allow himself to be loved. The dissatisfactions of romantic relationships are more often not being allowed to love rather than not being loved. Some are obvious: he will not let me love him; she will not let me help her. Others need to be read: he will not listen; she won't respond to my touch.

Problems arise when someone is so compelled to try to heal a problem that he pays little attention to rest of the person. For example, a man finds himself repeatedly in a relationship with a woman who is not sexually responsive to him. He so needs to cure her problem to make himself feel whole that he ignores that, for her own reasons, she does not want to be touched. Sometimes a couple like this will get married, thinking they will work it out later. In my experience they almost never do.

An emotional knower

David kept choosing the same woman over and over again. When we first met, thirty-eight-year-old David had already married two versions of her and was now, rather miserably, working his way through a long parade of post-divorce versions. Although David's particular rendition of *Ground Hog Day* was interestingly multi-cultural—one wife had been Jewish, the other Italian, and his current girlfriend Hispanic—whatever their ethnicity, all of David's wives and girlfriends were chronically worried, intensely anxious, and clung to him for help

"Why do I always end up with same woman?" he asked, in a half-joking, half-desperate voice one day.

In David's case, the obvious answer to this question also happened be true. Unconsciously, he was trying to recreate his relationship with his mother, a chronically worried and anxious woman herself. By soothing her, he could feel at one with her. David did not mind this particular problem in his wives. He took satisfaction in calming their fear and felt loved when he did. But his emotional style of knowing, which drew him instantly to worried women, did not allow him to see how troubled they were. He made the emotional equation: the more anxiety she suffers, the more she will need me and love me. In the thrall of his desire, he could not see that the women he chose were too troubled to be alone and could not be cured by his love. Eventually, he ended up feeling trapped and had to escape.

A cognitive knower

Linda grew up in posh suburbs, but her parents were working-class. Her mother worked at Kmart and her father tended lawns. At school, she felt humiliated, the child of servants dressed in Kmart clothes. In addition, her family was troubled. Her father drank and hit her mum. She was determined to escape and become like the people she envied. In Junior High School, the gym teacher noticed she was quick. She joined the track team as a sprinter and soon became a star. With her athletic ability and intelligence, she received a scholarship to an excellent college. She went on to graduate from a top law school and obtain a job in a prestigious firm.

She wanted to get married, move to the rich suburbs, and raise a family. She did not so much want it as think it was the right thing to do. Early in her childhood, she had stopped feeling to avoid the pain. She made all of her decisions by weighing all the facts. Linda chose her lovers based on their resumés. She had found several who seemed right. They were Ivy League and athletic, from wealthy families with good connections. She thought they would help her feel authentic, not like an impostor covering her past. After several painful break-ups, she came to see me not knowing what to do. When I listened to what happened, it seemed like the men had done just the opposite of what she wanted them to do. They teased her and let her know she was not good enough for them. They threatened her with exposure if she did not defer to their needs. Blocked from her emotions, she could not know that out of her awareness they felt quite familiar—like Daddy, they were mean and drank too much.

It took a few years before she could know what she felt. I must have said a thousand times—and I said little else—"you are detaching" or "you are not feeling" when I sensed her withdrawal. Then one day she surprised us both, "You're so boring. Can't you say something new?" Shocked, we both smiled broadly.

"You're angry."

"Yes," she said happily.

Notes

1. The Concise Oxford Dictionary of English Etymology.
2. www.sciencedaily.com/upi/index.php?feed=Science&article=UPI-1-20070705-16363500-bc-us-talkers.xml
3. http://www.abc.net.au/rn/science/mind/stories/s1244802.htm
4. Probably first used in the clinical context by Fred Pine (1984).
5. In some studies just the words were presented. The word "mommy" sometimes was changed to "mamma" in the South.

CHAPTER NINE

Why we don't know what we know

Denial

D eniers fly under all flags. They can be emotional knowers, cognitive knowers, even balanced knowers. But they are united in a desire to avoid other minds for fear of what they will find in them. Ruby J is a case in point. Few black children from rural Florida grow up with the dream of becoming a psycho-analyst, but one day when Ruby was fifteen, she came across a magazine article in the school library that literally changed her life. The subject of the article, Erik H. Ericson—Ruby still remembered her reaction thirty years later—seemed as distant from her world as the Man in the Moon, but the way he talked about analysis, as if it were a religious calling, struck a chord in the pastor's daughter. Walking out of the library that day, Ruby knew what she wanted to do with the rest of her life.

When I met her, Ruby had already received a doctorate in psychology and was in training at a prominent psychoanalytic institute. Our meeting had been arranged by the Dean of at the institute. Ruby had capped a difficult academic year by failing to pass the division boards—a requirement for advancement—and the institute was concerned that she might have to be dropped from the programme or that she would quit. "That wouldn't serve anyone's interests," the Dean said, when he called to make a referral for Ruby, "She's our first African-American student." A few days later, Ruby arrived in my office, full of anguish and self-reproach. The test—all her failures of the past year: they were all her fault, she insisted. For her teachers, whom she felt she had disappointed, Ruby had nothing but the highest praise. They were brilliant, warm, supportive, and sensitive—everything she had always imagined psychoanalysts to be. During our next few conversations, however, a more complicated picture of the institute teaching staff began to emerge.

One of the most durable findings about academic performance is that in an environment of low expectations, students underperform. It's called stereotype threat (Steele & Aronson, 2005), and it is a particular problem for black students at white institutions, though other people of colour and women are victims as well. In ways both big and small, Ruby's instructors were sending her a message of low expectations. There was, for example, the overly helpful teacher who kept pushing "special tutorials" on Ruby; and there was the forgetful teacher who would credit Ruby's most astute classroom observations to other students when he recalled them later, as if he thought Ruby incapable of intelligent comment. And there were the polite smiles and condescending remarks of a half dozen other instructors. The psychoanalysts at the institute were not aware of what they were doing. They were not consciously racist—on the contrary, many saw themselves as civil rights advocates—but they had little or no experience of working with black students or black patients, and their perception of Ruby was distorted by their unconscious stereotypes. They were not seeing her for who she was—and Ruby didn't want to know what was on their minds.

During our second meeting, when I asked Ruby if she thought her academic problems might be related to the environment at the institute, she looked genuinely surprised. "But everyone there is so nice," she said.

It was not hard to identify the source of Ruby's denial. To admit that her teachers were condescending and dismissive might throw into question her life's dream. More difficult was finding a way to help her quickly. Ruby would not be able to escape the expectations of her teachers until she stopped idealizing them. But how could I help her to do that without souring her on the institute, or on her chosen profession?

We found the answer in three strategies based on theory of mind. With the first, called contextualizing, the denier helps identify what she is really thinking and feeling by asking herself two questions. First: "Is there an experience in my past that is similar to the one I am having now?" And second: "How did I feel then, and why?" There was a parallel to Ruby's current problems at the institute. During her sophomore year as an undergraduate, Ruby's grades had also fallen off sharply. But back then she had not idealized her professors and teaching assistants at the prestigious university she had attended (that deference was reserved for psychoanalysts, who, in her mind, were far wiser than mundane academics), so she had no difficulty making a connection between their patronizing attitude and her poor performance.

"I felt I was being condescended to, and it made me furious," Ruby said, the day we talked about that earlier incident. "Eventually, my anger got in the way of my ability to study."

"Maybe you feel the same way now; you just won't admit it to yourself," I said.

The second theory-based strategy is called "bear in mind", meaning: bear in mind the deficits of the people you are dealing with. A denier has less incentive to hide and deny if she realizes that someone else's attitudes and opinions reflect that person's shortcomings, not her own. With some help from me, Ruby began to see that the institute teachers she worshipped as demigods were, in their own way, as provincial as the people she had grown up with in Florida. Many of her teachers shared a particular kind of upbringing and training, a particular mind-set and values, a particular ideology of life—and this densely shared culture made it difficult for them to see and appreciate the talents of someone as different as Ruby. She would have to educate them in order for them to be able to educate her.

The third theory-based strategy Ruby found useful was: act on distressing messages. As its name suggests, the technique requires confrontation. Instead of suppressing her anger when confronted with an unintentionally belittling or patronizing remark, I encouraged Ruby to act on the anger—not with finger pointing and accusations, but with polite yet firm observations designed to correct the speaker's mental image of her. Thus, when a teacher misattributed an astute observation of hers to another student, instead of suffering in silence, Ruby pulled him aside after class and reminded him who the real author of the observation was.

Ruby began to speak up more in class, not only demonstrating her sharp mind but also pointing out to her teachers and classmates the narrowness of their experience. Some were appreciative and took the opportunity to examine how their unconscious stereotypes influenced their judgement; not surprisingly, some were defensive and denied even a modicum of prejudice. Ruby came to understand that several of them would have preferred to keep the institute comfortably removed from the difficult realties of today's world, and that they had little desire to use their skills to try to understand the persistence of racism and oppression. She saw, too, that their defensiveness was in part due to their own experience of exclusion and prejudice. Some were immigrants or children of immigrants and had suffered real hardships; others felt that as psychoanalysts they were pushed aside by biological psychiatry and academic psychology.

No longer in denial, Ruby could now see her teachers as the conflicted human beings they were, not as the idealized figures she wished them to be. She could allow herself to read their minds. More importantly, she saw how they could misread hers; she let go of the belief that they were infallibly accurate. She did not have to become who they thought she was. She could be herself. After a few months of weekly meetings, Ruby took the qualifying test again—and passed.

We are all in denial

Most of us at some time or another have been in a position like Ruby's, where we really didn't want to know what others were thinking. We have seen with reading minds in general, and detecting lies in particular, that anxiety about what we may learn inhibits us, even though what we fear is often only in our memories. We fear we will discover something that is overwhelming or incomprehensible, in the way a child is afraid to know what may be on his parent's mind; we fear we will discover something that makes us feel shame and humiliation in the way a child is afraid to find her excitement is unnoticed or unreflected; we fear discovering no one cares in the way a child fears being alone. Perhaps in your family your parents were thinking of splitting up and you didn't want to know about it because there was nothing you could do. Perhaps at your job you were not doing your best and didn't want to know if everyone knew. Perhaps at a party you didn't want to know what others were thinking so you could continue to drink more than you should.

But our denial goes beyond particular situations—I suspect that more often than not, we do not want to know what is going on in other people's minds because it feels like too much to care about. Newborns cry in response to the cries of other babies. Before their second birthday, babies try to help others in distress (Zahn-Waxler, Radke-Yarrow, Wagner, & Chapman, 1992). But by the time they reach first grade, children's concern for others has decreased—they seem to have learnt not to notice or to care. To understand others you have to undo the denial: to read other minds, you need to think about other minds.

I don't know. When I ask a student to read my mind, to try to assess what I am thinking and feeling, the typical response is an anxiously stated, "I don't know. How should I know?" I answer, "I bet you have more of a sense of my thoughts and feelings than you suspect; maybe you're worried that if you try, you will be wrong or you'll embarrass me if you're right. But I'm sure you are much more likely to be right if you try something rather than nothing. What would you feel in my spot?" Any theory is better than none.

He's nice. If you ask someone what he thinks of a new acquaintance, the most common response is, "He's nice." What this means is that there was nothing glaringly out of the ordinary, nothing obviously dangerous or threatening about the new person. But people often report that someone who turned out to be a serial killer "seemed nice". Think about the last time you said, he's nice or she's nice. Now think about the person you were talking about and try to describe him more detail. You don't have to go right to his mind. Think about his dress and demeanour: what he was wearing? How did he hold himself? How did he move? What was the tone of his voice? The expressions on his face? Picture him as vividly as you can in your mind. Try to mimic his expressions and move as he moved. What do you feel? Now I'd bet you can say more about him than that he is nice

A patient recalled seeing a nice-looking man walk towards her in the park. As he approached, she felt increasingly frightened and "creeped-out". She cut a wide path and ran by him to the nearest exit to the street. Later she learnt that the man was Ted Bundy, the preppy serial killer. "Something about the way he carried himself seemed wrong," she shudders as she remembers.

Don't lose sight of the facts. Pay attention to your gut when it warns of danger, but pay attention as well when it says things are OK, and don't lose sight of the facts. Remember, when information is lacking, paranoia is the default position because the mind is designed to think, better safe than sorry. We are bombarded with frightening images and too often do not examine the data and needlessly keep our distance from those we have no reason to fear. Years ago, my wife and I travelled along the coast of southern Italy with our son, who was almost two. One warm evening at dinner at a dockside café, my son was fussing when a man in an elegant white suit swept him off my lap and into his arms. "Let me take him to my boat across the way so you can enjoy the beautiful night," he said.

My wife and I looked at each other and—though we knew we each felt some irrational concern—together nodded OK. A quarter-hour later, we followed, and found our son playing happily on the man's yacht. We had been warned about the wave of Italian kidnappings. We knew that, in fact, in twenty-three years ten children had been kidnapped in Italy—and most were children of wealthy parents held for ransom.[1] Based on our feelings and on the facts, we had no reason to fear the man in the white suit.

Beware of flatness. For emotional knowers especially, not feeling is a warning sign. It means something is interfering with their emotional antennae. The something could be a medication like Prozac—as it was for Nicholas (Chapter Five)—or it could be extreme fatigue or stress. But everyone should feel something before taking significant action. If you don't, you are losing important information. If you are a cognitive knower, don't dismiss feelings as untrustworthy. Attend carefully to even a small buzz of emotion. Several million years of evolution have made our heart and our gut useful guides.

Check it out. We all tend to hear what they want to hear, just as we tend to see what we want to see. I especially advise people who tilt strongly in one direction or another—towards head or heart—to enlist a spouse, friend, or colleague to act as a reality checker when they are making important decisions about others. Try to find someone who thinks not like you—a gut man or a cool-headed thinker as the case may be—to corroborate or challenge your impressions. Be aware of your deficits. We all have them. Don't try to do it all on your own.

Revelations fade

Fifty days after Jesus' resurrection many of his disciples—including his apostles, and his mother and family—hid together in a house in Jerusalem. Though many had heard him preach, witnessed his miracles of healing, and his resurrection, they were dispirited. The streets were thronged with pilgrims celebrating the feast of the harvest, yet the disciples were afraid to go out and spread the word. Without warning, a roaring wind swept over them and the sky filled with tongues of fire, and the Holy Spirit inspired them to preach, and when they spoke everyone—no matter what their language—understood.

Revelations fade is my motto. We have all had powerful epiphanies, seen the truth, understood something important, only to soon forget. Among the many revelations I hear from patients are: I want to spend more time with my family; I want to be more giving and caring; money doesn't buy happiness; I can let go of my anger: I can be grateful; love is the most important thing. Patients say these things with conviction, but they are usually soon forgotten. So I remind them of what they said. That's part of my job. Long ago psychoanalysts realized that simply having an insight is not enough. Eureka moments that in themselves change lives exist only in the movies. Insights are often forgotten; they have to be dug up and revived; they needed to be restated again and again in different ways and with feeling; and if they are really going to stick, they need to be practised. The technical term for this process is working though.

That's why psychoanalysts like to meet with patients several times a week. It provides an opportunity for practising insights. It doesn't surprise anyone that learning a new language or a new skill requires a great deal of practice, a few hours a week at a minimum. Yet people seem bothered by the fact that learning a new psychological approach and new social skills requires practice as well. You don't need to practise with a therapist, but you do need to practise.

In a similar vein, patients sometimes sheepishly confess that they have discovered a self-help book, DVD, or a guru that feels helpful and works quickly. They think I'll disapprove or think they are naïve for believing in a seemingly simple approach. I'm never discouraging and make it clear that I am interested in their experience. Many of the approaches share similar methods: (1) regularly scheduled time, free of distraction; (2) a method of relaxation; (3) a way of thinking about goals; (4) a way of feeling connected to a larger group. Why should I disapprove? It would be like disapproving of exercise or good nutrition.

Unfortunately, after a few weeks or months, I often find myself asking, "What's going on with yoga, Tony Robbins, meditation . . .? You felt it was helpful, what is stopping you from continuing?"

"I don't have time," is the usual reply, which is almost never really true. Why do people stop doing things they want to do? Whether it's exercise, a self-help programme, going to church, practising a sport, finding time for sex, doing charitable work, people often find it hard to keep doing it—even when it feels good. It is one of the most important unanswered questions in psychology. One of the very few scientific studies about the subject (Aarts, Custers, & Holland, 2007) came to several interesting conclusions: (1) often people don't even notice when they stop pursuing a goal; only in retrospect to they realize that they've stopped practising, exercising, studying, etc.; (2) bad feelings—fear, guilt, shame, etc.— made them stop, but they don't know it. For example, Jane started practising piano regularly. As she improved, she imagined playing for an audience and felt both excited by the idea and embarrassed at the thought she might make a mistake. She pushed these thoughts aside and without realizing she was doing it or why, she stopped practising. When a friend asked what happened, she replied with the common lament, "I don't know why I stopped doing it when it felt so good."

It's too hard and too lonely

Often when people see others performing something expertly—a graceful dancer, a concert violinist, a professional athlete, a champion chess player—they comment to themselves that they wish they had the talent to perform in that way. With certain activities like golf or poker, it is sometimes possible to imagine having the ability to play at a professional level. Most golfers have at least a shot or two each round worthy of a pro; and most poker players have played a few hands with the skill of an expert gambler. Yet many people feel they lack the talent to be expert at anything or even proficient at many things; and feel that whatever it is comes easier to those who are good at it than it would to them. Research conclusively demonstrates that is not the case. It takes effort and time to become expert at most things; but most people could do it if they were motivated; talent seems to be of little consequence.

Professor K. Anders Ericsson, Conradi Eminent Scholar and Professor of Psychology at Florida State University is almost sixty, and though he has lived in the USA since he was invited to study at Carnegie-Mellon University thirty years ago, he's still a Swedish citizen. With sparkling eyes, a full beard and still thick grey hair, it's easy to imagine him as a formidable academic in an Ingmar Bergman film. His message, too, has a Scandinavian cast: if you practise consistently, working hard but with moderation, you can achieve excellence in almost anything.

Maybe it's not a sexy message, because though major academic reviews of his research started to appear in 1993 (Anders Ericsson, Krampe, & Tesch-Römer, 1993), there was nary a pip from the popular press until 2006. It may not be sexy, but there is no doubt that it is true. And knowing it can eliminate an often debilitating theory of mind—other people have it easy; which is often accompanied by a negative self assessment—so there must be something wrong with me. Ericsson has been studying how people get good at something since he was in college. One of his first studies was about memory. Good memory was believed by many to be something you were born with. If you read random digits out loud an average person can easily memorize seven, kind of like a phone number. Ericsson showed that with just practice—and no special instruction—an average person could get up to eighty-two!

Ericsson, of course, knew that some people claimed to have "photographic" memories and wanted to see if it was true. While teaching at the University of Colorado he heard of some folk who had the reputation of having memorized the Bible. He went after them:

> When I finally tracked the "exceptional" people down they rejected their claims of having effortless photographic memory and claimed to be merely above average—as I confirmed in a few experimental tests of memory. I could find nobody who had memorized the whole Bible; most of them confessed to only knowing a large number of quotations and declined any experimental tests. [Schraw, 2005]

Ericsson went on to study experts in a variety of areas including sports, music, chess, art, and writing. Over and over again he found practice was the key. He found the best expert musicians, such as those in international orchestras, had spent over 10,000 hours practising by the time they were twenty, which was about twice as much as other less accomplished professional musicians and five times as much as good amateurs. About 5000 hours of practice to become an expert kept coming up in whatever area he studied. With an occasional day off, 5000 hours is about three hours a day for five years. That is something kids have time for but not most adults; the idea that you have to start young is probably wrong— but you do need to have the time. And you need focus: when Tiger Woods was a kid he enjoyed baseball and golf. His mother said to him that if he wanted to get really good, he'd have to choose one, and he did.

Ericsson means something specific by practice; he calls it deliberate practice. It's not just doing the same thing over and over. He said in an interview,

> Deliberate practice is to repeat what you're doing so you can correct it. Experience does not improve performance. Some amateur golfers can play at the same level for 30 years, and they don't automatically get better. Once people reach some acceptable level, they seem to get stuck there. In order to keep improving, you need to structure your training around specific goals. If you are a golfer, you don't just stand there and hit balls as hard as you can. [Aschoff, 2006]

Experience is not the same as practice. Ericsson found that length of experience doesn't relate to improvement. Deliberate practice is usually solitary and feels like work. Recent studies show that for some deliberate practice can be fun, but that comes after you're already near expert at something. Then practice can be like play. Ericsson has spent a great deal of time with highly successful actors, chessmasters, athletes, and doctors and notes that for them, "Frequently, the boundaries between work and leisure disappear" (Schraw, 2005).

When you look closely at people who seem like "naturals", you invariably find they have been practising most of their lives. Sometimes it doesn't seem that way because it fits neatly into their lives. Many great golfers, like Arnold Palmer, whose father was a club pro, grew up on golf courses. Others like Sam Snead, Ben Hogan, and Chi Chi Rodriguez were poor kids who started to work as caddies before they were ten. Picasso's father was an artist who had Pablo drawing as soon as he could hold a crayon. "For the last 25 years I have been hunting down proposed evidence for innate talent . . . With the exception of height and body size, I have not encountered any firm evidence, at least so far . . ." (*ibid.*) said Ericsson. Ericsson concedes that there are no 200 pound jockeys and you have a better shot at being a professional basketball player if you're tall; but desire can overcome even some such physical hand-icaps. 5'3" Mugsy Bogues played fourteen seasons in the NBA; Billy Holiday—one of the greatest jazz singers ever—had just over a one-octave range.

You might think that the idea that just about anyone can do just about anything would be welcome, but it's not. Ericsson's findings are difficult for many to absorb. Many psychologists, including multiple intelligences guru Howard Gardner (2005) find it hard to believe that talent—if it exists at all—counts for so little. This disbelief persists despite the fact that Ericsson's thesis has not been seriously challenged even as he has extended his research into domains like law and medicine (Ericsson, 2004). It is reasonable to wonder why, if no special talent is required, why do so few people do the work necessary to become top notch? Most seem to want to hold on to the theory that others have it easier. Why?

"No strain, no gain!" coaches commonly shout, and Ericsson's research shows that it's true. But what motivates some people to do it—to strain themselves to gain—and others not? Recall from Chapter Four that the line between stress and trauma is not so clear, and whether you learn from an experience or never want to do it again depends on many things, including temperament and attachment.[2] Here's where Ericsson's views on moderation come in. Experts, he has found, practise about 3–5 hours a day. More is too much.

> most students have perfected the short-term habits of cramming for tests and for concentrated work when preparing papers and reports. They work until they are completely fatigued. After that, they need many days of rest before taking on new tasks. I have talked to many people who prematurely terminated their pursuit of expertise because of prolonged fatigue, stress, and unrealistic goals about rate of improvement . . . One has to build up daily habits for working and practice with full concentration slowly to reach the experts' levels of 3–5 h per day. [Schraw, 2005]

Here Ericsson offers one explanation for the curious fact that most people have the ability to achieve an expert level of performance but very few do. People daydream about being accomplished athletes and musicians but few really try. His theory is that having pushed themselves beyond the point of growth-inducing stress into trauma, they become wary of trying again. I've seen former athletes who had never been taught when to stop. Several burned out in college sports and cannot face ever playing again. But most people never get to that point. For many, leaning and work are painful, not something to master and enjoy, but something to avoid. They cannot imagine the minds of those for whom work and the rest of their life are seamless, not workaholics who torment themselves and those around them, but those who enjoy their work and share their enjoyment with friends and family. Most people do not get expert at anything and many do not even get proficient.

Has practice become painful for so many because they were pushed beyond stress into trauma when very young? That's what Ericsson's theory would suggest. It would explain why so many feel that other people have it easy because in a sense they do: not because they have greater innate ability or talent but because they do not associate hard work and practice with trauma and pain. Clinically, I see something else that Ericsson does not discuss, though I think it's related. Feeling shame, as we've seen, is a powerful inhibitor. Expert achievement and performance go hand and hand. For most, practice is a lead-up to competition or exhibition. I think many have suffered the trauma of repeated shame and cannot even allow themselves to feel the full excitement that comes with achievement of a goal. It is one thing to be a star in fantasy; it is another to try when fear of shame is a constant companion. I think many are drawn to *American Idol* not as much to see the stars as to marvel at those brave souls who fail yet survive their public humiliation. Those who think that others have it easier are correct, but only in part. It is not that others have some special talent or ability; for those not traumatized by shame, failure is not so painful.

Ericsson also found that practice can sometimes be too lonely to bear. I started playing golf about fifteen years ago and decided to take Ericsson's work seriously. I haven't been able to devote three hours a day, but often put in one or two. Maybe it's trite to say it, but practising alone gets lonely. As a child, if you're lucky, a parent sits close by as you practise your scales or free throws, or pitch shots; and even if he is reading or knitting or chatting with a friend, as long as she looks up admiringly from time to time and smiles you know that she's there. I coached Little League for thirteen years and I saw what a difference it made for kids to have someone who loves them hang around. As an adult, on occasion I practise with a friend or a coach, but no one is going to sit near me even an hour a day; I don't need that but it does feel lonely sometimes. I think the loneliness is particularly poignant when you accomplish something new for the first time. You want someone who cares to be watching; to let you know it's really happening and share your joy. When I am on the driving range and suddenly find myself hitting some shot better than I ever imagined, I'll look around to see if someone is watching; of course, no one is, and I get a fleeting peevish childish thought—if no one cares I'm just going to pick up my clubs and go home. During his endless hours of practice, I bet Tiger Woods feels his father beside him.

My father was a plumber and he taught me how to fix things and I went on to learn how to fix almost anything, but if I had a plumbing problem he'd usually fix it or tell me how. After he died, I found myself haunted by one leak after another from plumbing problems that I couldn't fix. I eventually realized my ineptitude reflected my wish for my father to be there and take care of it for me. To do it myself meant to acknowledge he was really gone.

How many people on encountering a computer glitch throw up their hands in despair and say "I just don't get computers." I fix a lot of my friends' computers and they often comment on my "talent". I tell them about the hours spent on help lines, the frustrating days ripping apart and putting together old machines, but they seem unconvinced that they could do the same. I think they don't want to. Helplessness is often rewarded by help, whether in reality or fantasy.

Look at me!

Andy Warhol's 1968 prediction that "In the future, everyone will be world-famous for 15 minutes" has not yet come to pass, but the desire to be famous is stronger than ever. We live in an age of exhibitionism. From the talk shows and reality programmes of television, to the social meet markets, show-and-tell video sites, and blogs on the Internet, technology has allowed ever increasing numbers of people to display ever more themselves to the world. As of October 2009, there are over 400 million active personal websites; Facebook alone has over 200 million

What used to be considered shockingly personal is no longer shocking; the bar for what needs to be exposed in order to get even fleeting voyeuristic attention has been repeatedly raised. Self-exposure that used to be considered scandalous or a sign of mental illness is now the norm. Being seen has become an end in itself; and the desire to be famous for its own sake dominates many minds. Journalist and social commentator Jake Halpern examines this phenomenon in *Fame Junkies* (Halpern, 2007). With the help of Carol Liebler, Professor of Media Studies at Syracuse University, Halpern surveyed 653 teenagers attending middle school in Rochester, New York. Rochester was chosen because its population mirrors the US as a whole; for that reason it is often used in consumer product surveys. Halpern's results tell a startling tale.

"If you could push a magic button and become smarter, stronger, beautiful, or famous, which would you pick?" the students were asked. Fame was number one. Girls chose it more often than intelligence; for boys fame and intelligence were about equal. Students were asked to choose from a list of famous people who they would most like to have dinner with. The list included 50 cent, George Bush, Jesus Christ, Albert Einstein, Paris Hilton, Jennifer Lopez, and Shaquille O'Neil. Bush was the least favourite, followed by Einstein with less than 4% of the vote. Everyone else made it into the double digits, with Jennifer Lopez winning it among the girls and Jesus Christ winning among the boys.

Here's the one I find most distressing: another question asked, "When you grow up, which of the following jobs would you most like to have?: president of a great university like Harvard or Yale; the chief of a company like General Motors; a US Senator; a Navy SEAL; the personal assistant to a very famous singer or movie star." The overall first choice was personal assistant to someone famous, chosen among girls an overwhelming 43.4% of the time; almost twice as much as the next most popular job, university president. Boys chose Navy SEAL slightly more than personal assistant but tellingly, among boys and girls who were doing poorly in school and felt unpopular, a whopping 80% chose personal assistant.

The desire to be liked seems to be at the core of the wish to be famous or even just to associate with fame. One question was open-ended and asked, "If you suddenly became a celebrity—like a movie star or a rock star—what would be the best thing about being famous?" A typical response reads, "If I was to become famous, people would probably think I was sooo cool and they would all want to be my friend."

Halpern toys with the idea that fame is addictive, hence the title, *Fame Junkies*, Fame produces a rush, an adrenaline high, he says. But so does exercising political power, doing battle, climbing mountains, or diving beneath dark seas; and I can only imagine Einstein's rush when he grasped for the first time that energy and matter are the same. Addiction doesn't explain it. The mass media's focus may have more to do with it, but politicians are in the press a great deal, certainly more than college presidents or Navy SEALS, yet almost no teen wants to dine with the president and few aspire to public office. I think the kid got it right, "If I was to be famous … they would all want to be my friend." The famous are never alone, and— surrounded by sycophants and paparazzi—can never be alone. They are adored not for what they do but for who they are. It doesn't matter how someone becomes famous—through talent and hard work or by accident of birth or by mere association—fame is what matters; and the lonely and the lost can stare and imagine that some-day they will too will be discovered and thrust into the limelight.

People imagine they will be liked for who they are, not what they do. In truth, the only time we are ever loved purely for who we are is when we are infants, before we can do anything. As soon as we do, in one way or another we are judged. Once again we see the wish for return to our mother's arms is strong, so strong that many misread minds and confuse the motivations of groupies and hangers-on with real love and friendship. The motivation for this misread is so powerful that it persists despite all the sad but true tales of the famous feeling so alone and the formerly famous being abandoned by their crowd. Why does this near delusional misread persist so powerfully?

In the clinical setting, psychoanalysts have long recognized that some people derive little intrinsic satisfaction from their accom-plishments, and seem always in search of recognition and praise. No amount of praise, however, feels like enough, and even minor criticism causes great hurt. Success does not bring lasting satisfac-tion and feeling fraudulent and empty is common. People suffering from this disorder are called narcissistic, from the Greek myth of Narcissus—a handsome young man who was so captured by his image in a pond that he stayed riveted to the spot in awe of himself, eventually dying of starvation. He could not accept as valuable what others had to offer. Narcissistic problems exist in varying degrees from the occasional and mild to the all-consuming. Eric, in Chapter Six, is an example of someone with significant narcissistic problems. Analysts trace this difficulty to chronic mismatches between the child's experience and the parent's reflection of that experience. Often the child's accomplishments go unnoticed and her excitement unreflected, resulting in overwhelming shame. At other times the parents' excitement and praise may be all out of proportion to the child's accomplishments, so that no reliable inter-nal standard can be established. Even more damaging may be excessive and repeated praise for something the child has no sense of having accomplished, but makes the parent feel special: you are so beautiful; you are so smart.

"Every age develops its own peculiar forms of pathology", Professor of American History Christopher Lasch wrote in 1979.

The modern American only feels real if he is being broadcast and admired. Most people feel empty and unfulfilled, in chronic envy of those get such attention, Lasch observed. His book, *The Culture of Narcissism*, became a best-seller and was publicly endorsed by then President Jimmy Carter. Lasch blamed the epidemic of narcissism on children's other caretakers—their teachers—as much as on their parents.

The public school system had been transformed from disciplined institutions charged with creating educated and responsible citizens to daycare for the well-off and the lucky and dayprisons for the rest. America was locked in a forty-year-long cold war for world dominance in which technology seemed the key to victory. Especially after the Soviet Union launched its first space satellite far ahead of the United States, pressure was brought to bear on public education to teach more complex maths and science. It was never to happen. Instead, the public schools spiralled downward and the burden of education was left to be picked up by the colleges and universities. At the same time thousands of public school teachers, many without experience and inadequately trained, were recruited to educate the baby boomer generation. Our children's educators were given an impossible task: train the scientists and engineers of tomorrow but do not expect anything close to the resources required; expect large classes, little support, low pay, and no recognition. It should be no surprise that many teachers gave up their educational responsibilities and became frustrated babysitters, or guards—in the first case lavishing rewards and attention on all without regard to their actual accomplishments; in the second, trying simply to maintain order in the midst of chaos.

Building self-esteem and allowing students to find their own path, while often heartfelt goals, often served to cover the absence of education. As usual there was a confluence of factors. In the 1950s and 1960s, there was an increasing openness to progressive ideas about education. The philosophies of educators ranging from John Dewey and Maria Montessori to John Holt and Paul Krassner, among others, were hotly debated. All, however, agreed that education should be directed to the needs of the child. The implementation of such progressive education requires better educated teachers and greater resources than the standard approach; and when properly implemented it improves education by almost any measure

(Lillard & Else-Quest, 2006). When resources are limited and teachers not educated in the method, what gets called progressive education often deteriorates into relative neglect punctuated by empty praise.

At the time the self-esteem movement was in its ascendancy. Many psychologists and educators believed self-esteem could be raised by praise without reference to performance; that high self-esteem would lead to good performance and not the other way around; and that that low self-esteem was the root cause of individual and social problems. Now the myth of self-esteem is recognized even by one the movement's founders and advocates, Professor Roy Baumeister. Baumeister, one of America's leading social psychologists with over 250 publications spanning three decades, recently wrote,

> The modest correlations between self-esteem and school performance do not indicate that high self-esteem leads to good performance. Instead, high self-esteem is partly the result of good school performance. Efforts to boost the self-esteem of pupils have not been shown to improve academic performance and may sometimes be counterproductive.

> People high in self-esteem claim to be more likable and attractive, to have better relationships, and to make better impressions on others than people with low self-esteem, but objective measures disconfirm most of these beliefs. Narcissists are charming at first but tend to alienate others eventually. Self-esteem has not been shown to predict the quality or duration of relationships. [Baumeister, Campbell, Krueger, & Vohs, 2003]

Low self-esteem does not lead to crime or violence. In fact the opposite seems to be true.

Narcissists have high self-esteem—only consciously, I would add—and are prone to violent retaliation when they are shamed. Baumeister concluded, "little to be gained by raising self-esteem alone" (Baumeister, Campbell, Krueger, & Vohs, 2005).

Of late, many colleges have also abdicated their responsibility for educating their students. Grade inflation is rampant. Giving all students good grades lessens conflicts and the risk of puncturing already falsely inflated "self-esteem". Of course. it is possible to educate well without even giving grades—and some colleges do—

but that requires the time for close monitoring and personal engagement that most teachers lack. At some of the state mega-universities, students rarely meet a professor; there are hundreds of students in a class and the lectures can be viewed anytime on video. Graduating barely requires being there, much less real study. Time is often spent daydreaming or partying, engaged in an ever prolonged adolescent fantasy.

Many students and graduates never know the pleasures of education—the feeling of accomplishment that comes with working hard to solve a complex problem, the excitement that comes with learning something entirely new. Subsequently, careers are chosen based on ease, convenience, and financial reward without any thought that work can be meaningful and even fun. The only reasons for learning and working are external pressures to succeed and to make money.

Some people blame excessive praise for our culture of narcissism. For over forty years, educational psychologists have debated the value of praise, or, as it is technically called, extrinsic reward. In 1994, the prevailing view was that rewarding children for accomplishing a task was counterproductive, that it took away from their intrinsic motivation to do well and made them dependent on others for a sense of accomplishment. Then two Canadian researchers performed a meta-analysis of over 100 studies concerned with the effect of reward on learning and concluded that except for empty praise, praise didn't interfere with learning or desire (Cameron & Pierce, 1994). A meta-analysis is a complex statistical technique that allows the results of many different studies to be combined. A meta-analysis can be very useful, if the results are clear. For example. in the 1960s and 1970s, some famous behavioural psychologists claimed there was no proof that psychotherapy worked. Some studies showed it did, and others that it did not. In 1977, two sophisticated statisticians, Mary Lee Smith and Gene Glass, published a meta-analysis of psychotherapy that showed unequivocally that therapy works (Smith & Glass, 1977).[3] Theirs was one of the first meta-analyses and it changed the field. Researchers stopped asking if psychotherapy worked but instead asked how to make it work better. In the thirty years since there have been thousands of meta-analyses in psychology, most with results that are not so clear.

The 1994 praise meta-analysis was met by harsh criticism by psychologists who believed that praise was bad, and other praise meta-analyses followed (Tang & Hall, 1995). Some showed praise was good; others that it was bad. The same meta-analysis (Deci, Koestner, & Ryan, 1999a,b; Cameron, 2001; Deci, Ryan, & Koestner, 2001) has even been interpreted to support both positions illustrating the truth of Mark Twain's quip that there are lies, damn lies, and statistics. The obvious conclusion to draw is that praise is a complicated thing. Sometimes it motivates learning; sometimes it inhibits motivation and learning. It probably is affected by all the factors we have been discussing, including the relationship between giver and receiver of the praise, the age and temperament of the receiver, the truthfulness of the praise, its intensity, the setting, and more.

What is wrong with these researchers, you might wonder; can't they see the forest for the trees? Why does it have to one way or the other? What is wrong is that they too live in our culture of narcissism. Getting attention is more than getting it right. This distortion has become codified in the academic world. Academic jobs, promotions, and tenure decisions are heavily influenced by the citation index. The citation index, as well as the related impact factor, is the American Idol of academia. It measures how many times an article has been cited in other articles. It says nothing about the quality, originality, or daring of the author's work. What is wrong is that academics are driven by career pressure to publish studies that support their none-too-daring theories. If data doesn't fit, it often gets a new statistical analysis. If it still doesn't support the researcher's theory, it may be filed away forever. It is as true in psychology as it is in the pharmaceutical industry. Saying your theory is right gets more attention than saying it has got problems. Saying something simple like "praise is bad" gets more attention than saying praise is complicated.

Sigmund Koch, who moved from psychology professor to director of the Ford Foundation's Program in the Humanities and the Arts, was widely recognized as the most astute methodologist—an expert in research methods and data analysis—in the history of psychology. In 1952, Koch was asked to direct and to edit an extensive National Science Foundation-supported analysis of the status of psychology at mid-century. The result was the six-volume *Psychology: A Study of a Science* (1959–1963), described at the time as "probably the most important publishing event in psychology". Based on his close analysis of psychological research, Koch concluded that the vast majority of it was meaningless (Koch, 1999). No one has ever seriously challenged his conclusion. It was accepted as true, but it is a revelation that has faded.

Unfortunately, what gets transmitted to the general public is usually uncritical excitement about a particular researcher or theory, either by the researcher herself or by a busy journalist trying to tell a simple and engaging story. Journalists—whose job after all is to be noticed—usually accept without question what learned academics tell them; they are not trained in critical analysis. Of late, I see "meta-analysis" mentioned in the popular press as if it referred to the word of God and not a complex statistical tool that is subject to interpretation. When I was a publisher, I had the good fortune to meet noted researchers, theorists, and clinicians and talk with them about their ideas. I had the time to read across the different fields that study the mind and think about the connections between them. There's so much groundbreaking work being done. Trying to understand and connect even a small part of it felt both excitingly wonderful and awesomely complex, reflecting the wonder and complexity of the human mind.

Notes

1. http://www.guardian.co.uk/italy/story/0,,1724296,00.html
2. Ericsson has not investigated these factors.
3. Smith's own life-changing therapy in part prompted her to do the study.

REFERENCES

Aarts, H., Custers, R., & Holland, R. W. (2007). The nonconscious cessation of goal pursuit: when goals and negative affect are coactivated. *Journal of Personality and Social Psychology, 92*(2): 165–178.

Abagnale, F. (2005). *Catch Me If You Can*. Edinburgh: Mainstream Publishing.

Andersen, S. M., Reznik, I., & Manzella, L. M. (1996). Eliciting facial affect, motivation, and expectations in transference: significant-other representations in social relations. *Journal of Personality and Social Psychology, 71*(December): 1108–1129.

Aschoff, S. (2006). Anyone can have his shot. *St. Petersburg Times*, Sunday 28 May.

Attwood, T. (2007). *The Complete Guide to Asperger Syndrome* (p. 77). London: Jessica Kingsley.

Babiak, P., & Hare, R. D. (2006). *Snakes In Suits: When Psychopaths Go To Work*. New York: HarperCollins.

Baron-Cohen, S., Leslie, A. M., & Frith, U. (1985). Does the autistic child have a "theory of mind"? *Cognition, 21*(1): 37–46.

Bartholomew, K., & Shaver, P. (1998). Methods of assessing adult attachment: do they converge? In: J. A. Simpson & W. S. Rholes (Eds.), *Attachment Theory and Close Relationships* (pp. 25–45). New York: Guilford Press.

Baumeister, R. F., Campbell, J. D., Krueger, J. I., & Vohs, K. D. (2003). Does high self-esteem cause better performance, interpersonal success, happiness, or healthier lifestyles? *Psychological Science in the Public Interest*, 4(1): 1–44.

Baumeister, R. F., Campbell, J. D., Krueger, J. I., & Vohs, K. D. (2005). Exploding the self-esteem myth. *Scientific American*, 292(1): 84–91.

Bechara, A., Damasio, H., Damasio, A. R., & Lee, G. P. (1999). Different contributions of the human amygdala and ventromedial prefrontal cortex to decision making. *Journal of Neuroscience*, 19(13): 5473–5481.

Berns, G. S., Chappelow, J., Zink, C. F., Pagnoni, G., Martin-Skurski, M. E., & Richards, J. (2005). Neurobiological correlates of social conformity and independence during mental rotation. *Biological Psychiatry*.

Berns, G. S., Chappelow, J., Cekic, M., Zink, C. F., Pagnoni, G., & Martin-Skurski, M. (2006). Neurobiological substrates of dread. *Science*, 312: 754.

Blatt, S. J. (1998). Contributions of psychoanalysis to the understanding and treatment of depression. *Journal of the American Psychoanalytic Association*, 46: 723–752.

Board, B., & Fritzon, K. (2005). *Psychology, Crime & Law*, 11(1): 17–32.

Bowlby, J. (1982). *Attachment and Loss*. New York: Basic Books.

Bragg, M. (1983). A talk with John le Carré. *New York Times*, 13 March.

Bugental, D. B., Shennum, W., Frank, M., & Ekman, P. (2000). True lies: children's abuse history and power attributions as influences on deception detection. In: V. Manusov & J. H. Harvey (Eds.), *Attribution, Communication Behavior, and Close Relationships* (pp. 248–265). Cambridge: Cambridge University Press.

Cameron, J. (2001). Negative effects of reward on intrinsic motivation—a limited phenomenon: comment on Deci, Koestner, and Ryan. *Review of Educational Research*, 71(1): 29–42.

Cameron, J., & Pierce, W. D. (1994). Reinforcement, reward, and intrinsic motivation: a meta-analysis. *Review of Educational Research*, 64: 363–423.

Capote, T. (1965). *In Cold Blood*. New York: Random House.

Cary, B. (2009). In battle, hunches prove to be valuable. *New York Times*, 28 July.

Chomsky, N. (1959). A review of B. F. Skinner's verbal behavior. *Language*, 35(1): 26–58.

Chomsky, N. (1987). Equality: language development, human intelligence, and social organization, *The Chomsky Reader*. New York: Pantheon Books.

Chomsky, N., Foucault, M., & Rajchman, J. (2006). *The Chomsky–Foucault Debate: On Human Nature*. New York: New Press.

Coyle, D. (2007). How to grow a super-athlete. *New York Times*, 4 March.

Cringely, R. X. (1996). Triumph of the Nerds: The Rise of Accidental Empires. PBS Documentary.

De Bellis, M. D., Case, B. J., Dahl, R. E., Birmaher, B., Williamson, D. E., Thomas, K. M., Axelson, D. A., Frustaci, K., Boring, A. M., Hall, J., & Ryan, N. D. (2000). A pilot study of amygdala volumes in pediatric generalized anxiety disorder. *Biological Psychiatry, 48*: 51–57.

Deci, E. L., Koestner, R., & Ryan, R. M. (1999a). A meta-analytic review of experiments examining the effects of extrinsic rewards on intrinsic motivation. *Psychological Bulletin, 125*(6): 627–668.

Deci, E. L., Koestner, R., & Ryan, R. M. (1999b). The undermining effect is a reality after all-Extrinsic rewards, task interest, and self-determination: reply to Eisenberger, Pierce, and Cameron (1999) and Lepper, Henderlong, and Gingras (1999). *Psychological Bulletin*, Nov, *125*(6): 692–700.

Deci, E. L., Ryan, R. M., & Koestner, R. (2001). The pervasive negative effects of rewards on intrinsic motivation: response to Cameron. *Review of Educational Research, 71*(1): 43-51.

de Gelder, B., Morris, J. S., & Dolan, R. J. (2005). Unconscious fear influences emotional awareness of faces and voices. *Proceedings of the National Academy of Sciences, 102*(51): 18682–18687.

DePaulo, B. M., Kashy, D. A. (1998). Everyday lies in close and casual relationships. *Journal of Personality and Social Psychology, 74*(1): 63–79.

DePaulo, B. M., Kashy, D. A., Kirkendol, S. E., Wyer, M. M., & Epstein, J. A. (1996). Lying in everyday life. *Journal of Personality and Social Psychology, 70*: 979–995.

Doyle, J. (2005). Bodega Bay. *San Francisco Chronicle*, 21 October.

Dudas, J. (2005). Surfer's quick thinking saved her from shark, *UnderwaterTimes.com* (31 October). www.underwatertimes.com/ forum/viewtopic.php?p=1918.

Dunbar, R. I. M. (1993). Coevolution of neocortical size, group size and language in humans. *Behavioral and Brain Sciences, 16*(4): 681–735.

Ecoff, N. L., Ekman, P., Mage, J. J., & Frank, M. G. (2000). Lie detection and language loss. *Nature, 405*: 139.

Edelman, G. M. (1999). Building a picture of the brain. *Annals of the New York Academy of Sciences, 882*(1): 68–89.

Ekman, P. (1985). *Telling Lies*. New York: Norton.

Ekman, P. (1996). Why don't we catch liars? *Social Research, 63*: 801–817.

Ekman, P. (2003). *Emotions Revealed: Recognizing Faces and Feelings to Improve Communication and Emotional Life*. New York: Times Books, Henry Holt.

Ekman, P., & O'Sullivan, M. (1991). Who can catch a liar? *American Psychologist, 46*(9): 913–920.

Ekman, P., O'Sullivan, M., & Frank, M. (1999). A few can catch a liar. *Psychological Science, 10*: 263–266.

Ekman, P., O'Sullivan, M., Friesen, W. V., & Scherer, K. R. (1991). Face, voice and body in detecting deception. *Journal of Nonverbal Behavior, 15*: 125–135.

Elfenbein, H. A., Marsh, A. A., & Ambady, N. (2002). Emotional intelligence and the recognition of emotion from facial expressions. In: L. Feldman Barrett & P. Salovey (Eds.), *The Wisdom of Feelings: Psychological Processes in Emotional Intelligence*. New York: Guilford Press.

Ericsson, K. A. (2004). Deliberate practice and the acquisition and maintenance of expert performance in medicine and related domains. *Academic Medicine, 10*: S1–S12.

Ericsson, K. A., Krampe, R. Th., & Tesch-Römer, C. (1993). The role of deliberate practice in the acquisition of expert performance. *Psychological Review, 100*(3): 363–406.

Facts of Life: Issue Briefings for Health Reporters (1999) Mother's nurturing: medicine for life. 4(4) (May).

Feldman, R. S., Forrest, J. A., & Happ, B. R. (2002). Self-presentation and verbal deception: do self-presenters lie more? *Basic and Applied Social Psychology, 24*: 163–170.

Felmlee, D., Flynn, H., & Bahr, P. (2004). "Too much of a good thing": fatal attraction in adult intimate relationships. Paper presented at the Annual Meeting of the American Sociological Association, Hilton San Francisco & Renaissance Parc 55 Hotel, San Francisco, CA, 14 August 2004.

Fisher, P. M., Meltzer, C. C., Price, J. C., Coleman, R. L., Ziolko, S. K., Becker, C., Moses-Kolko, E. L., Berga, S. L., & Hariri, A. R. (2009). Medial prefrontal cortex 5-HT$_2$A density is correlated with amygdala reactivity, response habituation, and functional coupling. *Cerebral Cortex, 19*: 2499–2507.

Fiss, H., Ellman, S. J., & Klein, G. S. (1969). Waking fantasies following interrupted and completed REM periods. *Archives of General Psychiatry, 21*(2): 230–239.

Fonagy, P., & Target, M. (1996). Playing with reality: I. Theory of mind and the normal development of psychic reality. *International Journal of Psychoanalysis, 77*: 217–233.

Fonagy, P., & Target, M. (2000). Playing with reality: III. The persistence of dual psychic reality in borderline patients. *International Journal of Psychoanalysis, 81*: 853–873.

Fonagy, P., Gergely, G., Jurist, E. L., & Target, M. (2002). *Affect Regulation, Mentalization, and the Development of the Self.* New York: Other Press.

Forer, B. R. (1949). The fallacy of personal validation: a classroom study of gullibility. *Journal of Abnormal and Social Psychology, 44*: 118–123.

Fraley, R. C., Fazzari, D. A., Bonanno, G. A., & Dekel, S. (2006). Attachment and psychological adaptation in high exposure survivors of the September 11th attack on the World Trade Center. *Personality and Social Psychology Bulletin, 32*(4): 538–551.

Fresh Air (with Terry Gross) (1989). Radio interview with John le Carre, 30 May.

Freud, S. (1916d). Some character-types met with in psychoanalytic work. *S.E., 14*: 309–333. London: Hogarth.

Gallagher, H. L., Happe, F., Brunswick, N., Fletcher, P. C., Frith, U., & Frith, C. D. (2000). Reading the mind in cartoons and stories: an MRI study of 'theory of mind' in verbal and nonverbal tasks. *Neuropsychologia, 38*: 11–21.

Gallagher, H. L., Jack, A. I., Roepstorff, A., & Frith, C. D. (2002). Imaging the intentional stance in a competitive game. *NeuroImage, 16*, 814–821.

Gardner, H. (2005). Why would anyone become an expert? *American Psychologist*, September: 802–803.

Gergely, G., Nádasdy, Z., Csibra, G., & Bíró, S. (1995). Taking the intentional stance at 12 months of age. *Cognition, 56*: 165–193.

Gigerenzer, G. (2004). Dread risk, September 11, and fatal traffic accidents. *Psychological Science, 15*(4): 286–287.

Gladwell, M. (2005). *Blink: The Power of Thinking Without Thinking.* New York: Little, Brown.

Grandin, T. (2004). *Animals in Translation: Using the Mysteries of Autism to Decode Animal Behavior.* New York: Scribner.

Grandin, T., & Johnson, C. (2005). *Animals in Translation: Using the Mysteries of Autism to Decode Animal Behavior.* Harcourt.

Halpern, J. (2007). *Fame Junkies: The Hidden Truths Behind America's Favorite Addiction.* Boston: Houghton Mifflin.

Hamann, S., Herman, R. A., Nolan, C. L., & Wallen, K. (2004). Men and women differ in amygdala response to visual sexual stimuli. *Nature Neuroscience*, 7(4): 411–416.

Harlow, H. F. (1958). The nature of love. *American Psychologist*, 13: 573–685.

Harlow, H. F., Harlow, M. K., Dodsworth, R. O., & Arling, G. L. (1966). Maternal behavior of rhesus monkeys deprived of mothering and peer associations in infancy. *Proceedings of the American Philosophical Society*, 110(1): 58–66.

Harmon, A. (2004). How about not "curing" us, some autistics are pleading. *New York Times*, 20 December.

Hart, D., & Sussman, R. W. (2005). *Man the Hunted: Primates, Predators and Human Evolution*. Boulder, CO: Westview Press.

Hauser, M. D., Chomsky, N., Tecumseh Fitch, W. (2002). The faculty of language: what is it, who has it, and how did it evolve? *Science*, 298(5598): 1569–1579.

Hazan, C., & Shaver, P. (1987). Romantic love conceptualized as an attachment process. *Journal of Personality and Social Psychology*, 52: 511–524.

Høglend, P., Johansson, P., Marble, A., Bøgwald, K.-P., & Amlo, S. (2007). Moderators of the effects of transference interpretations in brief dynamic psychotherapy. *Psychotherapy Research*, 17(March): 162–174.

Jolij, J., & Lamme, V. A. F. (2006). Repression of unconscious information by conscious processing: evidence from affective blindsight induced by transcranial magnetic stimulation. *Proceedings of the National Academy of Sciences*, 102(30): 10747–10751.

Kassin, S. M., & Fong, C. T. (1999). 'I'm innocent!': effects of training on judgments of truth and deception in the interrogation room. *Law and Human Behavior*, 23(5): 499–516.

Kelly, J. (2005). *The Great Mortality, An Intimate History of the Black Death, the Most Devastating Plague of All Time*. New York: HarperCollins.

Kenny, D. A., Horner, C., Kashy, D. A., & Chu, L. (1992). Consensus at zero acquaintance: replication, behavioral cues, and stability. *Journal of Personality and Social Psychology*, 62: 88–97.

Koch, S. (1959–1963). *Psychology: A Study of Science* (Vols. 1–6). New York: McGraw Hill.

Koch, S. (1999). *Psychology in Human Context: Essays in Dissidence and Reconstruction*, D. Finkelman & F. Kessel (Eds.). Chicago. IL: University of Chicago Press.

Kohut, H. (1971). *Analysis of the Self: Systematic Approach to Treatment of Narcissistic Personality Disorders*. New York: International Universities Press.

Kramer, P. (1998). *Listening to Prozac*. Darby, PA: DIANE Publishing.

Kudo, H., & Dunbar, R. I. M. (2001). Neocortex size and social network size in primates. *Animal Behavior, 61*: 711–722.

Kuhn, T. (1996). *The Structure of Scientific Revolutions*. Chicago,IL: University of Chicago Press.

Lasch, C. (1979). *The Culture of Narcissism. American Life in an Age of Diminishing Expectations*. New York: W. W. Norton.

LeDoux, J. E. (1998). Nature vs. nurture: the pendulum still swings with plenty of momentum. *The Chronicle of Higher Education, 45*(16): B7–B8 (retrieved 18 April 2010 from Platinum Periodicals, Document ID: 36673010).

Lee, L. (2003). Theory of mind and clinical depression: the relationship between depression severity and mental state recognition. Unpublished MA dissertation, Queens University at Kingston.

Lerner, J. S., Gonzalez, R. M., Small, D. A., & Fischhoff, B. (2003). Effects of fear and anger on perceived risks of terrorism: a national field experiment. *Psychological Science, 14*(2): 144–150.

LeTourneau, N. (2002). Umass researcher finds most people lie in everyday conversation. www.Eurekalert.org (June 10); www.eurekalert.org/pub_releases/2002-06/uoma-urf061002.php.

Life Matters (with Norman Swan) (2000). Radio interview with Frank Abagnale, 17 March. http://anlimara.tripod.com/abagnaleintervw.html.

Lillard, A., & Else-Quest, N. (2006). The early years: evaluating Montessori education. *Science, 313*: 1893–1894.

Linley, P. A., & Joseph, S. (2004). Positive change following trauma and adversity: a review. *Journal of Traumatic Stress, 17*(1): 531–548.

MacDonald, D. J., & Standing, L. G. (2002). Does self-serving bias cancel the Barnum effect? *Social Behavior and Personality, 30*(6): 625–630.

Maguire, E. A., Gadian, D. G., Johnsrude, I. S., Good, C. D., Ashburner, J., Frackowiak, R. S. J., & Frith, C. D. (2000). Navigation-related structural change in the hippocampi of taxi drivers. *Proc. Natl. Acad. Sci. USA, 97*: 4398–4403.

Maguire, E. A., Spiers, H. J., Good, C. D., Hartley, T., Frackowiak, R. S. J., & Burgess, N. (2003). Navigation expertise and the human hippocampus: a structural brain imaging analysis. *Hippocampus, 13*(2): 208–217.

Mahler, M., Pine, F., & Bergman, A. (1975). *The Psychological Birth of the Human Infant*. New York: Basic Books.

Manes, S., & Andrews, P. (1994). Gates: How Microsoft's Mogul Reinvented an Industry and Made Himself the Richest Man in America. New York: Touchstone.

Marcus, B. (2005). Interview with a shark attack victim: Megan Halavais' close encounter with Mr. White. *Surfer Magazine: Online Exclusives*. http://www.surfermag.com/features/onlineexclusives/sharkmegan05.

McBride, J. (2006). *The Color of Water: A Black Man's Tribute to His White Mother*. New York: Penguin.

McKinney Jr, W. T., Suomi, S. J., & Harlow, H. F. (1971). Depression in primates. *American Journal of Psychiatry*, *127*(April): 1313–1320.

McKinney Jr., W. T., Suomi, S. J., & Harlow, H. F. (1972). Monkey psychiatrists. *American Journal of Psychiatry*, *128*(8): 927–932.

McLaughlin, J., Osterhout, L., & Kim, A. (2004). Neural correlates of second-language word learning: minimal instruction produces rapid change. *Nature Neuroscience*, *7*: 703–704.

Mechelli, A., Crinion, J. T., Noppeney, U., O'Doherty, J., Ashburner, J., Frackowiack, R. S., & Price, C. J. (2004). Neurolinguistics: structural plasticity in the bilingual brain. *Nature*, *431*(7010): 757.

Meeren, H. K. M., van Heijnsbergen, C. C. R. J., & de Gelder, B. L. M. F. (2005). Rapid perceptual integration of facial expression and emotional body language. *Proceedings of the National Academy of Sciences*, *102*(45): 16518–16523.

Mezzacappa, E. S., Katkin, E. S., & Palmer, S. N. (1999). Epinephrine, arousal, and emotion: a new look at two-factor theory. *Cognition and Emotion*, *13*(2): 181–199.

Mitchell, T. M., Shinkareva, S. V., Carlson, A., Chang, K.-M., Malave, V. L., Mason, R. A., & Just, M. A. (2008). Predicting human brain activity associated with the meanings of nouns. *Science*, *320*(5880): 1191–1195.

Paulus, M. P., Potterat, E. G., Taylor, M. K., Van Orden, K. F., Bauman, J., Momen, N., Padilla, G. A., & Swain, J. L. (2009). A neuroscience approach to optimizing brain resources for human performance in extreme environments. *Neuroscience and Biobehavioral Reviews*, *33*: 1080–1088.

Pavlov, I. (1904). Nobel Lecture, 12 December, 1904, http://nobelprize.org/nobel_prizes/medicine/laureates/1904/pavlov-lecture.html.

Pennebaker, J. W., Dyer, M. A., Caulkins, R. S., Litowitz, D. L., Ackreman, P. L., Anderson, D. B., & McGraw, K. M. (1979). Don't the girls get prettier at closing time: a country and western application to psychology. *Personality and Social Psychology Bulletin, 5*: 123–125.

Penton-Voak, I. S., Perrett, D. I., & Peirce, J. W. (1999). Computer graphic studies of the role of facial similarity in judgements of attractiveness. *Current Psychology, 18*(1): 104.

Peters, E. (Ed.) (1980). *Heresy and Authority in Medieval Europe*. London: Scolar Press.

Piaget, J. (1960) [1932]. *The Moral Judgement of the Child*, M. Gabain (Trans.). Glencoe, IL: Free Press.

Pierce, K., Haist, F., Sedaghat, F., & Courchesne, E. (2004). The brain response to personally familiar faces in autism: findings of fusiform activity and beyond brain advance access. *Brain, 127*: 2703–2716.

Pine, F. (1984). The interpretive moment. *Bulletin of the Menninger Clinic, 48*, 54–71.

Playboy Magazine (1994). The Bill Gates Interview.

Plato (360 BCE). Symposium http://classics.mit.edu/Plato/symposium.html.

Pollak, S. D. (2000). Recognizing emotion in faces: developmental effects of child abuse and neglect. *Developmental Psychology, 36*: 679–688.

Pryor, B., & Buchanan, R. W. (1984). The effects of a defendant's demeanor on juror perceptions of credibility and guilt. *Journal of Communication, 34*(3): 92–99.

Pulfer, L. (2003). Frank Abagnale Jr.: felon tells moral of his story. *The Enquirer Online* (27 February) [www.enquirer.com/editions/2003/02/27/loc_pulfer27.html].

Rhodes, R. A., Murthy, N. V., Dresner, M. A., Selvaraj, S., Stavrakakis, N., Babar, S., Cowen, P. J., & Grasby, P. M. (2007). Human 5-HT transporter availability predicts amygdala reactivity in vivo. *Journal of Neuroscience, 27*: 9233–9237.

Rizzolatti, G., Fadiga, L., Gallese, V., & Fogassi, L. (1996). Premotor cortex and the recognition of motor actions. *Cognitive Brain Research, 3*: 131–141.

Roisman, G. L. (2002). Earned-secure attachment status in retrospect and prospect. *Child Development, 73*(4): 1204–1219.

Sachs, O. (1998). *The Man Who Mistook His Wife For A Hat: And Other Clinical Tales*. New York: Touchstone.

Schachter, S., & Singer, J. (1962). Cognitive, social, and physiological determinants of emotional state. *Psychological Review, 69*: 379–399.

Schwartz, C. E., Wright, C. I., Shin, L. M., Kagan, J., & Rauch, S. L. (2004). Inhibited and uninhibited infants "grown up": adult amygdalar response to novelty. *Science, 300*(5627): 1952–1953.

Schwarz, J. (2004). "Parlez-vous français?" Study shows 14 hours to think in French. *University Week,* 24 June.

Science Daily (2005). "University of Chicago researchers find human brain still evolving. 9 September. www.sciencedaily.com/releases/2005/09/050909221043.htm.

Schore, A. N. (1994). *Affect Regulation and the Origin of Self: The Neurobiology of Emotional Development.* Hillsdale, NJ: Lawrence Erlbaum.

Schraw, G. (2005). An interview with K. Anders Ericsson. *Educational Psychology Review, 17*(4): 389–412.

Scorsese, M. (1976). *Taxi Driver* (film). Columbia Pictures.

Singleton, N., Meltzer, H., & Gatward, R. (1997). *Psychiatric Morbidity Among Prisoners in England and Wales.* London: The Stationery Office.

Smith, M. L., & Glass, G. V. (1977). Meta-analysis of psychotherapy outcome studies. *American Psychologist, 32:* 752–760.

Steele, C. M., & Aronson, J. (1995). Stereotype threat and the intellectual test performance of African Americans. *Journal of Personality and Social Psychology, 69:* 797–811.

Steele, M., Hodges, J., Kaniuk, J., Hillman, S., & Henderson, K. (2003). Attachment representations and adoption: associations between maternal states of mind and emotion narratives in previously maltreated children. *Journal of Child Psychotherapy, 29*(2): 187–205.

Stoléru, S., Redouté, J., Costes, N., Lavenne, F., Le Bars, D., Dechaud, H., Forest, M. G., Pugeat, M., Cinotti, L., & Pujol, J. F. (2003). Brain processing of visual sexual stimuli in men with hypoactive sexual desire disorder. *Psychiatry Research, 124*(2): 67–86.

Stouthamer-Loeber, M. (1986). Lying as a problem behavior in children: a review. *Clinical Psychology Review, 6:* 267–289.

Sullivan, H. S. (1953). *The Interpersonal Theory of Psychiatry.* New York: Norton.

Suomi, S. J. (1997). Early determinants of behaviour: evidence from primate studies. *British Medical Bulletin, 53*(I): 170–184.

Szecsody, I. (2008). A single-case study of the process and outcome of psychoanalysis. *Scandanavian Review, 31:* 105–113 [accessed online http://internationalpsychoanalysis.net/category/psychoanalytic-archives/].

Tammet, D., (2007). *Born on a Blue Day: Inside the Extraordinary Mind of an Autistic Savant.* New York: Free Press.

Tang, S.-H., & Hall, V. C. (1995). The overjustification effect: a meta-analysis. *Applied Cognitive Psychology, 9*: 365–404.

The National Autistic Society, London (2007). www.nas.org.uk/.

This American Life (2006). Weekly public radio broadcast. Episode 317—Unconditional love. 15 September.

Tronick, E., Als, H., Adamson, L., Wise, S., & Brazelton, B. (1978). The infant's response to entrapment between contradictory messages in face-to-face interaction. *American Academy of Child Psychiatry, 1*: 1–13.

Van Willigen, M. (2000). Differential benefits of volunteering across the life course. *The Journals of Gerontology, 55B*(5): S308.

Vogel, C. (2005). Rock, paper, payoff: child's play wins auction house an art sale. *New York Times*, 29 April.

Wellman, H. M., Cross, D., & Watson, J. (2001). Meta-analysis of theory-of-mind development: the truth about false belief. *Child Development, 72*(3): 655–684.

Werner, E. A., Myers, M. M., Fifer, W. P., Cheng, B., Allen, R., & Monk, C. (2007). Prenatal predictors of infant temperament. *Developmental Psychobiology, 49*(5): 474–484.

Wilson, A. E., Smith, M. D., & Ross, H. S. (2003). The nature and effects of young children's lies. *Social Development, 12*(1): 21–45.

Wilson-Smith, A. (1999). *Maclean's*, The Canadian Encyclopedia Historical Foundation of Canada (5 April).

Winston, J. S., Strange, B. A., O'Doherty, J., & Dolan, R. J. (2002). Automatic and intentional brain responses during evaluation of trustworthiness of faces. *Nature Neuroscience, 5*: 277–283.

Wootton, A. (2002). John le Carre at the NFT. The *Guardian Unlimited* (5 October) [http://film.guardian.co.uk/interview/interviewpages/0,,809419,00.html].

Zahn-Waxler, C., Radke-Yarrow, M., Wagner, E., & Chapman, M. (1992). Development of concern for others. *Developmental Psychology, 28*: 126–136.

Zanarini, M. C., Frankenburg, F. R., Bradford Reich, D., Silk, K. R., Hudson, J. I., & McSweeney, L. B. (2007). The subsyndromal phenomenology of borderline personality disorder: a 10-year follow-up study. *American Journal of Psychiatry, 164*: 929–935.

ACKNOWLEDGEMENTS

I started this book over five years ago. It has been a long journey of reading, writing, and re-writing many times; times of excitement and wonder; times of hellish anxiety and sleepless nights; and times of intense self-absorption that I know were not easy to bear for those around me.

I want to give great thanks to my friends and family—especially my wife Sally and my sons, Peter and John—for their help, support and love. I want to thank my teachers, especially Steven Ellman and Anni Bergman, whose careers exemplified courage in the face of conformity. I want to thank my many editors, especially John Kelly, Michael Denneny, Gottfried Röckelein, Anthony LaBruzza, and Sondra Tuckfelt (who I could call any time, even in the middle of the night) for all their help along the way.

Among the joys of being a psychoanalyst is learning from patients: meeting as strangers and then getting to know them in more detail and depth than anyone else in your life, except perhaps your closest friends and family. I want to thank my patients for teaching me so much and let my readers know that most of the brief clinical examples in this book are composite creations. In some of the longer illustrations, I have either thoroughly disguised my patients' identities or obtained their permission to say what I have said about them.